fP

HEAD, HAND, HEART

WHY INTELLIGENCE IS OVER-REWARDED,

MANUAL WORKERS MATTER,

AND CAREGIVERS DESERVE MORE RESPECT

DAVID GOODHART

FREE PRESS

New York London Toronto Sydney New Delhi

Free Press
An Imprint of Simon & Schuster, Inc.
1230 Avenue of the Americas
New York, NY 10020

First Free Press hardcover edition September 2020

FREE PRESS and colophon are registered
trademarks of Simon & Schuster, Inc.

For information about special discounts for bulk purchases,
please contact Simon & Schuster Special Sales at 1-866-506-1949
or business@simonandschuster.com.

The Simon & Schuster Speakers Bureau can bring authors to
your live event. For more information or to book an event, contact
the Simon & Schuster Speakers Bureau at 1-866-248-3049
or visit our website at www.simonspeakers.com.

Interior design by Kyle Kabel

Manufactured in the United States of America

1   3   5   7   9   10   8   6   4   2

Library of Congress Cataloging-in-Publication Data is available.

ISBN 978-1-9821-2844-9
ISBN 978-1-9821-2847-0 (ebook)

To my children,
in the hope that they might finally read
something I have written

Contents

Preface

I wrote most of this book before the Covid-19 crisis struck. Yet the crisis and its likely consequences have a direct bearing on its main theme: the lop-sided distribution of status that has become such a feature of rich societies in recent decades. For one thing it has made the unthinkable thinkable. If we can close down society and economic life for months and collectively underwrite at least some of the cost, then it becomes a little bit easier to imagine that we might adjust the status balance in our educationally stratified, postindustrial societies by a few degrees.

Most of us have wanted things to return to normal as swiftly as possible, but these coming years will also surely prove a hinge moment for politics in those rich countries in Europe and North America that have been overwhelmed by the crisis. There are several ways in which the crisis will enable, in the language of this book, Hand (manual work) and Heart (care work) to claim back some of the prestige and reward they have lost to Head (cognitive work) in recent decades.

At the most macro level a new version of globalization is now possible, summed up in one of the wittier slogans of the crisis: workers of the world unite, you have nothing to lose but your supply chains. Full-scale deglobalization is highly undesirable and is not going to happen; we have learned the lessons of 1930s protectionism. But some restraints on what economist Dani Rodrik has called "hyper-globalization"—the globalization that has favored large corporations, financial markets, and mobile skilled professionals—can be put in place.

The crisis has been the hour of the nation state and national social contracts at least in Europe, though in the United States it is the relative weakness of the central state that has been exposed. National democracies are likely to claim a greater say in the next phase of globalization. There will be some reshoring and shortening of those long, vulnerable supply chains. Lowest-cost globalization, which regrets the closure of the Midwest manufacturing plant but sees it as a price worth paying for cheaper goods in Walmart, will no longer win the argument so easily. Most of us are producers as well as consumers, and we might be prepared to pay a few dollars more for a smartphone produced closer to home.

Some of this sentiment was strengthening before the crisis. World trade fell slightly in 2019, partly as a result of the argument between the United States and China about what constitutes fair trade arrangements. The existing model of helter-skelter globalization has been producing too many losers, not least the global environment.

Western society has been dominated in the past two generations by *centrifugal* forces that have spread global openness and individual freedom but weakened collective bonds and enabled Head work to claim undue reward while Hand and Heart work has diminished in dignity and pay. The knowledge economy has placed cognitive meritocracy at the center of the status hierarchy, and the cognitively blessed have thrived—but many others feel they have lost place and meaning.

Recent political trends, surely reinforced by the pandemic, suggest we are moving into a more *centripetal* phase, in which the nation-state will be consolidated and economic and cultural openness will be a little more constrained. This phase will place more stress on localism, social stability, and solidarity, it will be more skeptical of the claims of the Head and more sensitive to the humiliations built into modern, achievement societies, including for minorities.

As I was writing the book in 2019, I would not have dared to imagine the public appreciations of the Hand and Heart workers that became such a dominant image of the early weeks of the crisis. People were applauding not just those working in health services but also those who maintain the hidden wiring of our everyday lives—the supermarket shelf stackers, the bus drivers and delivery people, those who maintain the food and drug supply chains and remove household waste. Not all of them are manual workers in a literal sense but all of them do essential jobs. In a partial inversion of the status hierarchy, many of the truly key workers turned out to be people who did not go to college and were less adept at manipulating information. Not all are hand workers in a literal sense, nor the factory workers of old, but all do essential jobs, and in the United Kingdom and United States at the height of the crisis it was males, especially older ethnic minority males, in those frontline jobs who were twice as likely to die from Covid-19 as the wider working population.

The pause for reflection that the lockdown imposed on normally hectic, achievement-orientated societies and individuals may leave the deepest traces of all. Many of us, perhaps especially the privileged and highly educated, have been forced to reconsider what we value most deeply and, having looked up from our busy, mobile, existences, often met a neighbor for the first time and actually felt rooted in a physical community. And then, stepping out from our immediate neighborhoods, we have smiled and nodded at strangers even while politely giving them a wide berth.

This new sense of rootedness and connection, along with the heightened awareness of our mortality, can spill over into a mawkish sentimentality and a "safetyism" that eschews all risk and refuses all trade-offs. At the other end of the spectrum many people desperately want to enjoy their old freedoms, including the freedom to treat our fellow citizens with normal indifference. Some predict not so much a gentler, more caring society emerging from the crisis but a wilder and angrier one, a new roaring twenties. Perhaps the Black Lives Matter eruption was a premonition of that.

But the care economy has been at the center of the crisis, and that in itself is likely to prompt some reevaluation of mainstream economic and political thought. Just as old attitudes to large-scale government

debt, and even printing money, have had to be revised even by con-
servative-minded politicians, so we may be pushed to reconsider our
attitudes to productivity and even the very idea of the economic sphere.

Rich Western societies already spend a large part of GDP on care,
health, and welfare; this share is likely to increase another step in the
wake of the crisis. And surely we need to more openly acknowledge
that what we want in many parts of the care economy, from ICUs to
elderly care homes, is *lower* productivity, not higher. We want fewer
beds per nurse not more. This is true in large parts of the Heart economy, in health, and in education. And if we are to upwardly revalue
the public care economy, and fund better the Cinderella parts such
as elderly care, then what about the work done in the private care
economy of the home looking after the young and the old? Should that
not also be valued more too and not seen as a domain of oppression
and limited opportunity?

That raises big questions about the gender division of labor and
how to revalue domesticity without undoing the freedoms that women
have achieved in recent decades. Our enforced confinement in the
home caused much family tension, couple separation, and even vio-
lence. But it was also a reminder to many people of the primary value
of family and the hard work of nurture and education that takes place
within its walls. If Britain's health service is, as the Conservative Prime
Minister, Boris Johnson, declared, "powered by love" then how much
more so the private realm of the family.

This is how I see the crisis as strengthening the Hand and Heart
and readjusting the status balance somewhat with Head. To put it in
political language, I see the crisis, particularly in Europe, as reinforcing an unusual coalition—a conservative preference for the local, the
national, the family, along with a liberal preference for higher social
spending and modest collectivism, combined too with a renewed
concern for the environment. But that is what I thought before the
virus struck too, as you can see from reading this book, so I have to
plead guilty to Covid confirmation bias—the tendency to see your

own assumptions about how the world should evolve confirmed by the crisis.

There are two counter arguments to these claims. The first is that contrary to Head being reined in by the crisis, the Head experts—whether highly educated medics or vaccine scientists or epidemiologists—have proved their vital importance and therefore dispatched the populist disdain for expertise. The second points out that the institutions that have become even more central to our existence during the crisis—the big-tech digital platforms—are the epitome of the disembodied world of data manipulation that tend to reinforce a Head worldview.

Both points have validity but I don't think they carry enough weight to dislodge my Covid-19 rebalancing thesis. Moreover, the first claim misunderstands the complaint against experts. Only a rather small number of people in what one might loosely call the populist movement—though more in the United States than in Europe—have ever been against the "hard" scientific, technical, or medical experts. Their argument was, and is, against economists, social scientists, and highly educated people in general passing off their often liberal presumptions as neutral truth.

And while the digital platforms have indeed proved their worth in the crisis, they have often done so not by reinforcing the "belong anywhere" message we have associated with them in the past, but rather by making it easier for real local communities to support each other via Facebook or WhatsApp groups. Indeed, so successful have they been that they have truly established themselves as utilities comparable to water and electricity and they will thus surely come to be subject to some of the same degree of regulation as the traditional utilities. But that is another story.

In the meantime, I think there are some grounds for optimism emerging from the crisis. In our open, fractious societies, divisions and disagreements have noisily continued—not least in the reaction to the killing of George Floyd in Minneapolis—yet below the surface, there has also been a greater sense of common destiny than usual, in Europe if not the United States. Arguments between liberals and conservatives, and left and right, will continue, as they should, yet I think there is a decent chance that one legacy of the crisis will be to acknowledge a wider range of human aptitudes in our allocation of reward and prestige—and thus a better balance between Head, Hand, and Heart. The bleak alternative is that the scars left by the epidemic will generate an even more divided and resentful politics.

PART ONE

OUR PROBLEM

Chapter One

Peak Head

We . . . need to apply ourselves to something we do not yet quite know how to do: to eradicate contempt for those who are disfavoured by the ethic of effortful competition.

Kwame Anthony Appiah

What has gone wrong in rich, Western democracies? Political polarization. Economic stagnation. A weaker sense of common interest. Disappointed expectations among the university-educated mass elite. A rising tide of depression and loneliness. A crisis of meaning.

Even before the Covid-19 crisis struck there was a mood of despondency in our politics—a sense that losers were outnumbering winners in nations buffeted by anonymous global forces, that the public realm was being slowly poisoned by social media, and that mainstream politics was failing to recognize the widespread yearning for stability and belonging.

But there's an overarching explanation for some of these discontents that was, and still is, hiding in plain sight. In recent decades, in the interests of efficiency, fairness, and progress, Western democracies have established systems of competition in which the most able succeed and too many of the rest feel like failures.

Who are the most able? People with higher levels of cognitive ability, or at least those *certified* as such by the education system. One form of human aptitude—cognitive-analytical ability, or the talent that helps people to pass exams and then handle information efficiently in their professional lives—has become *the gold standard of human esteem*. Those with a generous helping of this aptitude have formed a new kind of expanded cognitive class—a mass elite—who now shape society, and do so broadly in their own interests.

To put it more bluntly: smart people have become too powerful. How is this different from the past? Seventy years ago, just after the Second World War, when we lived in less complex societies, the people who ran government and business were generally brighter and more ambitious than the average—as they still are today.

What's different is that, back then, skills and qualities other than cognitive-analytical intelligence were held in higher regard. Education had not yet emerged as the primary marker of social stratification. In the 1970s most people in rich societies left school with no qualifications at all, and as recently as the 1990s many professionals lacked university degrees.

In the language of political cliché, the "best and brightest" today trump the "decent and hardworking." Qualities like character, integrity, experience, common sense, courage, and willingness to toil are by no means irrelevant, but they command relatively less respect.

When such virtues are undervalued, it can contribute to what socially conservative critics call a "moral deregulation" in which simply being a good person is valued less and it becomes harder to feel satisfaction and self-respect living an ordinary, decent life, especially in the bottom part of the income spectrum.

Without us noticing it, something fundamental has got out of kilter. It is too early to tell whether the Covid-19 crisis will contribute to a better balance between aptitudes based on "Head," "Hand," and "Heart." But we need one. The three aptitudes overlap to a degree, but the modern knowledge economy has produced ever rising returns for Head workers—who are highly qualified academically—and reduced the relative pay and status of much manual (Hand) work.

At the same time, many aspects of caring (Heart) work, traditionally done by women in the gift economy of the family, continues to be undervalued even as care work has become an increasingly critical part of the public economy and was so widely applauded (literally) at the height of the crisis.

An economic and social system in rich countries that once had a place for a range of aptitudes and abilities—in the skilled and semi-skilled jobs of the industrial era, on the land, in the military, in the church, in the private realm of the family—now favors the cognitive classes and the educationally successful.

The diminishing sway of those older structures and ways of life are a necessary condition of freer, more open societies, especially for women. But what many of those institutions also provided were forms of unconditional recognition based simply on being you, and a role and a purpose for the people, both men and women, whose strengths lie elsewhere than in the cognitive-analytical. Just doing your duty and making a contribution brought a degree of respect.

Moreover, whereas until recently different social classes and groups and regions had their own separate leaders and hierarchies and measures of prestige, today in most developed countries there is something more like *a single, common elite* that has passed through the same funnel of higher education and then into the top quartile of professional and managerial occupations. At the very top, these national elites merge into a semi-global one that studies at the same universities, works at the same corporations and institutions, and consumes the same media.

For most of human history, cognitive-analytical ability was scattered more or less randomly through society, with only a tiny minority attending university, religious seminaries, or similarly elite academies. But in recent decades in rich countries, a huge sorting process has taken place in which most of the young exam passers are swept up and sent into higher education. This has triggered a significant decline in the status of much nongraduate employment and also made promotion from below much harder for those without the passport of a university degree.

This does not mean that we now live in a true meritocracy. Family income and the educational background of your parents still correlates strongly with educational and career success, and indeed with performance in IQ-type tests.

The children of two-parent professional families are far more likely to be brought up by parents who are well-connected, understand what is required for children of even middling academic ability to enter good universities and obtain high-status professional jobs, and have the means to invest heavily in them.

The evidence also suggests that most rich societies are at least somewhat open and that many of the cognitively able from lower social classes can and do rise via higher education (thereby helping to legitimize the status quo).

The end result may be the emergence of a partially hereditary meritocracy, especially in the United States, although a few seem to get there by egregiously playing the system.* Many people, particularly members of the cognitive class themselves, may protest that progress has always been driven forward by the cognitively blessed and that modern, technologically advanced societies simply need more clever people—especially in software and computer science—than ever before.

Moreover, they may add, the so-called Flynn effect (named after the New Zealand academic James Flynn) shows that *everyone* is getting brighter—that average IQ levels have been rising throughout the twentieth century as a result of improved living conditions and human minds adapting to a more demanding cognitive environment.[1]

They argue that as long as the social biases mentioned above are ironed out, through spending on education and a sustained effort to give people of all backgrounds a fair chance at joining the cognitive class, all will be well.

---

* This was placed in the spotlight in early 2019 when overt corruption, including getting other people to take applicants' exams, was uncovered by the US Department of Justice to get undeserving candidates into top colleges, including Yale and Stanford.

This book disagrees. In the tradition of Michael Young's *The Rise of the Meritocracy*, his dystopian satire on rule by the cognitive elite, Daniel Bell's *The Coming of Post-Industrial Society: A Venture in Social Forecasting*, and Charles Murray's *Coming Apart: The State of White America, 1960–2010*—a socialist, a centrist, and a conservative—it argues that today's "achievement society" has replaced one system of domination by another.

It is true that the knowledge created by human reason continues to drive civilization, and in our data-based economies this is not about to decline in importance. The Covid-19 crisis underlined the vital significance of cognitive virtues such as medical expertise, pharmaceutical innovation, and the mathematical modeling of epidemiologists. (Though it has also revealed our dependence on those performing vital noncognitive Hand and Heart functions.) It is also true that the opening up of the cognitive class through the expansion of higher education has broadened the base of privilege.

IQ + effort—in Michael Young's formula for describing what is required to excel in the meritocracy—is undoubtedly a better selection criterion than nepotism or patronage. A cognitive class that puts innate talent to good use in invention and innovation is obviously preferable to a hereditary one and certainly produces more prosperity. So a meritocratic society has a lot to be said for it: by putting human ability to work, it creates a dynamic and wealthy society that appears to be fair, or at least fairer than the alternatives, and creates opportunities for some people born into disadvantage.

But inclusions often require new exclusions, in this case those who do not have the good fortune or aptitude to acquire a university degree—which is a majority of adults in most rich countries. And people no more *earn* their upbringing or innate intelligence than they earn being born into a rich family.

Although IQ-type tests and exams measure raw cognitive ability, they do not capture things like social intelligence and imagination that we today associate with a rounded, capable person. Intelligence is a complex, fuzzy, and often highly context-dependent phenomenon, as

I will unpack in Chapter Three, but in the United Kingdom, United States, and France—though less so elsewhere in continental Europe—it is the most abstract forms of reasoning that have historically attracted the most prestige.

Michael Young argued sixty years ago, in his critique of meritocracy, that people blessed with advanced cognitive skills can feel *less* obligation to those of below-average intelligence than the rich felt traditionally to the poor. Meritocracy sharply divides winners from losers in the education system while giving losers less psychological protection from their low status.

There will, of course, always be hierarchies of competence. But it is important to distinguish between meritocratic *selection systems* for highly skilled jobs and a meritocratic *society*. The former is necessary and desirable: you want capable nuclear scientists running your nuclear program. But the latter is not the hallmark of a good society and is potentially a source of mass resentment.

There are two challenges to this critique. Can you have meritocratic selection *without* a meritocratic society? I believe you can, because there is no single scale of human worth. A broader valuation of human qualities and aptitudes than those promoted by a cognitive meritocracy is an achievable goal. Human flourishing is compatible with a wide range of abilities and aptitudes.

The second challenge, often expressed by people who have risen into the elite from ordinary or disadvantaged homes, runs like this: I agree that meritocracy is not perfect, but can we have a proper one first before you start attacking it? Do you really want to go back to a dominant class selected on the basis of inherited property and status?

No, of course, I do not want to turn the clock back, I want an elite as open as possible and as much social fluidity as a fair society requires. And in principle it ought to be possible to have plenty of upward (and downward) mobility based on cognitive selection while also respecting and rewarding those who have other skills and aptitudes.

But in practice this is hard to achieve. And if high mobility is the mark of the good society, as both center-left and center-right politicians have argued in recent years, then we are in trouble, because mobility slows when "smart produces smart."

How close we are to that point and how much mobility we can expect in a fair society is contested, as I will show in Chapter Three. It depends on how much family, class, and environmental factors can tilt the system in favor of the only moderately able and how much ability is heritable. Given that both of those factors are clearly of significance, and assuming we continue to live in relatively free societies that allow families to pass on advantage, the meritocracy will be partial at best or will ossify into a hereditary system. In practice, meritocracy tends towards oligarchy.

One of the most difficult balancing acts of open, modern societies is seldom articulated: namely, how to constrain our partial cognitive meritocracies in a way that prevents disproportionate levels of status and wealth from going to high-cognitive-ability jobs without at the same time disincentivizing the cleverest and most ambitious. To some extent intelligence should be its own reward, but the contribution some of the most talented people make requires some special recognition.

The pleasure of mastering a task and performing it as well as you are able is available to people of all abilities. It is properly the case that more complex and difficult tasks, such as designing a building or helping to invent a new drug, will receive, and deserve to receive, more esteem and reward than delivering parcels or cleaning offices.

But it is also the case that a significant proportion of jobs that require high levels of academic qualification are demonstrably less useful and productive than many low-qualification jobs. Can we really argue that the work of a junior account manager in a financial PR firm is more useful than a bus driver or an adult care worker? Moreover, many jobs in law, finance, and other highly remunerated professions are often zero-sum: one individual or corporation wins and another loses. Public welfare has not been enhanced.

A successful society must balance the tension between the *inequality of esteem* that arises from open competition for highly rewarded jobs and the ethos of *equality of esteem* that flows from democratic citizenship. It is a tension that pits economic inequality against political equality.

A democratic society that wants to avoid a powerful undercurrent of resentment must sufficiently value and reward a broad range of achievement embracing both cognitive and noncognitive aptitudes and must provide meaning and respect for people who cannot—or do not want to—achieve in the examination room and professional career market. After all, half the population must always by definition be in the bottom half of the cognitive-ability spectrum, or indeed any spectrum you care to choose.

In recent years we have failed to get the balance right. Indeed, it may be the case that industrial societies, for all their failings, were better at distributing status and self-respect, especially for men, than the postindustrial societies we have become.

For many people on the left, this is mainly a problem of income and wealth inequality that can be solved by more redistribution and greater investment in education. Yet, despite noisy claims to the contrary, income inequality has not been rising sharply in many of the countries, including Brexit Britain, where there has been the biggest pushback against the cognitive class status quo.[2] If income inequality is the driving force behind political alienation and national populism, how come it is also thriving in the most equal societies on the planet: in Scandinavia?

It is true that slow or nonexistent wage growth is harder to bear when a small minority, most notably those in the financial industries, seem insulated from austerity. And thanks to the rise and rise in house values in certain parts of rich countries there is a lottery aspect to wealth distribution, in the United Kingdom one in five baby boomers is worth £1 million ($1.2 million) or more[3]—while younger people struggle to get on the housing ladder.

But this misses an even bigger though less measurable story about esteem and how valued people feel in the world. Angus Deaton, the

Nobel Prize–winning economist, who has pioneered the work on "deaths of despair" in the United States (suicides and deaths from drug and alcohol abuse), says he is struck by how *little* money has to do with such deaths. Recent happiness research, similarly, finds income to be of little significance in levels of well-being.

I call myself a social democrat and would like to live in a fairer and more equal society. But I think a big part of our problem lies in the undervaluing of everything that is not cognitively complex. If we attached more value, both in terms of prestige and income, to the caregivers and the skilled trades, income would naturally spread more evenly across society and economic growth would be more consistent and stable.

Western rationalist philosophy, from Plato to Descartes, reinforced by Christianity, has tended to privilege the mind as the source of immutable truth and understanding and looked down upon the body as the source of irrational appetite and moral inconstancy. For this reason embodied, emotional labor like nursing and care for the young and old has suffered lower prestige, along with the fact that they are overwhelmingly female occupations.

And all too often, cognitive ability and meritocratic achievement is confused with moral worth. The Latin root of "meritocracy"—*meritum*, for "merit"—means worthy of praise. It creeps into the language of everyday life. Newspapers are far more likely to highlight the accidental death of a promising twenty-two-year-old medical student than a twenty-two-year-old hairdresser. And how often, when you hear someone describing positively a new friend or work colleague, will they say before anything else, "Oh, he/she is so smart"? How often do you hear people described as generous or wise?

There's also a clear trend in modern politics to place special value on cognitive skills. High cognitive or analytical ability and success in the knowledge economy correlates strongly with support for the modern liberal virtues of individual autonomy, mobility, and hostility to tradition—the opposite of parochialism. Creative and intellectually gifted people tend to have an interest in the free flow of ideas across borders and boundaries. They may also have an interest in the relatively free flow of people across borders, providing them with multinational career options. These habits of mind dominate in the expanded higher-education sector of modern societies making, it hard for highly educated people to understand small-*c* conservatives.

"Anywheres" and "Somewheres"

This was one of the themes of my last book, *The Road to Somewhere: The Populist Revolt and the Future of Politics*, in which I described the value divides in British society, revealed starkly by the Brexit vote. On the one hand is the group I describe as the "Anywheres." They make up about 25 to 30 percent of the population, are well educated (mainly with at least an undergraduate degree), often live far from their parents, tend to favor openness and autonomy, and are comfortable with social fluidity and novelty.

On the other hand is a larger group of people I call the "Somewheres." They make up about half of the population, are less well educated, are more rooted, and value security and familiarity. They place a much greater emphasis on group attachments (local and national) than the Anywheres. (There is also an in-betweener group who share the two worldviews almost equally.)

Anywheres are generally comfortable with social change because they have "achieved identities," a sense of themselves derived from educational and career achievements, which allows them to fit in pretty much, well, *anywhere*. Somewheres, on the other hand, tend to have "ascribed identities," rooted more in place or group, which means that they are more easily discomforted by rapid change to those places and groups.

The Anywhere-Somewhere divide is very loose and fuzzy and does not map neatly onto the high-low cognitive ability divide. There are Anywheres of below-average cognitive ability and Somewheres of very high cognitive ability. In any case, as we shall see, there is some disagreement about what cognitive ability actually is and whether it is well captured in IQ tests or exams. Most of us know highly able people who have been poor at passing exams, and people with impressive academic credentials who appear dim.

Both the Anywhere and Somewhere worldviews are decent and legitimate, but the values and priorities of Anywheres have come to dominate modern politics and all mainstream political parties. And the Anywhere answer to everything from social mobility to improved productivity has been the same: more academic higher education in the quintessentially Anywhere institution of the modern university.

The Anywhere-Somewhere divide has certainly been exacerbated by the narrow focus on cognitive ability of recent decades. Yet, as David Lucas, the children's author and illustrator, has persuasively argued, society needs the cognitive skills of the knowledge economy, but we also need the craft skills of artisans, technicians, and the skilled trades, the imagination of artists, and the emotional intelligence of those in caring jobs.[4] He observes that the chronic undervaluing of Hand and Heart skills has unbalanced our societies and alienated millions of people. It also lurks beneath the surface of many contemporary crises, from mental health to recruitment problems in nursing and adult care.

Of course, bright people from whatever background should travel as far as their talents will take them, and, for many of the very brightest young people, attending an elite research university is the most appropriate way to nurture their abilities. There are also many other people, some smart and creative, whose intelligence manifests itself in a nonacademic way, who are not suited to higher education, and would do better going straight into jobs.

But today's American, British, and indeed European "dreams" have become too narrowly defined as going to university and into a professional job. This isn't surprising when in the United States 93 percent of congresspeople and 99 percent of senators hold at least bachelor degrees, compared to a national US average of 32 percent, and more than 90 percent of British MPs are graduates, up from less than half in the 1970s.

Politicians of all stripes make the same point. In his celebrated speech about inequality at Osawatomie, Kansas, President Obama said that "a higher education is the surest route to the middle class." Left Democrats like Bernie Sanders and Elizabeth Warren go even further and demand "college for all."

Not everyone can be a winner, however you design the game. In some fields such as law, medicine, technology, and some corners of business, "winner-takes-all" markets have provided exceptional rewards to exceptional people—people like Mark Zuckerberg, Jeff Bezos, Elon Musk—who have both high cognitive skills and practical knowledge of something that gives them a big first-mover advantage in new digital markets.

Below them is a wider group of highly educated—and highly credentialized—people from top universities who have the intelligence and personality attributes to propel them into the top layer of jobs.

Another level down is what one might call the rank and file of the cognitive class, the mass elite. These are people who have, in recent years, been directed into the expanded higher-education sector by parents, teachers, financial incentives, and, too often, by the lack of other post-school options (at least in the United Kingdom and United States). In the United Kingdom there are now more graduates than nongraduates among the under-thirties. Many have earned valuable qualifications and launched successful professional careers, yet too many others find themselves with degrees of little value in jobs with only high school graduate cognitive requirements (and student debts to pay off).

It is not clear that people in these last two groups are necessarily cleverer than the average citizen. After all, the majority of people achieve average or above-average scores on IQ-type tests. Their entry into the cognitive class is just as much attributable to background, social convention, and the character traits—self-discipline, application, and so on—that make academic success possible. Nevertheless, they often acquire expectations of professional status that, especially in the case of the mass elite group, are not satisfied by the relatively routine jobs they often go into.

Studying Sanskrit or *Middlemarch* at university can be a personally enriching experience, but, looked at through another lens, many university degrees, especially in the humanities, are not so much about what you know but a signal to employers that you have certain attributes. And from the point of view of the individual graduate, your degree level is something that fixes you in a hierarchy above or below your peers.

Making many occupations like nursing and policing graduate-only is not necessarily wrong, but there is an element of "If you can't beat 'em, join 'em" about it: if an undergraduate degree has become the only route to respect and prestige for an occupation, then why should nurses and police officers be denied it?

But as Randall Collins, the sociologist of education, has pointed out, this can lead to a cycle of credential inflation that "could go on endlessly, until janitors need PhDs, and household workers and babysitters will be required to hold advanced degrees in household appliances and childcare."[5]

In the United Kingdom there has been an attempt in recent years to offer better options to the half of high school graduates who do not go on to university, with a training levy on bigger employers to promote apprenticeships. But in the United Kingdom, unlike in many continental European countries, it is almost impossible to compete with the prestige of the university route, and the lack of a well-trodden, properly funded, sub-university vocational/technical route has left the economy starved of essential workers. In 2017, 42 percent of UK employers said they were struggling to fill vacancies for skilled trades jobs.[6] It is a similar story in the United States.

Meanwhile, Heart jobs in social care for the elderly, early-years education, and child care continue to be undervalued and often underpaid. Most nursery workers earn around £17,000 a year and a baby-sitter, even in London, is paid about £6 an hour per child.

Today's women's equality movement has focused primarily on breaking glass ceilings and competing equally with men in the world of professional careers. It has been more ambivalent about trying to raise the status of caring and nurturing occupations, which are associated with traditionally female roles. Women now have many more opportunities than in the 1950s or 1960s and fewer are volunteering for caring roles. Not many men are picking up the slack. In part, this explains the crisis in social care and in nurse recruitment.

Of course, as noted, Head, Hand, and Heart are always interacting. The Heart and Head are combined in the modern graduate nurse who has become a quasi-doctor. And many skilled-trade Hand roles, like plumber or car mechanic or IT support worker, require cognitive diagnostic skills that are not that different from the problem-solving abilities of a medical consultant.

Belong Anywhere

Yet, Head abstraction and detachment increasingly dominate our culture. The ethos of digital giants like Google and Facebook is self-consciously unrooted and global. It is best summed up in Airbnb's oxymoronic slogan: "Belong Anywhere." The internet and social media kept us connected in the Covid-19 crisis, and even in normal times these can help friends and communities come together more easily. But the advance of digital platforms into our lives has tended to reduce opportunities for craft and the need for human contact or attachment to specific places. By contrast, it is the undervalued *embodied* skills of Hand and Heart that promote belonging and attachment.

Across the developed world, the one quality-of-life indicator that is said to be *declining* is mental health. Mental well-being depends on a sense of meaning and purpose and a feeling that we are part of something larger than ourselves, useful to and needed by others (as confirmed by happiness research). It is our attachments that give us meaning and purpose. The most powerful route to meaning is through love, mutual dependence, and serving others. In other words, the realm of the Heart.

This can apply to the Hand too. Productive work with your Hand and Head on a farm or in a bicycle repair shop produces the pleasure of being immanent, in this place and time, the awareness of being much more than a disembodied intellect, a brain in a jar. The American philosopher Matthew Crawford wrote a book—*The Case for Working with Your Hands: Or Why Office Work Is Bad for Us and Fixing Things Feels Good*—that is partly about the *intellectual* satisfaction of Hand work.

Yet, especially in the Anglo-Saxon countries, achievement, success, even happiness, have increasingly become associated with physical mobility and disconnection from presence and place, custom and practice.

The fact is that joining the world of cognitive achievers often does require geographical mobility, especially in the United Kingdom, where this is reinforced by residential universities. In a speech in 2017, Justine Greening, the United Kingdom's former secretary of state for education, said: "All the years I spent growing up in Rotherham . . . I was aiming for something better . . . a better job, owning my own home, an interesting career, a life that I found really challenging . . . I knew there was something better out there . . ."[7]

The longing to spread your wings and seek fame and fortune in the big city is a common enough impulse across all times and in all places. Yet the unselfconscious way in which a (then) British cabinet minister doubts whether it is possible for an able, ambitious person to live a fulfilled life in a town of 120,000 people that is a thirty-minute commute from Sheffield, a city of more than half a million, reveals something flawed about modern Britain. Many towns like Rotherham lose 20 to 30 percent of their brightest eighteen-year-olds every year to university. Many of them never return, exacerbating the country's geographical divisions.

The American writer Michael Lind has described this as Hubs versus Heartlands: the former are home to most of the professional class and are where high-end business and professional services are located; the latter are where you find most goods production and mass services. The Hubs are socially liberal, home to most ethnic minorities, and astonishingly unequal: the gap between richest and poorest in New York City is comparable to that of Swaziland.[8]

The Heartlands are particularly neglected in Britain thanks to an over-mighty capital city, but there are similar patterns in parts of the ex-industrial United States, France (where the *gilets jaunes* [yellow vests] movement was a cry for recognition by the French heartland), and Germany, especially the former East Germany. (The so-called red wall of traditionally Labour seats that turned Tory in the 2019 UK election were Heartland seats; the Hubs remained mainly Labour.)

Peter Lampl, of the United Kingdom's social mobility charity the Sutton Trust, says that "it is often those who are most mobile who are most likely to find success" and wants to encourage more people from lower socioeconomic groups to enjoy what a Sutton Trust report refers to as the "migration premium."[9] But not everyone wants or needs to uproot themselves. Even if they did, there are limits on how many people can rise up into the cognitive class. Yet all of us need to feel we have a valued place in society from where we can participate and contribute even if we are not mobile high achievers.

As Joan C. Williams pointed out in her book *White Working Class: Overcoming Class Cluelessness in America* for many perfectly able working class people "their dream is not to join the upper middle class with its different culture but to stay true to their own values in their own communities, just with more money."[10] And physical mobility has in fact been declining sharply in the United States in recent decades. Michael Lind, in his book *The New Class War*, says that 57 percent of Americans have never lived outside their home state and 37 percent have never lived anywhere but their hometown. And according to an Upshot analysis published in the *New York Times* in 2015 the typical American adult lives only 18 miles from his or her mother.[11] The number of people crossing a county boundary for work has halved since the 1950s and now stands at just 4 percent of the working population.[12]

seventy years. I will also sketch out some of the heated debates about the nature of cognitive ability, how it is distributed, and whether it is properly measured in IQ tests.

The book will trace my own journey, too, from a leftish journalist who saw politics mainly through the prism of economic motivations—and for whom data was key—to my growing sense, in the last decade or so, of people's need for meaning and recognition, and the power of emotion and storytelling, in our politics and daily lives. As the Israeli historian Yuval Noah Harari has put it, in the modern world we exchanged meaning for power. But too many people feel they have lost meaning without acquiring power.

Questions of value underpin all these arguments. What is human worth? What is cultural worth? As Jonathan Sacks, the United Kingdom's former chief rabbi, has complained, without God we have increasingly adopted a utilitarian and economic definition of human worth, and questions of meaning and value have been relegated to the private sphere.

One reason why the language and methods of cognitive assessment have swept all before it in recent years is because they appear to make selecting people fair and easy to measure. Indeed, one of the reasons for the academic drift in education is that it is easier to mark and measure *written* tests than tests of manual skill or speaking ability.

This means that people with reasonable ability in writing skills and a university degree are often preferred even in forms of employment, such as a manager in a department store, suitable to someone with high social intelligence or so-called domain-specific skills derived from long experience of doing one thing.

Is a better balance between Head, Hand, and Heart achievable? Yes. Human norms and values lie behind the market signals of supply and demand, and they can change with surprising speed as we may witness in the aftermath of the Covid-19 crisis. In most European countries at least 40 percent of the economy is under direct or indirect public control (the figure is a bit less in the United States), and the corporate sector is sensitive to shifts in public attitudes and values. Consider the way in which environmental or gender equality concerns have impacted the business plans of big corporations in recent decades.

One of the forces driving change is political pressure from voters who don't share the interests of the cognitive classes. And there are other trends that suggest the Head will soon face a more even contest with Hand and Heart.

A dystopian trend was suggested by American journalist Nicholas Carr in his book *The Shallows: What the Internet Is Doing to Our Brains*, in which he argued that we are all being made dumber by the Internet.[13] Carr argued that sustained exposure to the Internet is reordering our synapses in ways that make us crave novelty and struggle to focus. This may bring improvements in some fields, but overall it means significant losses in linguistic facility, memory, and concentration.

Consider, too, that when people retire, they invariably engage in something embodied and rooted: a sport or a hobby that involves making something. Similarly, consider the centrality of sport and acting/singing celebrity in our public culture. Although these activities often require significant cognitive ability, they are rooted in Hand and Heart—closer to craft or artisanal skills than essay writing/analytical ability. And still a way out of the working class for men is the skilled physicality of becoming a sportsman, and for women it is beauty: the working-class schoolgirl spotted by the modeling agency or entering the world of stylists, high-end hairdressers, Instagram influencers, and so on.

In fact, human leisure, recreation, and ritual are almost all Hand and Heart based, though with significant aspects of Head too. Artisanal skills are also being rediscovered in some corners of the economy, especially in food and drink production, often by affluent young professionals.

Indeed, a shift away from Head and toward Hand and Heart seems to be programmed into many of the biggest social and economic trends: in the knowledge economy's declining appetite for all but the most able knowledge workers; the growing concern for place and environmental protection, including more labor-intensive organic farming; and the inevitable expansion of care functions of various kinds in an aging society. These are trends that are likely to be reinforced by the Covid-19 crisis, which revealed that most of the "key workers" who support our daily lives were Hand and Heart workers, mainly people without university degrees.

There is one very big fact that modern politics will need to confront in the next decade. Political parties of both the center-left and center-right have taken as axiomatic that modern society will see a continuing expansion of secure, middle-class, professional graduate jobs. Both education and social mobility policy are based on this assumption. Yet it is almost certainly wrong.

The knowledge economy does not need an ever-growing supply of knowledge workers. (See Chapter Nine.) It still needs a top layer of the cognitively most able and original, but much of the work required of middle ranking professionals is already substantially routinized, a kind of digital Taylorism.

The American economist Paul Krugman spotted this back in 1996. Writing for the *New York Times* but imagining himself looking back from one hundred years in the future, he saw that manipulating information was going to lose its value: "The long-ago prophets of the information age seem to have forgotten basic economics . . . A world awash in information is one in which information has very little market value. In general, when the economy becomes extremely good at doing something, that activity becomes less, rather than more, important."[14]

According to the British academics Phillip Brown and Hugh Lauder, the proportion of jobs in big corporations requiring a significant application of cognitive skill and judgment is in sharp decline, with as few as 10 to 15 percent of staff having "permission to think." And it is precisely the more routinized aspects of professional work in the law, accountancy, medicine, public administration, and so on that will in the near future be vulnerable to both artificial intelligence and to being exported to low-wage economies. It is much easier for an algorithm to replace a mid-level accountant than a garbage collector or a child-care giver.

This suggests that the rapid expansion of the traditional university sector over the past thirty years is likely to stop and go into reverse. Already in the United Kingdom nearly one-third of graduates are working in nongraduate jobs five years after graduating (the percentage is similar in the United States) and the graduate pay premium over those who don't go to university is dwindling to almost nothing for young men from non-elite universities. The disappointment of a substantial section of young people who felt that they had been promised entry, via higher education, into a secure, high-status world of professional accomplishment is one of the factors behind Labour's shift to the left in the United Kingdom and the Democrats' shift to the left in the United States.

The neglect of higher Hand skills, especially in the United Kingdom and the United States, will have to be reversed. Britain in the last two decades has overproduced general bachelor's degrees and basic apprenticeships and neglected the technical skills that are still required to make the world function smoothly. In the United Kingdom this has partly been obscured by free movement of people from the EU, which has helped to plug the gap.

Similar trends are observable in the United States, though less so in continental Europe, especially in Germany, Austria, and the Netherlands, where employer-based vocational training remains strongly embedded. Even in Germany, however, there has been a sharp rise in university participation in the past decade.

Automation has been cutting mainly blue-collar jobs, but artificial intelligence is now coming for the more routinized end of professional jobs. The disruption experienced by relatively well-educated professionals could lead to a new sympathy for people performing Hand and Heart work, partly because many former accountants and lawyers will find themselves doing those jobs. The educated people who voted against populism will be far more open to reallocating status when automation has abolished their jobs, as Richard Baldwin predicts in *The Globotics Upheaval: Globalization, Robotics, and the Future of Work.*

At the same time, the pay, conditions, and training of Hand and Heart jobs are likely to improve because of the simple operation of supply and demand. And most of these everyday face-to-face service and care jobs, from car mechanic to mail deliverer and nursery nurse, cannot be exported or done by a robot.

Low-skill work is not, as widely predicted by economists, disappearing. In Gordon Brown's penultimate budget speech as chancellor of the exchequer in 2006, he predicted there would be just 600,000 low-skill jobs in the United Kingdom by 2020. Depending on how one defines "low-skill," there are likely to be at least 8 million low-skill jobs in the British economy next year.

Indeed, one of the explanations for the slowdown in productivity growth in rich economies in recent years, associated with the theory of economist William Baumol, is that workers no longer needed in the more automated sectors end up in low-productivity jobs. Or as the *Economist* put it: "Technological progress pushes employment into the sectors most resistant to productivity growth. Eventually, nearly everyone may have jobs that are valued for their inefficiency: as concert musicians, or artisanal cheesemakers, or members of the household staff of the very rich."[15] Or, indeed, as medical staff in an intensive-care unit.

People will always be needed to clean offices, work in supermarkets and cafés, deliver things, work in fields, and fix your car and computer. Digital platforms like Amazon may be reducing jobs in shops, but they are creating them in warehouses and delivery firms. Some of these functions will be automated and some can be done by immigrants, allowing rich country workers to move up the employment chain. But given the unpopularity of large-scale immigration, especially in Europe, it makes more sense to try to make these jobs more attractive to national citizens.

There is an unavoidable element of drudgery to some of these roles, but if they are decently paid and people feel fairly managed, respected, and useful (as many delivery drivers and supermarket staff did during the Covid-19 crisis), they can provide sociable, purposive activity without necessarily providing meaning and identity in the way that professional jobs can—but people find meaning in other areas of life: family, sport, hobbies, and so on.

The final relevant trend—one that will surely raise the status of Heart work—is linked to two irreversible social facts: the increased numbers of older people, who will need significant levels of care in their final years—2020 is the first year in human history when the number of people over age sixty-five exceeds the number of children under age five—and the more prominent place of women in the public realm.

The #MeToo movement, which exposed the predatory behavior of men in the entertainment industry, politics, and elsewhere, didn't happen thirty years ago because there were simply too few women in positions of authority in the media and politics.

One of the most important questions in developed countries over the next generation will be whether women's greater political weight will be wielded to increase the limited market power of women now doing most Heart jobs. The women doing these jobs, many of whom work part-time or as agency staff, usually have strong obligations to those they care for, so they cannot easily apply pressure on those who employ them. Strikes by care home workers are rare.

Professional women have successfully de–gender segregated the upper end of the labor market in areas like medicine and law, but the middle and bottom end of the labor market remains highly gender segregated in most rich countries. Will the greater power of highly educated professional women in due course mean a $25-an-hour minimum wage in adult social care? Or are such professionals too detached from the interests of the kind of women who might be employed part-time in a nursing home?

The Anywhere, liberal professional worldview is public realm focused and tends to look down on domesticity. Yet it is hard to imagine an upward revaluation of care work in the public economy without valuing it more in the home, too, whether it is done by women or men. Britain and America are outliers among rich countries in their laissez-faire approach to support for families with children, and both experience high levels of family breakdown, one big factor behind the increase in deaths of despair in the United States.

Placing greater value on care, whether of young children or elderly parents, in the private realm raises the question of who does the caring. Many women feel, reasonably, that they already perform the burdensome "double shift" at work and home and want men to bear a fairer share of domestic care. This does seem to be happening, albeit rather slowly, but survey evidence in the United Kingdom also shows that most women with children would like to spend more time at home caring for preschool children if they could afford to, and work either part-time or not at all.[16] And yet family and gender policy, especially in the United States and United Kingdom, focuses on making it as easy as possible for both parents *to spend as little time as possible with their families.*

Every day in rich countries there are more hours spent caring, in its many forms, than in any other activity. And caring work is some of the most emotionally and physically draining labor of all. Yet as the writer Madeleine Bunting, author of *Labours of Love: The Crisis of Care*, argues, the ethos of care does not sit easily with the ethos of an individualistic, achievement-driven society. Care, especially in the private realm, is about duty to others, and its results are sometimes nebulous and hard to measure. (See Chapter Eight.)

There is some potential for the use of smart technologies in elderly care, with more remote monitoring and so on (and this could draw more men into the sector). But most caring jobs cannot easily be automated or performed by machines. Even in aging Japan, with its antipathy to mass immigration, Filipino caregivers are preferred to robots and are gradually being welcomed in larger numbers.

The rise of cognitive-analytical ability—Head work—as a measure of economic and social success, combined with the hegemony of
cognitive-class political interests, has led to the current great unbalanc-
ing of Western politics. The disaffection of large minorities, even majorities, in many countries is linked intimately to the declining status and
self-respect attached to work associated with the Hand and the Heart.

Status is a slippery concept: it is both highly subjective—how
we feel about ourselves and where we think we stand in the eyes of
others—and objective: people in higher professional jobs (a surgeon, a
lawyer) and celebrities of most kinds are almost universally recognized
as having more of it. And status usually follows the money (with some
exceptions, such as in the cases of priests or artists), although they
can be more or less closely aligned at different times.

The substantial element of subjectivity in the concept of status
makes it hard to measure the decline that I believe has been suffered
by many people in postindustrial societies, although I have grappled
with it in Chapter Seven.

Income inequality is easier to measure, and many people, especially
on the left, find it more comfortable to focus on because it points the
finger of blame at the rich and big business. But the preferences of the
cognitive class—especially the "creative class" cohort in the arts and
universities—for openness, autonomy, and change is also a source of
discomfort and conflict.

There is a broad agreement in developed societies about the importance of individual freedom and social justice, although there is also
fierce disagreement about the exact contours of both. There is much
less consensus about cultural-psychological issues—the security, status, respect, and identity themes—that shape how people feel about
themselves in daily life. For example, some people on the left would
question whether it is legitimate for someone to feel discomforted by
a neighborhood rapidly changed by immigration.

It is these psychological issues that cause so many people to feel
unmoored from a sense of meaning and belonging—the same people

who tell pollsters that the past was better than the present. A renewed respect for aptitudes connected to Hand and Heart as well as Head—a triumvirate instead of a cognitive meritocracy—is at least part of the answer to their discomfort.

Let's aim for a society as open and mobile as possible but not restrict our political ambition to designing a better ladder up. Instead, our politics should place more emphasis on a wider spread of respect, dignity, and regard, and on offering a valued place to people who play by the rules but do not excel cognitively. We need, in other words, to treat people democratically. It is an adjustment our democracies are now demanding.

Chapter Two

The Rise of the Cognitive Class

Recruits should be segregated at entry into a hierarchy of grades, ranging from clerical officers who conduct routine tasks, through to those who provide policy advice to ministers . . . Promotion should be on merit, not preferment, patronage, purchase, or length of service.

Conclusions of the Northcote-Trevelyan report
into civil service reform in Britain (1853)

In the rich, liberal societies of Europe and North America, many of the things that we value have become less self-evident. We are free to value radically different things from our fellow citizens, even from our close relatives (especially across generations). In the United Kingdom an institution like the BBC increasingly struggles to speak for, and to, the whole country. In the United States, a trusted national media voice no longer exists

But there are still plenty of assumptions that most people hold in common and are reinforced in the public and political conversation forming the collective "common sense" of a society—albeit one that is constantly, imperceptibly shifting.

This is sometimes hard to be precise about until an unexpected event reveals something that has been evolving below the surface. I am writing this in the middle of the Covid-19 crisis, so it is too early tell what, if anything, that will reveal, but the reaction to the death of Princess Diana revealed a country that was far more emotional and far less wedded to the stiff upper lip than most people, including most British people, expected.

The Brexit and Trump protest votes in 2016 were another crystal-lizing moment revealing not so much a shift in values as a value *divide* based on different attitudes and intuitions, arising in part from differ-ent experiences of education and the processes of cognitive selection. About 75 percent of people with minimal educational qualifications voted for Brexit, and about the same proportion with degrees or more voted to remain.[1] Similar divides were reflected in the Trump vote.

It is the central claim of this book that the protest vote was in part an understandable reaction to a profound status shift that has been gathering pace for over fifty years, one that has bestowed an increasing amount of recognition on cognitive-related aptitudes and jobs—what I call the Head—and quietly sucked it away from most others, above all those related to the Hand and the Heart.

This has been happening in most rich societies as the pyramid-shaped industrial society, with its large number of people doing man-ual jobs or working full-time in the home, has given way to a more lightbulb-shaped postindustrial society and a more knowledge-based economy.

Until recently almost everyone worked in order to support their family. Work was a means to an end found in the domestic realm. But in the latter part of the twentieth century, work, especially higher-status professional work, came to be a source of esteem and self-worth and self-expression—an end in itself.

This has coincided with rising concern for gender equality that has focused on enabling women to compete more equally with men in the public sphere of work and the professions. This has contributed to a devaluing of the private realm and the traditional caring func-tions for the young and elderly, mainly carried out by women. The proportion of families in which one parent stays at home full-time when the children are young is one-quarter in the United Kingdom and only slightly higher in the United States.[2] (The unexpected and prolonged refamiliarization with the private realm as a result of the Covid-19 lockdown came as an unwelcome shock to many people.)

In recent decades education systems have expanded, the years people spend in school have increased, and a quasi-meritocratic education system—above all in the modern university—has become the main distributor of status and position.

It is true that some of the richest and most powerful modern businesspeople, such as Bill Gates, dropped out of higher education, but the ethos of these "cognitive entrepreneurs" is certainly not hostile to the increased status of "nerdy" cognitive aptitudes—in fact, quite the opposite. Digital giants such as Google, Facebook, and Amazon recruit their senior people overwhelmingly from elite universities. Indeed universities are increasingly complaining that they are losing their best researchers, especially in AI, to Big Tech.

Postindustrial Disenchantment

This cognitive shift is a surprisingly recent thing in developed societies. It is hard to speak with any confidence about the mentalities or levels of contentment of people in earlier eras. But it may be that industrial society, especially in its most recent phase in the second half of the twentieth century—including democratic equality and welfare states—was better at distributing self-respect and status than today's cognitively stratified postindustrial society, especially for men. We are richer and freer but often more adrift and resentful.

The movement from the country to the town in Britain in the early nineteenth century was often traumatic and involved an increase in suffering and reduced longevity. But life soon became better in the town than the countryside. Indeed, 1845, the year that Friedrich Engels published his description of industrial misery, *The Condition of the Working Class in England*, was just about the point when things started to improve.

Improved public hygiene, the spread of literacy, and the arrival of cheap food from Australia and the Americas were just three ways in which lives were transformed for the better in the second half of the nineteenth century. This was not just about incomes and living conditions; new forms of meaning and self-respect soon established themselves too. The urban identity itself quickly came to be seen as superior to the rural one; indeed, the term "peasant" was soon adopted as a term of abuse, and there was no discernible movement back from the town to the country. New forms of skilled and semiskilled work in the factories and workshops conferred status and respect on both men and women.

Urbanization was associated with education and betterment, as opposed to what Marx called "the idiocy of rural life." Therefore it is no surprise that when, in Britain, the franchise was extended to the ordinary man (at this stage not the ordinary woman), it was the urban householder who was entrusted with the vote almost two decades before his rural cousin.

For all of the external upheaval in the early decades of industrialization, people's inner lives and moral universes often remained surprisingly unchanged. There was significant continuity in traditional understandings of the world and in social and gender roles.

Christianity remained the central belief system for most people, although it took new forms in the expanding urban centers in Low Church Methodism and radical forms of Protestantism. Women worked outside the home in larger numbers but family life was strengthened with the movement into towns as rates of illegitimacy fell throughout the nineteenth century, at least in Britain.[3] In the United Kingdom and the United States the multigenerational extended family remained the most common form well into the twentieth century. In 1850, 75 percent of Americans older than sixty-five lived with relatives; by 1990 only 18 percent did.[4]

It is in the nature of class stratified societies for status—meaning your place in the pecking order of social respect—to be a powerful *given* that few people can escape. This restricts human opportunity but also gives people an explanation for their position in the hierarchy that has little bearing on their abilities or intelligence. In the relatively immobile class society of the nineteenth and much of the twentieth century, if you failed to rise from the working class into more genteel society, it was no reflection on your own aptitudes; it was just the way things were.

Immobility can also consolidate a sense of group solidarity and make a project of *collective* advance, such as trade unionism or socialism, seem more relevant than individual aspiration. Trapped in steerage together, passengers will probably develop a sense of common interest. Given a ladder to the upper decks, and people are more likely to elbow each other out of the way.

And this is partly what has happened in our postindustrial societies. The main distributor of status and income is *individual* educational achievement, and the ethos, if not the reality, of the society is open and meritocratic. Those who do not enter into the cognitive class by taking A levels at school (or graduating from high school in the United States, or taking the *baccalauréat* in France or the *Abitur* in Germany) and going into higher education have, in the main, more restricted opportunities and lower social status than those who do. And this lower status is partly the result of their own cognitive limitations, or at least is widely perceived to be so by society and by many of the individuals themselves.

Some people have the resilience to avoid feelings of failure and may achieve a degree of success despite being in society's slow lane, but many others internalize a feeling of low self-respect that creates a pervasive sense of anxiety and uselessness.

There are several compounding problems that contribute to postindustrial disenchantment.

- Postindustrial society has eroded the compensating belief systems provided by religion, which recognizes you for your moral character, not your ability, and (in theory) sees everyone as equally valued in the eyes of God. It has done the same to the traditional roles in the private realm—such as male breadwinner or nurturing mother and homemaker—which constrains opportunity, especially for women, but also confers meaning and purpose. The institutions that have historically accepted you as a member unconditionally—family, church, nation—are all weakened in a freer, more mobile and more individualistic society. Achieved identities based on educational and career success have eclipsed ascribed identities based on attachment to place and group. (Of course, those are not always good roles: the serfs of premodern Europe or the Dalit—"Untouchables"—in India.)

- Postindustrial society elevates the values and priorities of the highly educated to a more dominant position, and those views tend to be secular, individualistic, anti-traditional, and anti-authority. Postindustrial modernity is often fluid and disorientating—more wealth, but less meaning, as Yuval Noah Harari says—and it is not so easy for some people to adapt to.

- Since the advent of mass higher education, we now have a *single* route into a *single* dominant cognitive class. This is a problem that I mentioned earlier. And although the graduate cognitive class is now much bigger, more open, and more democratic than it was fifty years ago, it passes through a narrower funnel: one goes to a good university and then into a professional middle-class career. Until recently there were many more routes to achievement and respect. There were many short ladders up, some of which led to taller ones. There was a working-class elite, for example, in the trade unions, friendly societies, and parties of the left, and different regional elites in provincial cities. At a workplace level, meaningful progression from below was possible without higher educational qualifications.

- It looks increasingly likely in today's economy that the cognitive class, at least in occupational terms, is going to stop growing. This will undermine the central promise of developed societies that everyone can, and should, become a middle-class professional. We will continue to need a layer of highly talented people who write the relevant software and provide the top professionals in everything from law and medicine to engineering, design, and finance. But the next round of AI is going to cut a swath through the middle ranks of professional life and potentially create an even bigger status gulf between the most able and the rest.

- The frame of comparison that people use to evaluate their lives has become much wider. People used to compare themselves in terms of wealth or talents of various kinds to people in their own village. Even after urbanization, people in a stratified class structure would mainly compare themselves to people a few rungs above or below them on the social ladder. For many, the shop steward, the supervisor, or the lay preacher was a figure of respect and an achievable model for emulation. With mass media—especially television and radio—and now social media, it is harder for people to avoid comparing themselves unfavorably with the brightest, most beautiful, and most talented in the world, which is thought to be one of the causes of rising mental stress.

People seek meaning in their lives and a sense of being useful to others as well as material comfort, freedom, and justice. It is not desirable or possible to go back to a past when social horizons and life chances were far more limited, but a recognition of some of the merits of earlier eras may help us to perceive the biases and failings of today's postindustrial achievement society.

The idea of being a successful or unsuccessful person is a comparatively recent one outside of the elites, and even now most people do not think of their lives in these terms. Yet, in more fluid, individualistic, competitive, and transparent societies, it is increasingly hard to protect oneself from such status judgments.

The sorting house for higher-status opportunity has increasingly become higher education, with a university degree serving as the passport to recognition. Theoretical or abstract reasoning, as opposed to merely empirical knowledge of facts or practical intelligence, is the aptitude that increasingly determines life chances. Practical "knowing how" has traditionally been seen as distinct from, and inferior to, abstract "knowing that," in the distinction made famous by the philosopher Gilbert Ryle, especially in England.

Our societies depend now not only on relatively high levels of general education, especially in literacy and math, but also on a significant number of specialist cadres in scientific, technological, legal as well as generalist analytical and administrative fields. And the proportion of Head jobs has grown disproportionately relative to Hand and Heart jobs in the course of the twentieth century.

Head work and professional jobs are not exactly synonymous, and as we will see later many apparently professional jobs involve relatively little cognitive ability or independent judgment. Nonetheless, "professional" status does act as a rough proxy for Head, so it is worth looking at how the numbers of professional jobs have expanded in the last two hundred years.

In Britain in 1841 it is estimated that just 2.5 percent of adults were in higher or lower professions, rising to 4.3 percent in 1911. The proportion for France in 1911 was roughly the same as in Britain, and for the United States it was slightly higher at 6.2 percent. By 2018 those numbers had risen to over 30 percent in Britain, 36 percent in the United States, 38 percent in France, and 41 percent in Germany.[5]

The world has become more complex and abstract, and it makes sense that those with the greatest facility for hypothetical reasoning and symbolic thinking should dominate the most important and prestigious positions. But politics and the wider culture are sending the signal that this cognitive revolution has gone too far for the countervailing democratic ethos of equal human worth and self-respect to bear: we have reached "peak Head."

Rather reassuringly, about 70 percent of us are in the middle range of the cognitive ability spectrum as measured by IQ tests. Yet, as already noted, half the population will always, by definition, be in the bottom half of that spectrum, and a system that rewards too generously the top 10 to 15 percent of the most cognitively blessed will run up against a mass democratic resentment.

Before considering the cognitively blessed more closely, we need to pause to consider some history and some definitions. The next section of this chapter examines the historical emergence of the cognitive class, in Britain and the United States in particular, and its methods of selection. The following chapter then considers the arguments about what cognitive ability actually is, how it is measured, how innate it is, and what this means for meritocracy and social mobility. The next three chapters will then look at the consolidation of cognitive domination in recent decades in the worlds of education, the economy, and politics.

Professions and Universities

Social selection based on intelligence rather than manual skill or physical strength or beauty has existed from the beginning of human society itself. Counselors to the powerful were not chosen for their looks or their athletic prowess. In Christian Europe, advisers such as Cardinal Thomas Wolsey, the son of an Ipswich butcher, emerged from ecclesiastical selection systems. In China more than 2,000 years ago, the Han dynasty introduced competitive exams, testing knowledge of Confucian principles of government, to determine entry to the higher bureaucracy.

Some professions that require a high degree of abstract reasoning, such as physician, lawyer, priest, teacher, architect, and diplomat, have long histories stretching back into the mists of time. In early modern Europe most of these roles were still connected to the church, and most people seeking advancement in them took holy orders too.

But gradually the professions secularized, and in the twelfth century the clergy were prohibited from practicing law and medicine in England. This was an important step. Law was the first organized secular profession with judges appointed by the crown and the Inns of Court established in the fourteenth century.

The Royal College of Physicians of London was established in 1518, but training and selection by examination was not institutionalized in medicine or law until the nineteenth century. In the meantime both professions—and indeed most skilled occupations—adopted a system of pupilage, with students of medicine or law becoming the pupil of an established practitioner.[6]

The Enlightenment in the eighteenth century carved out a bigger role for human reason in the most developed societies of Europe. It helped to challenge and weaken traditional religious belief and opened the intellectual space for modern science and technology to thrive. Knowledge was no longer derived from ancient texts but could be *created*.

Two hundred years later, in the year that I was born, 1956, cognitive selection via higher education still played only a minor role in the lives of most people in rich countries. It was still possible then to walk straight into an apprenticeship or a decently paying job without any exams or other qualifications to one's name. And the more able and ambitious could rise up the ranks by supplementing basic education with qualifications gained at night school or other part-time study.

Late entry into professional jobs—accountant, lawyer, engineer—was commonplace. British banks used to recruit mainly from high school graduates well into the 1980s. According to the 1991 UK census, fewer than half of people in professional, managerial, and technical positions held college degrees.[7]

How different the world looks today with the onward march of cognitive selection for all schoolchildren, with a university degree an increasing necessity for almost all jobs in the top 40 percent of the occupational hierarchy and around one-third of all jobs in Europe and North America loosely categorized as "professional"!

In Britain this story of educational selection, even of meritocracy itself, is often seen to have begun with the publication of the Northcote-Trevelyan report on civil service reform in 1853. The Northcote-Trevelyan Report, following an earlier initiative from Thomas Babington Macaulay at the East India Company, recommended the principle of competitive exams for entry into an expanded civil service, replacing earlier systems of nomination, patronage, and even purchase of positions.

It began to be widely accepted that expertise and ability should replace patronage and nepotism—that the well-trained professional should replace the gentleman amateur, especially after the failures of the Crimean War (1853–56) and the Indian Mutiny (1857–59), both of which were seen at the time as illustrating the limits of the amateur, aristocratic ethos.

The report, which now seems like common sense, was greeted with some hostility, including from Queen Victoria herself. And at the time its most important consequence was not so much in entrenching meritocratic selection but in enabling the creation of a politically neutral senior civil service.

The principle of entry into elite jobs by competitive exam or educational qualification rather than nepotism became more common in Britain, America, and continental Europe in the second half of the nineteenth century and start of the twentieth.

The industrial revolution created a demand for technical and scientific institutions and places of learning across Europe and North America, and the second industrial revolution of the 1880s, followed by the two world wars of the first part of the twentieth century, reinforced the expansion of a scientific-technical class increasingly drawn from non-elite backgrounds.

In most countries touched by industrial takeoff, the universities initially had little to do with the training of the new scientific and technical class, and this was especially true of England, where Oxford (established in 1096) and Cambridge (established 1209) remained the *only* universities for more than six hundred years, well into the nineteenth century.

Most of the innovations associated with the first industrial revolution in Britain—from the formation of the Royal Society in 1660 to key inventions such as James Hargreaves's spinning jenny (1764) and James Watt's steam engine (1775)—had nothing to do with England's fossilized "Oxbridge duopoly." Learned societies like the Lunar Society of Birmingham were far more intellectually significant.

And although the philosopher John Locke graduated from Oxford in the mid-seventeenth century after having studied medicine, natural philosophy, and philosophy, the Enlightenment, too, had only a limited impact on the two institutions, which remained dominated by the Anglican church and the teaching of theology and the classics (with some mathematics and natural sciences) until the latter part of the nineteenth century. Both Newton in the seventeenth century and Darwin in the nineteenth century attended Cambridge, but it left little intellectual mark on either of them. In the mid-eighteenth century, Adam Smith found Oxford intellectually stifling compared with Glasgow.

There were no formal entrance examinations for Oxford or Cambridge colleges until the mid-nineteenth century, but from the early nineteenth century you had to pass an exam in order to receive a degree. In the case of Oxford you had to show a knowledge of the gospels in Greek, the Thirty-Nine Articles, and Joseph Butler's *The Analogy of Religion*.

The development of the vocational professions (apart from clergymen and civil servants) and their training and examination systems happened largely independent of the two universities.

The first half of the nineteenth century in Britain saw the establishment of the Royal College of Surgeons, the Institution of Civil Engineers, the London Law Institution (forerunner of the Law Society), the Royal Institute of British Architects, the Pharmaceutical Society of Great Britain, and the Institution of Mechanical Engineers. The 1858 Medical Act established a national register of doctors, the qualification for which was a university degree or equivalent. And the 1860s, 1870s, and 1880s saw more such bodies established: the Royal Institution of Chartered Surveyors, the Institution of Electrical Engineers, the Royal Institute of Chemistry, and the Institute of Chartered Accountants in England and Wales.[8]

These bodies were responsible for professional standards and ethics and in most cases for entry into the profession via public examination. By the 1880s exams had to be passed to become a barrister, solicitor, doctor, surgeon, clergyman, pharmacist, merchant navy officer, mining engineer, architect, chartered accountant, and many more professions. Competitive exams were also conducted for admission into the Home and Indian Civil Service and for a commission into the armed services.[9]

The story was broadly similar in the United States, with local professional associations established in the first half of the nineteenth century and national ones in the second half of the century. Curiously, despite America's reputation in the nineteenth century for a rough-and-ready social equality and a weaker class structure than Europe, it was not until 1883 that civil servants were hired on the basis of exam results.

The American openness and opportunity that so appealed to French observer Alexis de Tocqueville writing in 1835—"The first thing that strikes one in the United States is the innumerable crowd of those striving to escape from their original social position . . . Every American is eaten up with a longing to rise"—was not especially connected to educational achievement. Benjamin Franklin began his career as an ordinary apprentice.

Nevertheless, the United States did pioneer free elementary education in the middle of the nineteenth century, several decades before most European countries, and then free secondary education (normally to the age of sixteen) at the start of the twentieth century, with nearly half of the population graduating from high school by 1940. In 1944, as Britain's Education Act was catching up with America's mass secondary education system, America was pulling ahead again, with

President Roosevelt signing the GI Bill that ushered in mass *higher* education.

By the latter part of the nineteenth century and early twentieth century, academic selection and educational qualifications had become part of everyday life in much of Europe and North America, at least among the elites.

The respective roles of professional associations, universities, and the state in certifying membership of the cognitive class played out differently in different countries—similarly with the different degrees of prestige attached to the academic and the technical.

While in Britain and America, with their shared common law heritage, the formation of professional organizations was largely a bottom-up story, in Germany and France it was more top-down, with the state and universities playing a bigger role. In France this was via the elite universities, the so-called *grandes écoles* established by Napoleon and in Germany via civil service licensing. There was also more stress in those countries on technical and industrial disciplines inspired by the national goal of catching up with the first industrial pioneer over the channel in England.

In England, as we have seen, most of the important developments were happening outside higher education, which remained subject to the stranglehold of Oxford and Cambridge. The numbers attending the two universities remained tiny, with the proportion of young people remaining roughly constant between the end of the English Civil War and the end of the First World War.

Oxford and Cambridge used their political influence to stifle the creation of any rival institutions until the early nineteenth century. Mathematics was introduced at Cambridge in the eighteenth century, but Oxbridge remained for most students a sort of upper-class finishing school. Instead of a network of local universities and colleges, as in most of the rest of Europe and the United States, England had just two socially prestigious *national* seats of learning that students traveled to from across the country and then boarded at.

Yet, despite the irrelevance of Oxford and Cambridge in relation to the industrial revolution, the Enlightenment, and the development of the professions, their social and political prestige—almost all British prime ministers were educated at one or the other in the eighteenth and nineteenth centuries—allowed them to establish themselves in the latter part of the nineteenth century (when they did finally modernize) at the center of academic and educational life.

By the 1870s, Oxford and Cambridge had succumbed, like other national institutions, to the reforming zeal of the Victorian upper-class moralists. They also became more affordable for the business and professional classes, although an Oxbridge education still cost around £200 ($240) a year, more than the annual income of a manual worker. The curriculum, too, began to modernize, especially at Cambridge, which became a key center of scientific research after the foundation of the Cavendish Laboratory in 1874. The great economist Alfred Marshall started teaching economics at Cambridge in 1884, although there was no official economics course there until 1903.*

This modernization was also in response to the challenge to Oxbridge dominance from London. University College London was established by radical liberals, followers of Jeremy Bentham, in 1829 as a rational, secular, nonresidential, meritocratic alternative to conservative, Anglican, residential, privileged Oxbridge. Influenced by both German and Scottish higher education models, UCL, and later King's, required both entrance exams and graduation exams. In 1858, London University external degrees were created so anyone in the country could get a high level qualification, and in 1878 it admitted women to full degrees.

Following this breakthrough, the end of the nineteenth century and start of the twentieth century saw the establishment of several new

---

* My American grandfather eagerly signed up for one of the new economics courses at Cambridge, England, just before the First World War, only to be told that his proposed tutor at Trinity College was away for the year. Trinity suggested an alternative young economist at King's but warned that he was not "sound"; his name was John Maynard Keynes. My grandfather decided to study law instead.

"redbrick" universities serving the industrial cities of Manchester, Liverpool, Leeds, Sheffield, and Birmingham. (The more traditional, clerical, and residential University of Durham had been founded in 1832.)

The 1870 Education Act in Britain introduced free elementary schooling for the whole population for the first time, catching up with the United States, and the rest of Europe did the same around the same time (although literacy was already high in Britain and America prior to universal basic education). Secondary schooling was patchy in Britain even after the 1902 Education Act established a national system, but around this time both public schools for the wealthy and state-aided schools of various kinds started to formalize syllabuses and exams in conjunction with the universities.

This was a mainly top-down process, with the pinnacle of Oxbridge and the London universities essentially standardizing learning lower down the system to fit with their own academic ethos and requirements. It is a story that remains true to this day in England with the continuing domination of A levels in the school system, designed purely for the purpose of entry into university and academic study.

In 1873, the Oxford and Cambridge Schools Examination Board was established to administer the exams for public schools and the emerging state grammar schools. The dominance of Oxford and Cambridge was also reinforced through their scholarships for grammar school pupils, mainly to study classics.

England's historic bias against technical and vocational (Hand) education was evident not only in the universities but in the secondary schools, which established a curriculum based on the traditional public school academic model. Robert Morant, the permanent secretary at the education department at the start of the twentieth century, was an academic traditionalist who resisted attempts to introduce more vocational elements into secondary education.

There was, however, a parallel technical British tradition that worried about the educational roots of lost industrial competitiveness, especially after the Exposition Universelle in Paris in 1867 and the loss of the dyestuffs industry—an industry invented in England but developed by superior German chemists into an international monopoly. This technical tradition, often associated with protectionist thinking, had some influence too. In the late nineteenth century several official commissions expressed admiration for German technical education, and this influenced the curriculum at the new redbrick universities. It also led to the creation of several new technical colleges, in some cases opened by local authorities, and the founding of Imperial College in London.[10]

The trade unions were often hostile to technical education, preferring the time-served apprenticeship system. But a tradition of working class self-improvement and education as the route out of poverty was found in the Workers' Education Association and the idea of university "extension" colleges in the new industrial centers. Toynbee Hall was established in London's East End in 1884, to take the gospel of education to workers and artisans, and Ruskin College at Oxford was founded in 1899. But educational historian Robert Anderson points out that the ancient universities mainly failed to respond to the "yearning after knowledge of self-educated artisans" as described in Thomas Hardy's tragedy *Jude the Obscure* (1895).[11]

The tension evident in most education systems between prioritizing raising the general educational level and competence of the population and selecting an academic elite was largely resolved in favor of the latter in late nineteenth-century England. The English university system had established itself as socially exclusive, partly because it was overwhelmingly residential and therefore expensive, and national as opposed to local in character. And the pedagogical tradition was theoretical and general rather than vocational and specific—"knowing that" rather than "knowing how."

American writer Matthew Crawford describes the distinction: "[It] corresponds roughly to universal knowledge versus the kind that comes from individual experience. If you know *that* something is the case, then this proposition can be stated from anywhere. In fact, such knowledge aspires to a view from nowhere . . . Occupations based on universal, propositional knowledge are more prestigious, but they are also the kind that face competition from the whole world as book learning becomes more widely disseminated in the global economy."[12]

The higher education story in America and the rest of Europe was somewhat different from England. At the time of the Enlightenment at the end of the eighteenth and the beginning of the nineteenth century, the best universities in Europe were probably in Scotland—St Andrews and Glasgow had both been established in the fifteenth century, Edinburgh in the sixteenth—although Germany was catching up fast as the different states and principalities competed with each other to create the most prestigious seats of learning.

After Prussia's defeat by Napoleon, Wilhelm von Humboldt, the education minister, proposed a new type of university—the prototype of the modern university—that did not just teach a social elite but also undertook research. The Humboldt University of Berlin was founded in 1810 on these principles.

Meanwhile, in France, the French Revolution simply abolished the existing system of universities replacing them with the so-called *grandes écoles*, specializing in different skills such as engineering, which continue to exist today, alongside the public university system, educating much of the French higher elite, most notoriously in the tiny École Nationale d'Administration (ENA), established in 1945.

America's Ivy League emerged in colonial times partly because of the stranglehold of Oxbridge in England; Harvard was established in 1636. The Test Acts that restricted Oxford and Cambridge to members of the Church of England meant that non-Anglicans often looked to America for higher education, and in 1790, after the War of Independence, there were already nineteen institutions called "college" or "university."

The US system in the nineteenth century was decentralized and market-driven. Local civic pride and religious diversity created the incentive for a rash of smaller colleges to spring up all over the country.

As David Labaree puts it: "Colleges were founded with an eye toward civic boosterism, intended to shore up a community's claim to be a major cultural and commercial center rather than a sleepy farm town."[13] The total number of colleges in 1880 was an extraordinary 811—at a time when England had fewer than 10—but the average number of students per institution was just 130.

Some of America's great universities, like Johns Hopkins, founded on the German research university template, were already up and running at the end of the nineteenth century, but most universities avoided Oxbridge-style elitism and were middle-class institutions, relatively easy to get into and extensions of the local community. The Morrill Acts of 1862 and 1890 established American public state universities by granting land to states who used it to establish colleges. Most of the "land-grant" public colleges subsidized tuition, which further opened up higher education. Like the redbricks in England, the land-grant colleges tended to pursue a more applied curriculum than the private liberal arts colleges.

Technical and vocational education in the United States had its strong supporters but tended, as in England, to play second fiddle to academic education. In 1917 the Smith-Hughes Act gave a big boost to vocational education, including federal funding. But John Dewey, the American philosopher and educationalist, in a famous debate with "social efficiency" advocate David Snedden, was hostile to narrow skills training in favor of nurturing the intellectual capacity and critical spirit of all citizens. A version of the Dewey spirit has broadly prevailed in the United States.

In England, more than in continental Europe (or Scotland), the idea of the gentleman generalist scholar pursuing knowledge for its own sake, as described by Cardinal John Henry Newman in *The Idea of a University* or Matthew Arnold in *Culture and Anarchy*, trumped that of the vocational specialist. The generalist intellectual tradition was also reinforced by the demands of empire. Colonial administration required capable polymaths—"training the whole man," as a training manual for the Colonial Service described it—something that Germany with only a small overseas empire did not have to concern itself with.

The United States, too, had a bias toward the generalist. People should be selected for higher education "not for their suitability for specific roles but for their general worth, as if they were an updated Puritan elect," wrote Nicholas Lemann in his gripping account of the rise of the American meritocracy, *The Big Test*.[14]

But England lagged way behind Germany and the United States in sheer numbers going to university and in the numbers doing technical subjects. At the turn of the twentieth century England had six universities compared to Germany's thirty and America's several hundred. Oxford remained strongly attached to the classics: in 1900, 136 of its 297 academic fellowships were still in classics.

In the United States the shortage of labor meant more capital-intensive industry. At the end of the nineteenth and start of the twentieth century the United States roared ahead in mass production and machine tools and the engineer, and technical education enjoyed high status for a few decades. By contrast, England had a surplus of workers arriving in the cities from the depressed countryside, which helped to create a more labor-intensive economy that was less mechanized and with less prestige attaching to technical education.[15]

The United States also benefited not only from secondary education to age sixteen from the end of the nineteenth century and a tradition of excellence in engineering but also in its pioneering management and business schools.

England on the eve of the First World War had roughly 25,000 university students, compared with 60,000 in Germany and 150,000 in the United States. In 1910 there were 16,000 engineering students in German technical high schools and just 4,000 in British universities. There were 5,500 graduate chemists in Germany and just 1,500 in Britain.[16] (That said, the German population was around 25 percent larger than England's, and the US population, at 75 million, was almost twice as large.)

In England the domination of Oxbridge continued into the twentieth century; on the eve of the Second World War, the total student population had risen to 50,000, but 20 percent were accounted for by Oxford and Cambridge alone. The Oxbridge model of the residential academic community pursuing knowledge for its own sake (apart from obviously vocational courses like medicine) became the national ideal.

The so-called redbrick universities in England like the College of Science in Birmingham and Owens College in Manchester were mainly nonresidential, for local students, and sponsored by local industrialists. They taught practical subjects alien to Oxbridge, such as metallurgy and mining engineering. Yet there was never a concerted attempt to establish an alternative national ethos of higher education in the provincial universities.

Student numbers trebled in Europe between 1870 and 1914, but, with the exception of more open America, most students continued to be drawn from a tiny, almost all-male social elite. In England what they were studying, especially at the most prestigious institutions, was equipping them at best for the most traditional professions such as the law, the church, and the civil service. At the beginning of the twentieth century you needed Latin and Greek and sometimes Hebrew to get into most universities apart from the redbricks; Latin was dispensed with as part of the entry requirement for Oxford and Cambridge only in 1960.

The world and its wealth-producing machine do today make greater cognitive demands both on ordinary people and elites than in the nineteenth and early twentieth century. The British and American economies would not work with the literacy levels of 1800.

But at a time when we seem to fear for our national future if no more than half of high school graduates go on to university, it is worth noting that between 1800 and 1950 Britain gave birth to an industrial revolution, governed a far-flung empire, saw vast increases in per capita income, introduced democracy and a welfare state, and mobilized successfully to fight and win two titanic military conflicts (dominated by technological competition)—all with only the most rudimentary education for the vast majority of the population and very basic systems for selecting the most able. The most common selection system was life itself and how people performed in their allotted roles. Failure could be costly, as Admiral John Byng famously discovered when he failed to prevent the French from taking Menorca in 1756 and was court-martialed and executed by firing squad.

Much of the above list would also apply to the United States, minus the empire but with the added task of fashioning a new society from scratch. But some Americans worried that their country's democratic and classless character had curdled into something much less attractive at the start of the twentieth century. Frederick Jackson Turner, the historian of the American West, argued that what had made the United States a country of opportunity was the availability of land on the western frontier. With the frontier no more and cities filling up with collectivist-minded immigrants, this dream was over, he argued; moreover, America had also produced a distinct *Great Gatsby*–style upper class.[17]

Nicholas Lemann shows in *The Big Test* how this analysis motivated the men behind the Educational Testing Service and the introduction of the biggest IQ-style tests in the Western world, the Scholastic Aptitude Test (SAT), designed to create a new meritocratic leadership for American society as it became the most powerful country in the world.

Approaching the midpoint of the twentieth century, some of the groundwork has thus been laid for the great leap forward of the cognitive class that was to come in the latter part of that century, as I will describe in Chapter Four.

It was no longer a matter of merely "putting yourself down" for Harvard in the United States or Oxford in England; you now had to pass a competitive exam to get into elite academic institutions. Yet the social base of such institutions remained extremely narrow. As Charles Murray puts it, prior to the Second World War "Harvard was full of rich kids with a few really smart ones; fifty years later it was full of really smart kids with a few merely rich ones."[18]

England was even narrower in its elite university intake in the first part of the twentieth century and also had a more radical status divide than Germany or France between generalist academic forms of knowledge and specific practical forms.

Nonetheless, the exam principle was now firmly established in the lives of the upper and middle classes, and professional associations now monitored entry into both the higher and lower professions with tests of cognitive competence of various kinds alongside straightforward know-how.

By the 1930s the proportion of the adult male population in professional occupations remained below 10 percent in all rich countries. The cognitive class was too small to have significant political or cultural influence. The world was still largely ruled by tradition, religious belief, and the "practical men" who, according to John Maynard Keynes, writing in 1936, "believe themselves to be exempt from any intellectual influences, but are usually slaves of some defunct economist."

Keynes was a member of the loose grouping of English intellectuals and artists known as the Bloomsbury Group whose avant-garde ideas and ways of life—"they lived in squares, painted in circles, and loved in triangles," as Dorothy Parker is said to have put it—had almost no impact on British society in the 1930s. Today their ideas are commonplace, an apt metaphor, perhaps, for the rise and rise of the cognitive class through the latter part of the twentieth century.

But before considering that history, we need to pause to consider in greater depth what we actually mean by "cognitive aptitude."

Chapter Three

Cognitive Ability and the Meritocracy Puzzle

To equate IQ with human virtue or wisdom or character or a whole variety of other of the most important measures of a value of a person is ridiculous. IQ is equivalent to chip speed, and superior chip speed will enable things that inferior chip speed will not enable. The same is true about just about any human attribute you can think of . . .

Charles Murray

Human intelligence and ingenuity are at the core of modern civilization and will remain so. But it is *un*intelligent both for individuals and societies to attach too much prestige and reward to just one kind of human aptitude.

Why? Human dignity is part of the answer. Intelligence, for the first time in human history, has become central to social stratification, but this has happened in an era in which rich societies are more democratic than ever before and place a high value on equality. Given that intelligence, like wealth, is distributed unevenly, how can we ensure that those blessed with more modest levels of cognitive ability, or who prefer to develop other aptitudes, receive their fair share of dignity and respect without constraining human freedom or discriminating against the intelligent?

We cannot redistribute intelligence in the way we can wealth, but we can regard both as, in part, products of chance and only properly exercised in society. Polly Mackenzie, a British political commentator, puts it neatly: "There are endless debates about whether ability comes from our genes, or the environment in which we are raised. It doesn't matter. The one thing those two factors share is that you have no control over them. My parents gave me my genes, and they gave me my childhood. It would be as wrong for me to claim credit for my talents as it would be to let them go to waste. Talent, or merit, is an obligation as much as a gift."[1]

Another reason for wanting to reallocate prestige and reward away from cognitive ability is more pragmatic. If too many of those in the middle range of intelligence are encouraged to nurture mainly their cognitive skills, as has been happening with the rapid expansion of higher education in many rich countries, then the other aptitudes and skills that society needs will be neglected.

Placing a special value on cognitive ability in economically unequal societies seems fair and neutral, in part because it appears easy to measure. But it turns out that it is not so easy to measure. Or, rather, the qualities we admire in a rounded, intelligent person will only partly relate to raw cognitive functioning—what intelligence researchers call "general intelligence," or g—that is measured in IQ-type tests.

A person is unlikely to do well in exams or rise in an organization—whether an inner-city gang or a multinational corporation—without a decent measure of general intelligence. But that is a necessary, not a sufficient condition of what one might call general human *capability*, which also requires social intelligence, judgment, imagination, and so on.

These are qualities that are only partially captured by IQ-type tests—or, indeed, exams more generally. We know, for example, that some people with very high cognitive functioning, and usually very high IQs, are "on the spectrum" for autism and lack social intelligence.

Most of us have no idea of our own IQ or that of the people we work with and know well, but we do have a sense of some people being "brighter" than others. However, it is not a given that the people we regard as the brightest people in our social circles would also be those with the highest IQs.

There's no universally accepted definition of intelligence, but the following one, from the American psychologist Linda Gottfredson, is popular: "Intelligence is a very general mental capability that, among other things, involves the ability to reason, plan, solve problems, think abstractly, comprehend complex ideas, learn quickly and learn from experience. It is not merely book learning, a narrow academic skill, or test-taking smarts. Rather, it reflects a broader and deeper capability for comprehending our surroundings—'catching on,' 'making sense' of things, or 'figuring out' what to do."[2]

This is a wide and somewhat vague definition, but it points to something that varies between people, that allows people to function well in the real world and is concerned with mental abilities. It also distinguishes between a broader, more intangible notion of intelligence and quantifiable "test-taking smarts," the computational ability to retrieve, sift, and apply information.

General intelligence, *g*, is evidently a real thing, and I describe some of the history behind it and the arguments that swirl around it below. How much is innate? Can it really be measured without cultural bias? But we should, in any case, treat it with caution and regard it as our servant, not our master, in human selection systems. It is only *part* of the story of human capability, as almost all intelligence researchers would accept.

For intelligence in the broader sense is dependent not only on obvious things like the quality of your education but also on the general context of your life. Some examples.

Ben, the twenty-four-year-old son of an acquaintance, comes from a very academic family in London: both his parents are successful professionals and his three brothers all went to good universities. But he rebelled against the academic pressure and failed his A levels.

He ended up doing an aerospace apprenticeship near Bristol, leaving home to live in a bedsit. It was a trying time. He learned a lot during his three year apprenticeship and was keen to go on learning, but there seemed few opportunities to progress, and two years later he quit and decided to do an aerospace engineering degree at the University of the West of England in Bristol. In 2019, having failed his A levels only a few years earlier, he passed his foundation year exams with a first-class grade and now wants to train to be a pilot when he graduates.

Like the biblical parable of the sower, in which some seeds fall on stony or thorny ground and others on fertile ground, it is the context of our lives that so often decides whether intelligence or some other aptitude develops or shrivels. People of exceptional talent—Shakespeare, Mozart, Einstein—have some innate quality, some seed of greatness, inside them, but it still needs fertile soil in which to grow.

My friend David Lucas, the children's-book author and illustrator, describes the less happy experience of his own father. He was a bright working-class boy who got into grammar school at a time when new opportunities were opening up in the 1950s. But where he lived, in Middlesbrough, the only employer was heavy industry. He wasn't suited to that and managed to escape to art school in London in the 1970s, even though he was by then in his mid-thirties and had five kids in tow.

"Metrosexual, trendy, arty London was just a step too far for him. He did his best to try to find a place for himself. I remember him listening to jazz and buying modern furniture, trying to reinvent himself, but he couldn't really do it. He soon withered away; he couldn't get work and used to say, 'It's not what you know; it's who you know.' He retreated into bitterness and disappointment.

"My dad had the same genetic makeup at sixty as at thirty. But at thirty he had a wife who loved him, he had kids who looked up to him, he had his mum and dad rooting for him. He was on the up. He had none of those things at sixty. Our audience is crucial to how well we perform."

IQ, or raw ability of various kinds, has to be seen in many dimensions and across time: blossoming and fading. Or frozen until the sun shines and it can suddenly bloom. Or in many cases just never being given the right conditions to bloom at all.

I can, with some trepidation, also illustrate this point by reference to my own life. I think I count as a relevant case study in the fluidity and context-dependency of intelligence. As a child and adolescent I never felt clever and have a dim recollection of taking part in an IQ test at school and coming out just a smidgeon above average. I was easily intimidated by my more confident and articulate peers, although I had a good memory (which probably helped with the IQ test) and so performed well enough academically at school up to the age of sixteen.

A rebellious streak then appeared that contributed to a disastrous performance in my A levels (D, E, and fail) despite being educated at one of the most prestigious private schools in the country: Eton. I benefited from a second chance at a London crammer and squeezed into a decent university.

Five years after my A level disaster, I got a first-class degree in history and politics from York University thanks, in part, to my absorption in student Marxism. I was motivated to become interested in ideas and intellectual matters by guilt about my upper-class background and a vague desire to make the world a better place. Marxism provided an insecure and immature young man with a protective shield of certainty—and a reason to have a view about almost everything.

After getting a job as a trainee journalist on the local newspaper in York in my mid-twenties, a certain restlessness and maybe insecurity drove me to seek a higher-status job on a national newspaper in my late twenties, moving politically from far left to center-left (and now somewhere around the center, depending on the issue) along the way. That eventually gave me the confidence to think for myself for the first time in my life.

Thirty-five years later I write books and get invited to express my opinions on television and radio and at academic conferences. So what happened?

Was it the gradual emergence of some innate general intelligence, or the delayed influence of my privileged background? Clearly my background has helped in obvious ways. Not least, it gave me a second chance after failing my A levels, which many people don't have. Yet none of my six siblings have followed a similar path. My father was a Conservative politician of independent mind, though a notoriously poor public speaker, and not present enough in my youth to discuss politics or anything else. My mother was a pre-equality housewife who was capable and quick-witted but lacked much formal education.

The magic ingredient for my intellectual evolution was confidence, or what Carol Dweck calls the acquisition of a "growth mindset."[3] The belief—which so many people lack—that my own thoughts and ideas mattered acted as a kind of elixir, causing more and more of them to pop into my head.

Everyone comes alive if they feel someone is interested in what they have to say; it's a dynamic process between speaker and listener, performer and audience. We all know people who make us feel dumb, and our lasting friendships or romantic attachments are usually with people who make us feel smart and witty and admirable (at least initially!).

Was my evolution a kind of delayed onset of that infamous Etonian confidence? Or a need to prove myself to my high-achieving father? Maybe that is part of it, but I think just as plausible is that it resulted from achieving something in my own right, at least partly independent of the privileges of my background and schooling.

That something was leading a team that launched a monthly magazine of ideas called *Prospect* and finding for the first time in my late thirties something I could do really well: commission and edit essays on current affairs and intellectual themes. Successfully starting *Prospect* in 1995 also gave me a degree of personal prestige that I had never before enjoyed.

I now feel, in my early sixties, more intellectually alert than ever despite the fact that my memory is in decline and many of my other mental functions are slower and less reliable. But to offset that decline I have the accumulation of knowledge, and the lessons I have drawn from experience, to guide my thinking.

Other aptitudes, too, have taken time to reveal themselves. I've always enjoyed singing but never regarded myself as able to sing since being turned down for the choir at school. Confidence and encouragement from friends have helped put that tuneless failure behind me, and in recent years I've been an active member of several singing groups.

Thinking about my own life for the purposes of this book has also reminded me of the significant role played by chance in deciding a life course. One reason for that rebellious streak emerging in my late teens was the result of my first brush with failure: I failed to get into my school's top cricket team. (It was a weak response to a minor setback but I was glad to read many years later that John Strachey, a minister in the postwar Labour government, became a leading communist in the 1930s after also narrowly failing to get into the Eton cricket team!)

If I had been slightly better at cricket, my life might have taken a more conventional course into banking or law. Similarly, a few years later, while at university, I stood on the far-left ticket for a full-time student union job and lost by just six votes. If I had won that vote, I would have become immersed in the self-important world of left-wing student politics and might have ended up as a Labour MP or a full-time politician of some kind.

Can We Measure Intelligence?

Can intelligence, narrow or broad, be more or less accurately measured through tests? Most of the academics and researchers working in the field of cognitive intelligence are convinced that general intelligence, or g, is a real and partly innate thing, a product of biology and subsequent environmental influence with around 50 percent of the differences in g between people accounted for by genes.[4] They also think it can be measured accurately.

The most radical critics dismiss the whole idea of innate intelligence. But the more mainstream skeptics argue that *g* is only one aspect of a broader notion of human capability and that IQ-type tests are too narrow, too much of a snapshot, and too far removed from real life to properly capture something so complex and social context dependent, as I have argued above. Moreover, tests are biased toward those whose parents have been able to invest in them in various ways.

Let me be clear: this book is in part an argument about *the limits of cognitive meritocracy*. Even if intelligence of the most socially functional kind were something that is measurable and even if the cognitive meritocracy were fairly selected, without class bias, that would not in itself legitimize allocating such a disproportionate share of society's collective gains to the cognitive elite.

Nevertheless, highly intelligent people are also socially useful, and we all benefit from their work as we have seen in the Covid-19 crisis. They are also good at certain tasks—organization, innovation, scientific research—that are essential to modern societies and economies. Therefore, there is a utilitarian argument for rewarding smart people sufficiently so they will perform those socially useful tasks instead of loafing around or getting rich through socially predatory activities like crime.

Moreover, even in a society of the future that did spread reward and status more evenly across different human attributes, selection systems would still be needed to make sure the most appropriate people were being selected for the right jobs.

For these reasons it is important for nonexperts to try to understand at least some of the arguments that intelligence researchers make about cognitive ability and its distribution—and indeed to understand something of the history of intelligence research itself.

So what is *g*? It describes what is common in cognitive performance across a range of IQ-type measures. An analogy would be with sporting ability: at school there are some people who are good at sport, and if they are good at football, they also tend to be good at rugby and cricket. That would reflect a high level of sporting *g*. Similarly with musical ability.

Intelligence researchers say that test scores for cognitive *g* are more or less stable across a lifetime—unlike, for example, the Myers-Briggs personality tests—and that IQ performance has strongly predictive powers in many areas of life, including educational and career success. They point to the several cognitive domains underlying the tests, such as verbal comprehension, perceptual organization, processing speed, and working memory. And researchers typically claim that tests based on these domains are among the most accurate in all of psychology.

The critics, mainly outside the field of intelligence research, point to the narrowness of the activities measured by IQ and the potential circularity of the claims, arguing that IQ tests have evolved to measure a form of ability that is defined by the tests themselves.

Many critics also question the degree of innateness of *g* and want to place much more emphasis on the plasticity of intelligence and the importance of social class and other environmental factors, including pure chance, in shaping it.

They point, for example, to the likelihood that a family history of being read to and talked to when young (or not) is likely to have a significant impact on verbal abilities. Some research has also found that material incentives can significantly increase test scores.

James Flynn, the academic whose work has revealed the existence of significant global IQ gains over time, stresses the environmental influence on *g*, although he would not deny that some people have more efficient thought processes than others.

Flynn also points to the importance of human subcultures, both ethnic and class, some of which encourage cognitive pursuits more than others, in helping to explain average differences between groups. The assessment of average group IQ differences is probably the most controversial subject in the whole of social science and uncomfortably connects intelligence research to an earlier era when it was closely linked to eugenics and so-called scientific racism.

The study of intelligence in the nineteenth and part of the twentieth century did, indeed, attract people with a certain cluster of beliefs. "They thought of intelligence as being by far the single most important human trait, and therefore the one around which society should be organized; they believed it was genetically inherited; they believed that the world's darker-skinned races were inferior in intelligence to its lighter-skinned ones; and they were concerned that unintelligent people were reproducing at a more rapid rate than intelligent ones, which would eventually bring down the IQ of the entire human species," as American writer Nicholas Lemann sums it up in his book *The Big Test.*[5]

However, several generations later, intelligence research is now a respectable branch of psychology, and psychometric tests based on IQ are widely used in business and large organizations to select candidates for jobs. And the early twentieth-century origins of modern cognitive tests in Europe were actually provoked by a benign concern for children with learning difficulties at the dawn of mass free education.

The Binet-Simon scale was created in 1905 when French psychologists were asked to determine which children might need more assistance at school. American psychologist Lewis Terman at Stanford University then revised the Binet-Simon scale, creating the Stanford-Binet Intelligence Scale (1916). The concept of IQ (intelligence quotient) was introduced by William Stern and used in this test. It became the most popular test in the United States in the earliest part of the twentieth century and began to provide a single usable number.

The concept of g—that aspect of intelligence that can be detected in what remains constant between different tests—was invented in 1904 by British psychologist and army officer Charles Spearman.

The first large-scale use of intelligence testing was by the US Army in the First World War to screen out those considered intellectually inadequate. Like many tests it was criticized for class and racial bias, but the US military continued to use variations of it in the Second World War and the Korean and Vietnam Wars. Robert Yerkes and

Lewis Terman, the main figures behind the US Army testing program, also carried their methods into education, where they became the basis for the Scholastic Aptitude Test, or SAT, which continues to be central to entry into selective higher education in the United States.

Today, g is most commonly measured using the Wechsler Adult Intelligence Scale. The first version of this was published in 1955 by the American psychologist David Wechsler. The results from a ninety-minute examination of comprehension, vocabulary, and arithmetic are combined to derive a final IQ score.

The Wechsler test was substantially revised in the late 1960s by Wechsler in collaboration with Alan S. Kaufman in response to complaints of cultural and ethnic bias, especially from African Americans. Critics pointed to the fact that some test questions were merely testing acquired knowledge (for example: Who wrote *Romeo and Juliet?*) rather than raw ability, and that children with a good math education were going to perform better than equally bright children without one.

The revised tests turned out to be good at predicting certain things like school achievement, but the questions are: How useful is this and what does it tell us about something as big and fuzzy as intelligence? If g, as revealed by IQ-type tests, is just a form of pattern recognition should it be afforded such a large space in educational and career selection processes?

And that influence is still significant. In Britain, the eleven-plus is an IQ-type test, but since the abolition of most grammar schools and selection at age eleven, IQ tests are not used routinely in schools. Nevertheless, when most eleven-year-olds move to secondary school, they are given something close to an IQ test—a Cognitive Abilities Test, or CAT—which is then used to sort them into sets and predict their future exam outcomes.

In the United States some school districts do routinely use IQ tests for academic selection (though schools in California are barred from using them for certain placement decisions involving black students for fear of racial bias). And the SAT test in the United States is sometimes described as a "cousin" of the IQ test. It was first used in 1926 by the College Board, the association of twelve elite northeastern universities, and with the surge in college enrollment with the GI Bill after the Second World War, as many as 800,000 people were taking it a year in the early 1960s. The SAT is the subject of heavy and persistent criticism, particularly from progressive educationalists in the United States, but it is still widely used; more than 2 million students took the SAT test in 2018, the highest number ever.

Both Britain with the eleven-plus and the United States with the SAT test have a history of testing, or trying to test, for underlying *innate* ability rather than what you have learned. In the United States it is still the case that high school students are sorted according to "scholastic aptitude" as measured by the SAT, with the highest scorers going to the most selective colleges.

Exams of a more conventional kind as used in France, Germany—indeed, most countries—still select for an elite but not by trying to excavate some innate quality "analogous to taking a blood sample," as Nicholas Lemann puts it. France, like most countries, has an education ministry that controls the school curriculum and then tests students on their mastery of it.

Critics of the IQ/SAT test, like Lemann, say that the message of a national achievement test should be that life is about how hard you work and how much you learn—that is what you accomplish—rather than about innate ability or the manipulation of supposed measures of innate ability.

Nevertheless, as noted, many corporations and public bodies throughout the developed world do use psychometric tests, mostly based on IQ principles, when selecting candidates for senior jobs. About three-quarters of organizations in the United States with more than one hundred employees rely on aptitude and personality tests for external hiring, and the number is expected to rise in the next few years.[6]

Most mainstream intelligence researchers do acknowledge that *g* is just one form of intelligence that does not predict reliably for creativity, imagination, or what is sometimes called social intelligence. The American intelligence researcher Christopher Chabris argues that "there are neural systems which evolved for relating to other people which are distinct from the neural systems for more abstract reasoning."[7]

Then there are also the personality traits that contribute both to intelligence and to the broader notion of being an effective or successful person: energy, drive, conscientiousness, leadership qualities, the wisdom to draw the right lessons from one's experiences, and the ability to defer gratification. People who might excel in some of these latter qualities could have average IQs. One American psychologist, Angela Duckworth, who has written extensively about the concept of "grit," even claims that it is often a better predictor of success than IQ.

Most such challenges to the standard psychometric analysis of intelligence—James Flynn's observations about rising IQ scores around the world; Howard Gardner's theory of multiple intelligences; Daniel Goleman's notion of emotional intelligence; Robert Sternberg's concepts of practical, analytical, and creative intelligence; and Carol Dweck's ideas about mindsets—focus on widening the meaning of intelligence rather than on assaulting the idea of IQ.

The "Flynn effect" accepts that IQ tests have some utility but stresses the influence of the environment on test scores both for individuals and whole populations. Those who stress the environmental influence on IQ differences over time or between people often point to improvements to nutrition or health or education. Flynn goes further and argues that modernity itself confers cognitive skills relating to abstraction, symbolic thinking, and classification that our ancestors lacked.[8]

He showed that across a number of rich countries average IQ was rising at the rate of about 3 points a decade in the twentieth century.[9] His original paper showed an increase of 14 points over forty-six years (1932 to 1978) in the United States.[10] There is some debate as to whether the Flynn effect has halted or even reversed in recent decades, but no conclusive evidence.

The defenders of the innateness and heritability of IQ do not in general deny the reality of the Flynn effect, but they have a simple answer. IQ, they say, is like height: average height has been increasing around the world in recent centuries partly due to improvements in nutrition, but that does not affect differences in height between individuals or the innateness, or high heritability, of height.

Popular culture remains suspicious of the idea of the innateness of intelligence, preferring to attribute success to opportunity, luck, or self-improvement. Malcolm Gladwell's book *Outliers: The Story of Success* popularized the idea that 10,000 hours of practice was needed to become world-class in any field.

Intelligence levels can indeed depend on how much you actually use your brain. The American academic Melvin Kohn showed back in 1974, in a paper in the *American Sociological Review*, that dull, routine jobs really can make you dumber, while cognitively complex work makes the people doing it smarter—the test scores of people doing these different kinds of jobs falling and rising, respectively, over time. He and collaborators replicated it in Japan in the 1980s and Poland in the 1990s.

This also helps to explain the increase in average IQ in Ireland between the 1970s—when it was still an overwhelmingly agricultural country with a lower average IQ than England—to a highly educated, mainly urbanized society with a higher average IQ than England today.

Mainstream intelligence researchers are not opposed to the commonsense idea that talents and even IQ scores can be improved with training—just as muscles can be built up by weight lifting—but would claim that those with high innate ability would reach master level more quickly than those of lower ability.

All behavior is a mix of innate, inherited traits and the environment. Yet, to repeat: If the classic IQ tests and the exams that are based on them (like the SAT test in the United States) are testing just one network in the brain and are too narrow to have much to say about creativity, imagination, or empathy, then they are of limited use as a signaling device to employers or elite college admissions staff.

And what about the impact of personality traits on test and exam performance? Some people do less well in exams because they lack self-control or perform less well under time pressure.

The historical record is littered with highly successful and intelligent people who failed life-determining exams or who performed poorly at school or college.

Moreover, we also all know many people who are very capable in some areas of life and flail around in others—"kinda dumb and kinda smart" as Bobby Goldsboro sang of his sadly deceased Honey— perhaps especially men, who sometimes score highly on cognitive functions but are emotionally stupid in ways that are damaging to themselves and those around them.

And anyone who has spent time in a university will know that there are plenty of people with impressive academic credentials who do not seem very bright.

None of this is to deny that *g* captures *something* significant, nor is it to deny that there are real differences in more general intellectual aptitude between individuals; just ask anyone who has had long experience of teaching people or indeed managing people.

The standard bell curve for IQ in a country like Britain today has, as already mentioned, about 70 percent of the population hovering around the average in the 85 to 115 range, with about 15 percent highly gifted and 15 percent struggling to keep up.

Would we regard it as a successful outcome of our social and educational selection systems if most of the gifted 15 percent, at least in IQ terms, were finding their way into the most important jobs? Toby Young, the journalist and educationalist, has written: "All things being equal, a country's economy will grow faster, its public services will be run better, its politicians will make smarter decisions, diseases are more likely to be eradicated, if the people at the top possess the most cognitive ability."[11]

Surely that will not be the case if cognitive ability just means those who score highest on psychometric and IQ-type tests. Moreover, the

15 percent will have a very similar experience of the world and it will not be the same as the 85 percent, which is likely to be sub-optimal if you are creating policy for that 85 percent.

David Robson, the British science journalist, described in his book *The Intelligence Trap: Why Smart People Make Dumb Mistakes* how very smart people, by test standards, often have real problems understanding risks and weighing up evidence. This, he argues, is not just about "absent-minded intellectuals"; it is a case of "smart people, by test standards, often lacking *rational* judgement and common sense."[12] Indeed, people with high IQs can use their extra brainpower to rationalize erroneous beliefs and to dismiss the contradictory evidence that disagrees with their worldviews, which is why climate change deniers and conspiracy theorists are often people of higher cognitive ability.

Similarly, a Google engineer wrote a fascinating blog about the very smart, successful people around him whose overconfidence gave them the dangerous "ability to convincingly rationalize nearly anything."[13] And the idea that, even for highly educated people, our emotions and intuitions take precedence over our reason has become commonplace, thanks to the work of Jonathan Haidt (*The Righteous Mind: Why People Are Divided by Politics and Religion*), Daniel Kahneman (*Thinking, Fast and Slow*), and others.

To summarize: cognitive ability is a real and measurable thing, but the cognitive ability-based sorting machine does not always get things right because of the difficulty of capturing something as elusive as intelligence in narrowly based tests. Moreover, many of the qualities that even advanced technological societies need to function well, and to do so fairly—such as effort, empathy, virtue, imagination, courage, caring, and ability—do not feature at all in narrower definitions of intelligence.

Perhaps part of the answer is in our use of language and labeling. It would surely be sensible to distinguish between what Linda Gottfredson called "test-taking smarts" and a broader notion of human capability. If we called the first "cognitive function" and reserved the word "intelligence" for that broader notion of human competence and capability, it would capture more accurately the kind of distinctions we want to make in selecting people for different roles. Entry into the higher levels of the cognitive class would still require a high level of cognitive function, but that would be a necessary though not sufficient condition of success.

In the real world this is, in fact, what usually happens. Initial entry into an increasing number of jobs requires strong performance in exams and often IQ-type tests, too, especially in the United Kingdom and the United States, but thereafter success in an organization depends on a broader notion of emotional intelligence and psychological aptitude.

I now want to consider two enormous questions. How heritable is intelligence? And how open is selection into the cognitive class?

Nature and Nurture

First, to underline my main argument: whether a broad or narrow IQ-based form of intelligence is used to select for elites, whether intelligence (broad or narrow) is substantially heritable or not, and whether or not we are moving toward a self-reproducing cognitive elite, are all secondary issues compared with my main concern, which is to spread status and rewards more evenly across the Head, Hand, and Heart range of human aptitudes.

There has been a misallocation of financial and psychological rewards to cognitive ability, broad *and* narrow. Establishing a fairer scramble to occupy the senior positions within the cognitive class does nothing to increase the status and pay of an exceptional care worker. The American conservative Charles Murray puts it well at the start of the chapter: high IQ does not equal wisdom or virtue.[14]

One might also want to argue that if the evidence shows that the cognitive ability that leads to success is substantially *inherited*, either genetically or culturally, from parents, then society should not try to handicap the cognitively successful, in some parody of communism, but neither should it excessively reward them as if the outcomes are merited purely by individual effort.

In the ancient argument between nature and nurture, nature seems to have stolen a march on nurture in the past few years. Physical traits like height have always belonged to nature, but thirty years ago psychology and personality were thought to be mainly the product of environment.

Yet genes are now said to account for around half of psychological differences, from depression to intelligence and school attainment, and even weight is about 70 percent heritable, according to Robert Plomin, one of the leaders of the behavioral genetics movement.[15]

These things, Plomin says, have been long established by twin and adoption studies, but now, with the sequencing of the human genome, we can detect the actual genetic basis of human difference, not through a single gene for this or that, but through thousands of small differences that can be aggregated together to predict psychological propensities, or "polygenic scores."

This issue presents a challenge for our traditional thinking about many moral and political issues. The left's stress on the centrality of the social environment to individual outcomes and the right's ideals of personal responsibility are both discomforted by these findings.

Plomin himself is a politically liberal, soft-spoken American, and when I met him recently he came across as anything but an old-school "You can't buck nature" conservative. He strives to make us feel unthreatened by his claims by pointing out that if the first law of genetics is that like begets like, the second law is that like does not beget like, and genes are "probabilistic propensities, not predetermined programming."

He is, however, far too much of a genetic determinist for some fellow scientists, and a review in the journal *Nature* slammed his recent book, *Blueprint: How DNA Makes Us Who We Are*, pointing out that in education the significance of good teaching as well as diet and home conditions "have been established irrefutably." And surely childhood trauma, such as losing a parent, and plain bad parenting can leave a big mark too.

Plomin does not deny any of those points, but the argument with the *Nature* reviewer arises out of that contentious history, mentioned earlier, that still makes many people wary of the discipline of intelligence research in general and behavioral genetics in particular. Many early researchers into the heritability of human traits in the nineteenth and early twentieth centuries were proponents of eugenics and some were unashamed racists. The Nazi-eugenics association further discredited heritability research immediately after the war.

Then in 1963 an article in *Science* reviewed twin and adoption studies and concluded that genetic influence was important in IQ scores, tentatively restoring some respectability to genetic research into behavior.[16]

But this new respect for genetics was reversed in 1969 when the intelligence researcher Arthur Jensen published a paper that was skeptical about the impact of early-years education—something that had widespread bipartisan support in the US to reduce race and class inequality—and he went further and suggested that IQ differences between races might come down to genetic factors.

A few years later the late American psychologist Richard Herrnstein argued that IQ differences between classes might be genetic in origin too. These publications caused outrage and entrenched the hard environmentalist position for two decades or more.

One beneficial side effect of the decades-long pariah status of behavioral genetic research is that it raised the quality threshold for research in the field. Many more rigorous large-scale twin and adoption studies emerged in the 1980s and 1990s showing substantial genetic influence on intelligence. This was through studying identical twins, who share the same genes but when raised apart in very different environments often display similar aptitudes, interests, and personality traits.

The findings became hard to ignore and have been partly confirmed by the more recent sequencing of the human genome. It is now widely accepted that about half of the variance in measures of intelligence, as traditionally defined, is accounted for by genes.

For various reasons the genetic influence is only about 20 percent in infancy, rising to 40 percent in childhood and 60 percent in adulthood. This is partly because of what Robert Plomin has called the "nature of nurture," meaning that genes and environment interact with each other and that how we select, modify, and create environments is also based on our genetic propensities. So even something like the amount of television watching that a child does—which used to be seen as the classic example of an environmental influence—turns out to be partly attributable to heritable traits too.

Critics point to methodological problems with twin studies and the obvious influence of class and family background. But geneticists do not deny a substantial role for environment, nor that normal child development requires a basic level of responsible care. Seriously deprived or abusive environments are bound to have a negative impact on development, including intellectual development.

Indeed, Plomin and other geneticists stress that cognitive function is *only* about 50 percent inherited and point out that the principle of "reversion to the mean" means that very clever people often have only averagely clever children.*

It is also a commonplace among geneticists and intelligence researchers to claim that high IQ is associated not only with measures of socioeconomic status—education, occupational prestige, and income—but health and longevity too. The main debate is about the direction of causality, or how much the economic investment of affluent, well-educated parents contributes to the IQ scores of their children.

---

* The nineteenth-century polymath Francis Galton observed that the offspring of parents who lie at the tails of a distribution will tend to lie closer to the center.

An important recent study of the "genetics of success" that looked at genetic associations with educational attainment and social mobility provided a mixed picture. The study, led by Daniel Belsky, consisted of five longitudinal studies testing 20,000 individuals in the United States, Britain, and New Zealand.[17]

The authors concluded that participants with higher polygenic scores achieved most education and career success, but they also tended to come from better-off families. Nevertheless, participants with higher polygenic scores tended to be upwardly mobile compared with their parents, and siblings with the highest polygenic score were the most upwardly mobile. So polygenic scores are not merely the product of advantages provided by background.

The Flawed Meritocracy

So one might say that it is not private tutors or genes that determine your success but both. It is indisputably true that educational and career success remains strongly connected with privilege and class background in all developed countries, although in some more than others. In Britain, although the dominance of the privately educated in the political, economic, and cultural elite has weakened in recent decades, particularly in politics and business, it remains strong.

And most social mobility researchers would agree that the main advantage conferred by a privileged background is a high floor for those of average or below average ability. To express it as an equation: average cognitive ability + privilege = better chance of a high status occupation. As James Bloodworth has put it in his book *The Myth of Meritocracy: Why Working-Class Kids Get Working-Class Jobs*: "Environmental mechanisms exist that can turn a dull child into an average one and an average child into a successful one."[18]

Nevertheless, there is also strong evidence for Britain being a more socially mobile and, indeed, meritocratic society than most people realize. The most recent research by Oxford sociologists

Erzsébet Bukodi and John Goldthorpe finds that almost 80 percent of UK adults move at least one class category relative to their parents, either up or down. Britain, they conclude, is not a low-mobility country.[19]

A 2018 paper using the 1970 British Cohort Study also found that 63 percent of people in the highest social class originated from lower down the social scale. And those in the top quartile of cognitive scores at age ten were relatively likely to achieve top social class positions (28 percent) compared to those in the bottom quartile (5.3 percent).[20]

Long-range mobility is, of course, harder than short-range mobility, and people from higher-class backgrounds do have a significant advantage in achieving high-status positions. But Bukodi and Goldthorpe also find a significant role for both cognitive and noncognitive ability in determining mobility into the highest social classes.

They find that there has been no significant falloff in mobility in recent years, as is often claimed, but—thanks to a slowdown in the number of new middle-class professional jobs—there is "less room at the top," so there has been more downward than upward mobility.

Education, they argue, has not played a significant role in boosting mobility and indeed may have restricted it, partly because higher education has been so dominated by the middle class and because better-off families can buy extra educational support of various kinds. Formal qualifications are used by employers as a signal of competence but seem to be less important for long-term career success than demonstrating capability on the job.

Economists from the London School of Economics who looked at income rather than the occupational position favored by sociologists found 40 percent of children born in 1958 to fathers in the bottom income quartile rose to the top two, and for those born in 1970 the figure had fallen to 33 percent.[21]

That paper, published in 2005, helped to trigger a debate about a "slump" in social mobility in Britain when in fact what it revealed was a much higher level of it than most people would have expected.

One of the main reasons given for the fall in upward mobility was a middle-class monopolization of higher education, yet one of the main policy levers favored by politicians to *increase* upward mobility has been more higher education.

So there are moderate levels of social mobility in Britain despite the fact that average-ability children from more affluent backgrounds do better than they should in a true meritocracy. According to mobility researcher Peter Saunders, about 41 percent of middle-class children in the lowest IQ quartile end up in the top two social classes. But he also argues that almost 70 percent of people in the top IQ quartile reach the top two classes irrespective of class background.[22]

"Performance in an IQ test at age ten predicts a child's eventual social class destination about three times better than their parents' social class does. Class origins do have some effect on academic and occupational outcomes . . . but ability trumps class background," according to Saunders.

So, if social mobility is at least partly driven by cognitive function—and if, in turn, that is around 50 percent inherited—one might already expect a proportion of people at the top to be there on cognitive merit and for many of their children to remain there too. One might also, therefore, expect average ability levels to start to vary between broad social classes and for Michael Young's nightmare of a *hereditary cognitive elite* to have come closer.

Young's dystopian futuristic fantasy, *The Rise of the Meritocracy*, published in 1958 (after having been rejected by many publishers), describes Britain's progression to a radical meritocracy in the period 1870 to 2033 via extreme education reforms and annual IQ tests: "By 1990 or thereabouts all adults with I.Q.s of more than 125 belonged to the meritocracy. A high proportion of the children with I.Q.s over 125 were the children of these same adults. The top of today are breeding the top of tomorrow to a greater extent than at any time in the past. The élite is on the way to becoming hereditary; the principles of heredity and merit are coming together."[23]

This is in fact what psychologist Richard Herrnstein and political scientist Charles Murray *did* argue about the American experience in their controversial book *The Bell Curve: Intelligence and Class Structure in American Life* (1994). They said that the correlation between intelligence and socioeconomic status has become stronger in America since the 1950s as access to higher education has become broader and more competitive and the economy has become more knowledge based, and that this was particularly the case at each end of the IQ distribution curve. They did not claim that a person's IQ is the sole determinant of whether they succeed or fail, only that it's an increasingly important factor.

"Even as recently as midcentury, America was still a society in which most bright people were scattered throughout the wide range of jobs," Herrnstein and Murray wrote. "As the century draws to a close, a very high proportion of that same group is now concentrated within a few occupations that are highly screened for IQ."[24]

From the 1950s onward, college students were being selected ever more efficiently for their high IQs. By the beginning of the 1990s, about 80 percent of all people in the top quartile of IQ-measured ability continued to college after high school.

At the pinnacle of American society, Herrnstein and Murray argued, there is a "cognitive elite." Typically, members of this group possess IQs of 125 and above, have postgraduate degrees from good universities, and belong to a handful of "high-IQ professions"; they are accountants, engineers and architects, college teachers, dentists and physicians, mathematicians, and scientists. According to their analysis, someone with an IQ of 130 has a less than 2 percent chance of living in poverty, whereas someone with an IQ of 70 has a 26 percent chance.[25]

Others have found similar relationships. Tino Sanandaji, from the Research Institute of Industrial Economics, has drilled down into a data set to track a representative sample of the US population and discovered that those with IQs above 120 typically earn twice as much as those with average IQs. Christopher Chabris, professor of psychology at Union College in New York State, estimates that a random person with above-average intelligence has a two-thirds chance of earning an above-average income, while a random person of below-average intelligence has only a one-third chance.

So it seems that there is strong evidence that increased levels of cognitive selection into higher education and the higher professions has helped to shape a cognitive class over the past seventy years, reinforced by "assortative mating," in which like increasingly attracts like in marriage and partnering. Bright men and women were attracted to each in the past, too, but fifty years ago there were far fewer women at elite universities or in higher professional jobs, so the very brightest were less likely to meet up. Male doctors often married female nurses and male businessmen often married female secretaries.

According to the *Economist*: "In 1970 only 9 per cent of those with bachelor's degrees in America were women, so the vast majority of men with such degrees married women who lacked them. Now the numbers are roughly even (in fact women are earning more degrees) and people tend to pair up with mates of a similar educational background . . . And in 1970, fewer than 5 per cent of American lawyers were female. Now the figure is 34 per cent, and nearly half of law students are female. So highly educated, double-income power couples have become far more common. The children of such couples have every advantage, but there are not many of them."[26]

There has been a similar pattern in other rich countries. Social class and educational background have tightened their grip on marriage in the United Kingdom in recent decades. According to research by the think tank Institute for Public Policy Research, 39 percent of women born in 1958 married a partner in the same social class, rising to 56 percent for those born twenty years later.[27] David Willetts, the former Conservative minister, argued in his book *The Pinch: How the Baby Boomers Took Their Children's Future—and Why They Should Give It Back* that such assortative mating has contributed to a slowing of social mobility. "If advantage marries advantage then we must not be surprised if social mobility suffers . . . [I]ncreasing equality between the sexes has meant increasing inequality between social classes. Feminism has trumped egalitarianism."[28]

Charles Murray returns to this theme in his more recent book *Coming Apart: The State of White America, 1960–2010* (2012). "The reason that upper-middle-class children dominate the population of elite schools," he writes, "is that the parents of the upper-middle class now produce a disproportionate number of the smartest children."[29] He says that 87 percent of college-bound seniors who scored above 700 in their SAT in 2010 had at least one parent with a college degree, with 56 percent of them having a parent with a graduate degree. He concludes: "Highly disproportionate numbers of exceptionally able children in the next generation will come from parents in the upper-middle class, and more specifically from parents who are already part of the broad elite."

The children of those in the top 4 percent of earners in the United States—those earning at least $200,000 a year—score on average 250 points higher on SAT tests than the children of people on median incomes, who, in turn, score on average 125 points higher than those on low incomes. Princeton and Yale take more students from the top one percent of the income distribution than the bottom 60 percent.[30]

But it is the top 20 percent in the United States, not just the super-rich, who have enjoyed a disproportionate slice of the increased national income of the past forty years and dominated the highest rungs of the educational ladder, according to Richard Reeves. The children of the top income quartile are represented in the top 150 most competitive colleges in the United States by a ratio of 14 to 1 over those in the bottom income quartile.[31] It is a similar story in the United Kingdom, where the most advantaged 20 percent of young people are seven times more likely to attend one of the top Russell Group universities than the most disadvantaged 40 percent.[32]

So, the United States and the United Kingdom—where most of this research has been done—appear to have established very partial and flawed meritocracies. Higher socioeconomic status families tend to have higher polygenic scores on cognitive functions, which is what one might expect from a society that is at least somewhat meritocratic, given significant heritability of cognitive aptitudes *combined* with the ability of the affluent to invest in their children.

There is less of this kind of social mobility research in France and Germany. But the comparative work of Richard Breen, looking at the United States, France, Germany, the Netherlands, and Sweden, sees a broadly similar pattern between countries and, as in the United Kingdom, signs of the higher upward mobility of the 1960s and 1970s slowing down, thanks to fewer new professional jobs being created.[33]

There is some other comparative work that suggests a lower correlation between parental socioeconomic status and educational outcomes in Germany than in the United States. In the case of France, as we will see in the next chapter, there is evidence of a hereditary meritocracy emerging, with around two-thirds of students entering the most prestigious *grandes écoles* coming from the highest social class.

There is, as one would expect, a weaker correlation between IQ and educational success for children from disadvantaged backgrounds. The ability of the privileged to tilt the balance in their favor by investing more in their children means they can thwart the emergence of a more fairly meritocratic society, as we have seen.

But there appear to be natural limits on the extent to which the privileged can tilt the *genetic* balance in favor of their descendants. So the Michael Young nightmare of an ossified hereditary cognitive meritocracy is unlikely to fully materialize.

In *Coming Apart*, Murray estimates that there will always be 14 percent of children in the top 5 percent of the IQ distribution curve who are the offspring of parents with below-average IQs. Others argue for much higher levels of genetic shuffling.

Regression to the mean—meaning clever parents will sometimes have average children—still operates even if it has been slowed somewhat by assortative mating and educational investment. Overall, the evidence for the emergence of a hereditary cognitive meritocracy remains tentative and is contested.

For example, Andrew Hacker, a teacher of political science and math at Queens College in New York, writes: "We know that well-off and otherwise accomplished parents can give their children a good start, or at least try. So the next question is how these presumably favored offspring fare as adults. Such studies as we have suggest that early advantages don't always last."[34]

Ron Haskins at the Brookings Institution, following top-quintile youngsters, was surprised to find that only a little over half obtained college degrees. Tom Hertz, an economist at American University, found that of children raised in families in the top income quintile, only 38 percent were still there as adults.

A friend of mine who lives near Manchester and is himself an educationalist reported something comparable from his own experience: "My third son is fifteen and goes to a selective grammar school. I am sufficiently in favor of selection to allow him to go, but sufficiently cantankerous about fair competition to refuse to pay for a tutor. He passed the exam, and arrived at the school, and out of his whole year only he and one other boy had not had a tutor, with parents often hiring them for up to two years before the eleven-plus exam. But what subsequently happened is that some of the boys who passed the eleven-plus then struggled to keep up as they progressed through the school. They were already on the first rung of the cognitive elite ladder but in some cases were no cleverer than kids who failed the test."

Even for people who do score highly on IQ-type tests, there are usually so many other things going on in determining whether someone enjoys a successful career or happy life that IQ determinism is rarely justified.

David Robson, author of *The Intelligence Trap*, underlines the importance of factors other than cognitive function in successful careers: "If you consider surveys of lawyers, accountants, or engineers, for instance, the average IQ may lie around 125—showing that intelligence does give you an advantage. But the scores cover a considerable range, between 95 and 157 . . . And when you compare the individuals' success in those professions, those different scores can, at the very most, account for around 29 percent of the variance in performance, as measured by managers' ratings."[35]

But the most convincing recent challenge to the *Bell Curve* analysis of a self-reproducing meritocratic elite comes from American sociologists Dalton Conley and Jason Fletcher.[36] They argue that Herrnstein and Murray simply did not have sufficient data on population genetics in the early 1990s to come to some of the conclusions they did about meritocracy ossifying into a sort of "genotocracy." Conley and Fletcher look at whether genetic traits relating to intelligence have become more heritable over the course of the twentieth century as assortative mating has increased. In 1960, 32 percent of men with college bachelor's degrees married women with degrees; in 2000, 65 percent did.

But they conclude that there has been *less* sorting by genes as educational opportunity has risen. (They argue that is true of Sweden too.) The Conley and Fletcher findings suggest that there is less genetic stickiness between generations than assumed in the *Bell Curve*.

So the question of how fairly selected for and how fluid the cognitive class is remains messy and complex. Nevertheless, a combination of genetic inheritance, parental support of various kinds, and a much greater emphasis on educational selection processes for everyone is likely to be shaping a somewhat more entrenched cognitive meritocracy than fifty years ago.

To many meritocrats, and many of those who thrive in a knowledge-based society, this just seems like common sense. The meritocracy may always be tilted somewhat toward the affluent and well-connected, but so long as it is sufficiently open, the most able people will rise into the higher cognitive roles, benefiting themselves and the wider society.

But is that just the self-interest of a nascent cognitive caste speaking? The alternative view is put pithily by American philosopher Tim

Sommers: "Even if you don't mind the tyranny of the talented, just wait, it will become the tyranny of the talented's children." And, in any case, even a relatively open cognitive meritocracy still leaves a significant minority, if not a majority, in knowledge-based societies feeling excluded or with noncognitive aptitudes that do not command sufficient respect and reward.

What is to be done? One way of considering the issue is through listening in to a cross-generational debate within the Young family.

The Cognitive Veil of Ignorance

Toby Young, the British journalist and educationalist quoted earlier, has recently taken an intense interest in these debates on a different side to his father, the late socialist intellectual Michael Young, author of both the radical 1945 Labour Party manifesto and then twelve years later the anti-meritocracy satire *The Rise of the Meritocracy*. Young junior is a pugnacious fifty-six-year-old, educated at state schools and Oxford, who for the first part of his career was a troublemaking journalist. In recent years the bespectacled Young has appeared to want to follow in his father's intellectual footsteps, albeit espousing very different views, and has become a more serious if controversial figure in the London educational and political world, setting up his own state school in the capital.

Michael Young was an egalitarian who opposed the idea of equality of opportunity because it was about the opportunity to be unequal. He argued, like other egalitarians such as philosopher John Rawls, that the intelligence and capability you are born with is the result of a "natural lottery" and no more deserved than the wealth that a rich person might inherit.

Young junior is a classical liberal who believes in equal rights, equal treatment, and equal opportunities but not equality of outcome, because he believes the latter can only be achieved at too high a human cost: "I like meritocracy for the same reason that my father disapproved of it: because it helps to secure people's consent to the inequalities that are the inevitable consequence of limited government. I say this not as someone fond of inequality but as someone who believes limited government is preferable to a large, coercive state."

How does he believe that meritocracy achieves this goal? First, by creating a society that is dynamic and wealthy because talents are put to good use. Second, by allocating wealth and prestige in a way that at least appears to be fair, or fairer than the alternatives. Third, by creating opportunities for at least some people born on the wrong side of the tracks.

But there is also a danger that a creeping hereditary meritocracy and an overshoot in the status attached to cognitive aptitudes could destroy the consent for a free society just as his father predicted in the closing scene of his book *The Rise of the Meritocracy*, when the resentment of those excluded from the cognitive class boils over and they rise up violently against their oppressors.

So which Young is right, the elder or the younger? Looked at through one lens, the knowledge society, the expansion of higher education, and the creation of a large cognitive class of almost one-third of the population is a process of opening, democratization, and inclusion. And looked at in both historical terms or internationally— just consider the recent success of Singapore and China, which has been driven at least in part by the principle, if not the practice, of cognitive meritocracy—it should surely be considered a success.*

But, as Michael Young was keenly aware, one person's inclusion is another's exclusion. The psychological pain and resentment created by that exclusion, combined with the higher democratic expectations of modern citizens, is one of the factors behind the current political alienation.

Generally speaking, high cognitive ability is a desirable attribute. Indeed, it is such a desirable attribute that it might be said to be its own

---

* According to Professor David Goodman of the University of Sydney, a joint study conducted by researchers at Peking University and Australian National University found that Chinese women's occupation, status, and wealth is almost completely determined by their fathers' occupations and status. For men, that determination is about 80 percent.

reward. The ability to understand one's environment and to pick up new skills quickly does not necessarily require the additional rewards that society has been granting the cognitively able in recent decades.

In any case, to repeat: high intelligence may be a highly desirable attribute but it is not the only one. It does not make anyone a good or likable or honest or conscientious or compassionate or courageous or contented person. And yet, increasingly parents will go to great lengths to ensure that their children can pass into the graduate class even if they do not have the cognitive ability or personal attributes to properly benefit from a three- or four-year degree course. This is creating an epidemic of square pegs in round holes.

If respect for intelligence were tempered by a broader valuing of human abilities, then it might also be easier to be more honest about some of the discoveries about human aptitude emerging from genomics research. And that could, in turn, make it easier to help to fit peoples' cognitive and psychological propensities, as revealed by that research, to the most suitable jobs and occupations and for society more generally to be more accepting of people for who they are.

Natural abilities are distributed unequally, but in rich democracies the outcomes of such inequality are constrained by our moral and political beliefs and institutions—above all, our belief that all humans are morally and politically equal. A gradual rearrangement of current trade-offs to produce a more even distribution of status—while avoiding false egalitarian extremes—is the most desirable direction of travel for rich countries.

The philosopher Kwame Anthony Appiah has put it most eloquently: "The goal is not to eradicate hierarchy and to turn every mountain into a salt flat; we live in a plenitude of incommensurable hierarchies, and the circulation of social esteem will always benefit the better novelist, the more important mathematician, the savvier businessman, the faster runner, the more effective social entrepreneur. We cannot fully control the distribution of economic, social and human capital, or eradicate the intricate patterns that emerge from these overlaid grids. But class identities do not have to internalise those injuries of class. It remains an urgent collective endeavour to revise the ways we think about human worth in the service of moral equality."[37]

In *The Rise of the Meritocracy*, a manifesto is drawn up by opponents of the new meritocratic order that asks for a society with a different system of valuation. "Were we to evaluate people, not only according to their intelligence and their education, their occupation, and their power, but according to their kindliness and their courage, their imagination and sensitivity, their sympathy and generosity, there could be no classes . . . Every human being would then have equal opportunity, not to rise up in the world in the light of any mathematical measure, but to develop his own special capacities for leading a rich life."[38]

Meritocracy, like all social arrangements, is based on the idea of reciprocity: what you put in is connected to what you take out. But as Appiah points out, meritocracy then elides two different things: capability and human worth: "I know what it is for my life to go better or worse, but it doesn't make sense to ask whether my life is better than yours. And that means there is no comparative measure, no single scale of human worth . . . Indeed, because each of us faces a distinct challenge, what matters in the end is not how we rank against others at all. We do not need to find something we are best at; what is important is simply that we do *our* best."[39]

The egalitarian political philosopher John Rawls invented the idea of the veil of ignorance, asking people to imagine the social arrangements they would be most likely to favor if, behind the veil, they did not know what their position or status in society was going to be. This idea has often been applied to income distribution, class, race, and gender. But it should apply to cognitive ability too.

And if it were to be so applied, most people would surely choose meritocratic *selection systems* for the most important jobs to ensure that society made the best use of bright peoples' talents but not a meritocratic *society* that sharply divides winners from losers. This is a vital distinction, analogous to wanting a market economy but not a market society (in the phrase of French socialist Lionel Jospin).

Obviously, we want some of our most competent statisticians running the government statistical service. There is a commonsense case for cognitive meritocratic selection in education, science, professional organizations, and so on—and indeed for noncognitive meritocratic selection in sport and other areas of human endeavor.

And Young himself said this: "It is good sense to appoint individual people to jobs on their merit. It is the opposite when those who are judged to have merit of a particular kind harden into a new social class without room in it for others."

This is the crux of the matter and much easier said than done— maybe impossible. There will always be hierarchies of ability and competence across all fields of human endeavour and that means hierarchies of status too. But acknowledging that there is no single scale of worth and spreading status more evenly across a wider range of human aptitudes can help to dilute its overconcentration around Head capabilities. People want opportunities but not always the same kind of opportunities.

In politics and representative organizations there is a particularly strong case for cognitive *diversity* for people with a range of aptitudes and experiences to be making decisions and having their experiences taken into account.

This chapter has tried to navigate a route between describing some of the scientific consensus about cognitive ability while at the same time questioning both the possibility and desirability of a cognitive meritocracy.

A cognitive meritocracy is welcomed by most people as preferable to the hereditary ruling class of the recent past. But these are not the only two alternatives for democratic societies, and, as this chapter has shown, a *fair* cognitive meritocracy is almost as hard to achieve as a fair hereditary ruling class, because it is also too easy to pass on cognitive advantage through education, upbringing, and genes.

The other big problem with the cognitive meritocracy is that in a world that requires a diverse range of aptitudes to function well, it selects for and rewards—both psychologically and materially—just one cluster. The next three chapters will describe how that one cluster has become so dominant in the past two generations, in what I call the cognitive takeover.

PART TWO

THE COGNITIVE TAKEOVER

Chapter Four

The Era of
Educational Selection

Where is the wisdom we have lost in knowledge? Where
is the knowledge we have lost in information?

T. S. Eliot

Most people, certainly most politicians, regard formal education as an unquestionable good that helps economies to grow faster, societies to become more civilized, and individuals to earn more and become better people.

There is also a sense that a more educated population is part of a teleological story of human progress: that we all started as primitive people dominated by instinct, then reason began to play an ever larger role in human affairs. This was initially led by a small literate elite, but gradually literacy became the norm, at least in rich societies, followed by mass primary, secondary, and now higher education.

Given how much humanity has benefited from knowledge and its application in the last two hundred years, it seems counterintuitive to argue that education can produce diminishing returns. Yet the central claim of this book is that, at least in rich countries, we are now approaching "peak Head." Guiding more people into academic higher education made good sense in the latter part of the twentieth century, but today it is neither politically nor economically rational.

Most of the conventional assumptions about higher education and the benefit for individuals and whole societies are now at best only half-right: consider the fact that just as the graduate share in the workforce has been sharply increasing, productivity has been slowing in most developed economies, inequality has been increasing (or at least not declining), and political polarization is rising.

And the ideal that many of us might think of when we consider education in the abstract—say, studying medicine, combining vocational and academic learning and leading to an obviously useful and well-remunerated professional career—is a very long way from the reality for most people most of the time.

Many of the academic qualifications that people are working toward have a far more tenuous connection to future employment and are often a form of *credentialism*, signaling to employers where you stand relative to others rather than evidence of mastery of complex cognitive skills.

There can, of course, be valuable intellectual inquiry that is neither signaling nor vocational. A friend of mine says he studied the philosopher Kant for a year at university and now could not write a coherent sentence about him but he thinks it did help him to think—a kind of intellectual gymnasium.

But outside of core vocational subjects such as medicine or engineering, there is plenty of evidence that many students do not learn, or at least retain, much from their studies, and whether they learn to think critically is hard to measure.

Education can be "what is left after you have forgotten everything you were taught," in the old saying. The problem is this: education is in many circumstances a cultural good and an economic investment both for individuals and society, but it is also a signaling arms race that sorts people into different occupational streams. It usually makes sense at the individual level to invest in it, but some of the investment can be misallocated at the social level.

If, thanks to an oversupply of graduates, advertisements for teaching assistants or accounting technicians begin to routinely require a degree, it is common sense for individuals who wish to work in these fields to obtain one. But it would be better for both individuals and society if the arms race could be called off and access to such jobs restored to conscientious high school graduates, as used to be the case.

It is not that we are investing too much in education in general, but too much may be going on signaling efforts for the higher-level exam passers and not enough on the vocational, professional, and technical skills—and indeed the lifelong learning—that most of the population, and the economy, need to flourish. It is a bit like acquiring a state-of-the-art nuclear weapon while your tanks and artillery decay.

And it is worth recalling just how much our ancestors achieved in the nineteenth century and early part of the twentieth, most of them having received only the most rudimentary education. This was true as recently as the 1960s. As Mark Bovens and Anchrit Wille put it in their book *Diploma Democracy: The Rise of Political Meritocracy*: "The idea that success in school was the only road to achievement was absent in the 1960s. Many people who failed in school succeeded later, while the idea of success was broad and varied."[1]

By making academic achievement the only gateway to success, we are shutting out some of the most talented future leaders of our police force, legal profession, civil service, and private enterprise.

In 1972, more than 40 percent of pupils left school in the United Kingdom with essentially no qualifications (some with the basic Certificate of Secondary Education).[2] The figure was a bit lower in the United States, around 25 percent.

Even the elite public schools in the United Kingdom sent only about half of their pupils to university at that time.[3] The year I left Eton, in 1974, many of my fellow pupils were going directly into family businesses, professions, or the armed forces. Today the elite public schools send 90 percent or more of their pupils to top universities.

In the early 1970s most exams were still only for a minority even in developed countries. At that time in England just one-third of pupils took O levels (the main school exam for sixteen-year-olds) and about 15 percent took at least one A level (the high school graduate university entrance exam taken at age seventeen or eighteen). There were only about thirty universities, and 9 percent of high school graduates went to them.

In 1988, General Certificates of Secondary Education (GCSEs), designed for a wider ability range, replaced O levels and *all* pupils took them. Today about 47 percent of pupils take A levels and nearly half of the high school–graduating cohort go on to some form of higher education. That has inevitably led to some dilution in standards: an A at A level or a first-class degree from most universities is easier to achieve than in the 1970s.

The period since the Second World War, and especially since the 1970s, has become the *era of educational selection*. In the second half of the twentieth century, many developed countries led by America moved from being countries of mass literacy and numeracy, and mass primary and secondary education, to being countries of mass *higher* education.

It was the 1944 GI Bill for returning servicemen that set the United States on the path to mass higher education. Rewards for veterans was an established part of American politics, and the sense that the First World War package had been a miserly one prompted Roosevelt to agree to a much more generous package of benefits in 1944, including not just funding for college education but also cut-rate mortgages and medical care.

Nobody knew how many veterans would take up the offer, but well over 1 million did, doubling the already high number in higher education, at least compared with Europe, to 2 million in 1951, compared with barely 100,000 in the United Kingdom at the same time. The number had doubled again to 4 million by 1961. By the 1970s about 40 percent of high school graduates were experiencing some kind of higher education, but only around a quarter were taking four-year bachelor's degree courses, with the rest doing two-year courses at community colleges. By 2018 the percentage had risen to around 50 percent in total, but with only around one-third taking full four-year bachelor degree courses.[4]

This expansion of the cognitive class in all rich countries was initially a welcome and necessary change. The economy and the expansion of the public sector required more Head jobs and relatively fewer Hand ones, and as we shall see in the next chapter, the income returns to knowledge and education began to take off in the 1970s after almost a century of income compression between Head and Hand.

Frederick Winslow Taylor's theories of scientific management developed in the United States before the First World War had produced the giant mass-production factory by ending skilled workers' monopoly of production know-how and breaking it down into easy-to-perform functions. This required less manual skill but some degree of literacy and numeracy. Taylorist standardization and specialization hugely increased productivity. By the 1970s many corporations were employing many more people with college degrees in marketing, sales, engineering, IT, and management than on the increasingly automated production lines.

There was also a big increase in professional, high-cognitive employment—doctors, scientists, teachers, lawyers, accountants— as the proportion of the workforce involved in broadly professional work rose from low-single-figure percentages at the beginning of the twentieth century to between 30 and 40 percent today.

This was a common trend across all developed countries, but there were also distinctive attitudes to knowledge and to the relationship between Head and Hand in different national traditions as described in Chapter Two.

England opted at the dawn of the twentieth century for a socially exclusive, national higher-education system—dominated by Oxford and Cambridge—which imposed its ethos through exam boards and scholarships on the rest of the nascent education sector. Central to the ethos in higher education was the principle of the *residential* university.

This English ethos (Scotland was somewhat different) was not only socially exclusive; it also favored the generalist-academic over the specific-vocational at every turn with the partial exception of medicine and engineering. The domination of theoretical reasoning over knowledge of facts or practical expertise went furthest in the Anglo-Saxon countries, thanks in part to the cultural influence of Oxbridge in Britain and to John Dewey in the United States. Germany, Austria, the Netherlands, and the Scandinavian countries have continued to attach greater prestige to vocational and technical education.

The 1944 Education Act in the United Kingdom reinforced the separation of Head and Hand. It proposed a tripartite system of grammar schools, technical schools, and secondary moderns, but in most parts of the country the technical schools never emerged. The decision in 1992 to convert the thirty-five polytechnics—institutions established in 1965 that had given some prestige to technical skills—into universities represented another tilt in the direction of academic-analytical aptitudes.

Mass higher education in England was elite academic higher education writ a little larger, as higher education policy expert Guy Neave has put it. And since the postwar expansion—from just 4 percent of high school graduates going to university in 1962 to almost half today—the school system has become more and more focused on nurturing academic, analytical ability.

Academic A levels have been the one prestigious constant in the school curriculum as different vocational qualifications have come and gone. A levels were developed by the universities themselves in order to decide who to admit. But as David Willetts, former UK universities minister, puts it: "A finely tuned device for producing mini-scholars has become a de facto school-leaving exam, shaping the character of mass secondary education."[5]

Despite the abolition of most grammar schools, the school ranking system in the United Kingdom has become increasingly focused on the number of pupils schools are able to send to top universities. By contrast, those not in the academic A level stream and not heading to university have little incentive to apply themselves.

In countries like Germany, Austria, and the Netherlands, where academic schooling is combined with strong vocational tracks and an institutionalized school-to-work transition, pupils at the lower end of the academic ability spectrum still have incentives to work hard in order to get into the best vocational schools or to have the widest possible choice of apprenticeship. By contrast, in general-skills systems such as in the United States and the United Kingdom, there tends to be a big divide in the secondary-school population between those in the academic stream and those with a much less certain future in either the job market or some other form of post-school education. Many of them will already regard themselves as failures.[6]

As the British economist Paul Collier has pointed out, it is easier to move from the cognitive environment of the school to the cognitive environment of a college or university than into the noncognitive environment of an actual job, and yet in Britain there has been far more financial and institutional support for the first than the second.

By common consent, nonacademic post-school education remains poorly funded, complex, and often inadequate, in both the United Kingdom and United States. The Hand has been sorely neglected in school and post-school education, which has made both economies unusually dependent on foreign labor. One in ten adults in England have a technical qualification compared with more than one in five in Germany.[7]

Meanwhile, university expansion continues unabated in most rich countries (though it is likely to be at least temporarily set back by the Covid-19 crisis). In 2015 the British government abolished the cap on university numbers and allowed almost anyone who wanted to become an undergraduate to become one. Universities have a big financial incentive to cram in as many students as possible, lowering entry standards, inflating degree awards, reducing direct contact time with academics, and—in the case of some of the newer universities, which tend to attract less research funding—struggling to remain solvent. Germany is also now fast increasing the proportion of high school graduates going on to university.

University or Bust

The rise and rise of academic secondary education, and then higher education, really began in the UK with the aforementioned 1944 Education Act. It was the 1944 act that first introduced the exam principle into most households in the country with the eleven-plus exam that determined entry into the grammar schools.

After the war, grammar schools educated about 20 percent of the population, with the rest going to less academic secondary modern schools or technical schools. The eleven-plus was an intelligence test rather like an IQ test, with verbal and nonverbal reasoning, based partly on the work of Cyril Burt, the influential and controversial educational psychologist with a strong belief in the heritability of intelligence.

During the late 1960s the eleven-plus and grammar schools were phased out in most of the country, partly thanks to the influence of Michael Young's meritocracy skepticism on education secretary Tony Crosland. Young may have won this battle but he lost the war, as cognitive-based meritocratic selection increasingly became the symbol of national modernization—exemplified by Harold Wilson, the technocratic grammar school boy from Huddersfield, who won the 1964 general election for Labour and became prime minister.

The early 1960s saw the first big postwar expansion of higher education with seven new universities established to accommodate the surge of pupils coming out of the new grammar schools. The British universities had had a "good war,"[8] with university scientists playing a prominent role and academics occupying senior positions in Whitehall. And there was postwar political pressure to broaden the social base of higher education and catch up with the United States. The university sector was still tiny in 1945, with just eleven full universities with a further 150 technical colleges run by local authorities.

The 1963 report on the future of higher education, led by the economist Lionel Robbins, provided justification for further expansion with a view to making it available to all of those qualified "by ability and attainment." But Robbins also reinforced a traditional "Oxbridge" view of disinterested study for its own sake.

Indeed, Robbins provided a useful definition of what is distinctive about specifically *academic* learning: "While emphasising that there is no betrayal of values when institutions of higher education teach what will be of some practical use, we must postulate that what is taught should be taught in such a way as to promote the general powers of the mind. The aim should be to produce not mere specialists but rather cultivated men and women. And it is the distinguishing characteristic of a healthy higher education that, even where it is concerned with practical techniques, it imparts them on a plane of generality that makes possible their application to many problems—to find the one in the many, the general characteristic in the collection of particulars. It is this that the world of affairs demands of the world of learning."[9]

It is not at all clear that this is what "the world of affairs" does demand from the world of learning. But the universities that emerged in the 1960s borrowed heavily from Oxbridge in their structure and intellectual ethos—Sussex University was nicknamed "Balliol by the sea"—focusing on research as well as teaching, being overwhelmingly residential, and in most cases with a college system and a tutorial system and an offer of subjects that mimicked Oxbridge. Some Labour educationalists complained, too, that the new universities had reaffirmed the boarding school principle of the privately educated elite.

In one significant departure from Robbins's recommendations, Tony Crosland, the Labour education secretary, created in 1965 another tier of higher education—thirty-five polytechnics—that were technical and vocational in focus: engineering, computer science, management, architecture, town planning, and so on. They differed from universities not only in their STEM and vocational focus but also in the fact that they were not mainly residential, were governed by local authorities, did not (at least initially) do research, catered to part-time and mature students, and offered diplomas rather than degrees.

The university-polytechnic divide was found in France, too, with both the specialist technical elite *grandes écoles* and the Institut Universitaire de Technologie, and Germany with its *Fachhochschulen*, created in the early 1970s as distinct technical institutions of higher education (now classified as universities). The US community colleges are closer to polytechnics than universities.

The British polytechnics did not survive long enough to establish a tradition of excellence, and their distinct mission was in any case gradually eroding as the polytechnics drifted toward traditional academic subjects and away from their vocational STEM subject focus.[10]

The directors and senior staff of the polytechnics, themselves often Oxbridge trained, began to lobby for the higher prestige and greater independence of the classical university. And, in 1992, Kenneth Clarke, then Conservative education secretary and himself Cambridge educated, saw no reason to deny them this privilege. This left the UK as an outlier among rich countries in having no dedicated institutions of higher technical education.

This was the moment of real take-off for higher education in the United Kingdom, as the number of official universities rose from 40 in 1990 to around 130 today, while over the same period the proportion of young people going to higher education rose from 20 percent to nearly half—overtaking most other developed countries in relative participation rates.

The internal hierarchy of prestige within the university sector in both teaching and research also became more overt. In order to distinguish themselves from the former polytechnics, or "new universities," the so-called Russell Group of the most selective and research-intensive universities was established in 1994: eighteen universities, initially, now twenty-four, accounting for about 20 percent of all undergraduates—a larger version of the American Ivy League or French *grandes écoles*.

Raising the overall educational level of the population and selecting the most cognitively able to go into an expanded higher-education system were the two principal goals of the education system in all rich countries from the 1970s. Those two goals can, however, conflict, and schools—especially in the United Kingdom and United States—have been increasingly judged in official league tables by the second goal, their ability to find the most able pupils and send them on to top universities.

Between 1970 and today, the United Kingdom's spending on education has risen from around £30 billion ($39 billion) in today's prices to more than £90 billion ($117 billion), and as a proportion of total spending it has risen about 20 percent since the 1960s.[11] There has also been a steep change in direct state involvement from the 1980s with the creation of a national curriculum and then in the 1990s national accountability systems, notably the Office for Standards in Education, Children's Services and Skills ("Ofsted") inspection regime and the publication of exam league tables.

The spending increases have been similar in the United States, Germany, and France, with all four countries now spending between 5 and 6 percent of their GDPs on education, although as a proportion of public spending and per capita spending the overall spending numbers are a bit higher in the United Kingdom and the United States, probably because of the higher level of spending on higher education.[12]

More and more education came to be seen by politicians, who were now almost all graduates, as the answer to everything from a more productive economy to social mobility, if not equality. (One hundred and fifty years of mass public education has proved a disappointment to egalitarians.) Tony Blair's famous "Education, education, education" mantra of 1997 evolved two years later into the plan to send 50 percent of young people into academic higher education at a time when only about 30 percent were then attending.

This headlong rush into mass academic higher education, leapfrogging even the United States, happened faster in the United Kingdom than in most other comparable countries and it seemed to happen on automatic pilot, with remarkably little thought given to either the economic or social consequences. And in the Anglo-Saxon countries, which have long had weaker traditions of vocational and technical training, a status gap opened up, which sucked much of the remaining purpose and prestige out of non-university, post-school education. This was much less true in Germany, and to a lesser extent France, where there were still respected alternatives to higher education, but in the United Kingdom and the United States almost all the bright and ambitious kids now had only one goal: university.

In the United Kingdom the academicization of education and careers for something between one-third and half of the younger population was a quiet revolution. Yet the only thing about this revolution that was closely debated was the level of fees that UK students should pay.

There was a recognition that truly mass higher education in the United Kingdom could not be solely funded by the state, especially given the economic benefits of a university education to the individuals concerned, and tuition fees were introduced and raised rapidly to a ceiling (that became the norm) of £9,000 ($11,700) a year. But the loan and funding arrangements meant that university was free at the point of use, and the typical student is currently estimated to repay only a little over half the roughly £50,000 ($65,000) in loans that they are likely to acquire for tuition and living expenses.[13]* Higher education is now open to almost anyone who wants it, and, contrary to expectations, the number of students from low-income backgrounds has been going up, not down.

One reason that the rapid expansion of higher education to half of secondary-school graduates seemed desirable to those in the room when the decision was made is that all of them were graduates. One man in that room and closely involved in discussions over the Labour government's 50 percent target was David Soskice, the charismatic and original London School of Economics political economist and son of former Labour home secretary Frank Soskice.

---

* The current repayment terms mean that a student who studies an economically worthless degree and gains no career benefit from it will repay nothing, meaning the taxpayer provides the greatest subsidy to the least beneficial degrees.

When I spoke to him in his North London home about the target, he can remember nobody in government involved in the decision raising any objections. The economy seemed to want more graduates, judging by the graduate income premium, and university was regarded as a ladder of social mobility for those from middle- and lower -income groups.

What I call "the 15/50 problem" does not seem to have been considered: the idea that when 15 percent of people in your class or school or town go to university and you don't, it does not create a "left behind" problem; but when 50 percent go to university and you don't, it does create such a problem.

Soskice, who is himself an influential analyst of different models of capitalism, was convinced that there was no point in Britain trying to copy the highly regulated German market economy, with its apprenticeship system and commitment to long-term investment in manufacturing technology.

Rather, thought Soskice, the United Kingdom should follow the United States and play to its strengths in innovation, finance, and the service sector. He saw university expansion as producing the professional and managerial generalists to run the service economy.

This, he said, was merely going with the grain of the Anglo-Saxon road chosen back in the 1980s: the postindustrial route of deregulated, flexible labor markets and the teaching of general, transferable skills rather than the continental European model of more regulated, company-based skill training.

Just forty years ago Britain had a vocational training system that was patchy but worked pretty well, and followed a common European pattern: the largest bloc of secondary-school graduates went into employer-led apprenticeships; qualifications called BTECs (after the Business and Technology Education Council) provided a respectable classroom based alternative to A levels; and there was a dual higher-education system with polytechnics alongside universities, offering a range of higher technical and vocational qualifications, with further education (FE) colleges offering lower-level vocational qualifications.

This system has now largely disappeared. The apprenticeship system was the weak link in the chain and was seen by the free-market enthusiasts of the early Thatcher era as a source of protectionist labor movement power and also far too narrowly focused on disappearing manual skills.

The dramatic expansion of higher education from the early 1990s then obliterated the higher manual qualifications—particularly the sub-degree qualifications at so-called levels 4 and 5 Higher National Diplomas (HNDs) and Higher National Certificates (HNCs), the qualifications taken since the 1920s by technicians, non-university engineers, and skilled-trade people such as electricians and plumbers. These were being taken by 64,000 and 49,000, respectively, as recently as the year 2000, and the numbers were even higher in the 1980s. In 2016–17 just 15,000 students in England were registered for HNDs and 19,500 for HNCs. Only 4 percent of twenty-five-year-olds in England hold a sub-degree technical qualification as their highest qualification, compared with more than 20 percent in Germany.[14]

The technical training numbers have been falling further, despite recent concern about technician shortages, because of the way that funding and incentives in post-school education currently work hugely in favor of classical university degrees.[15] Meanwhile, anything between 30 and 50 percent of graduates in England are in nongraduate employment five years after graduating.

Supporters of the current version of mass university education in the UK argue that around 40 percent of university courses, and even more in the new universities, are essentially vocational, whether traditional, high-prestige, vocational courses such as medicine, law, and engineering or newer university degrees such as nursing, quantity surveying, and marketing.

Yet, thanks to its student demand–led higher education funding system, the United Kingdom was in the bizarre position, in the

2011–2017 period, of increasing university teaching funding per student in physics by just 6 percent, compared with 27 percent for business degrees and 34 percent for sports sciences.[16]

It is true that many of the new universities do an impressive job. Standards vary enormously, but some of them have retained a distinctive polytechnic-technical ethos and are good local colleges serving local students and the local economy. They often add more educational value than the elite Russell Group universities with a high proportion of students from selective or private schools.

The people who run these new universities bridle at the suggestion that they should abandon their university status and form a more distinctive technical or applied subset of higher education, yet they choose to play in a league where they are bound to be the losers.

The Missing Middle

The relevant question in most rich countries is this: Is a classical university—with its bias toward the academic, and lecturers who are often researchers first and teachers second—the best place to deliver the kind of higher vocational skills that many individuals want to acquire and that the economy, especially in the United Kingdom and United States, so badly needs? Public opinion in the United Kingdom clearly does not think so. A large-scale survey by the think tank Onward found that 66 percent of respondents agreed that more people going to university and fewer gaining technical qualifications had been bad for the country overall; only 34 percent said it was beneficial.[17]

Yet the current incentives in the United Kingdom, from very tangible financial ones to less tangible cultural ones, focus on three- or four-year full-time courses for eighteen- to nineteen-year-olds, usually at residential universities, old or new, which is very expensive both for the country and the individuals concerned and not always an effective use of someone's time. And those incentives tend to discourage part-time study, mature students, shorter diploma-type higher vocational courses, sandwich courses, and the more spread-out lifelong learning that is set to be increasingly important.

And the content of courses at universities lean toward academic-analytical essay-writing methods even in the vocational courses that many of the new universities in the United Kingdom teach. In the case of something like a construction management degree course, the emphasis is on general cognitive skills, critical thinking, and management theory rather than field-specific experience.

The overall economic effects of mass higher education is a mixed picture, but one thing that is worth noting is that much research has shown that the *technician gap* in middle and higher skilled manual occupations cannot easily be filled with graduates, partly because they have different expectations of work after studying for a degree.

Paul Lewis of King's College London has studied UK employers who have responded to shortages of genuine technicians by recruiting science and engineering graduates to fill technician roles. But the use of overqualified graduates often causes significant problems, and nongraduates are still preferred in many jobs like air traffic control.

As Lewis puts it: "Graduates may possess a higher level of *theoretical* knowledge than is needed to fill a technician role, they are also often *underskilled*, because they lack the *practical* skills required to do the job well. Also, graduates often quickly become dissatisfied, both with the mundane, highly routinised nature of technician work and also with their relatively low wages, and so often leave relatively soon after joining their employer. The education system is producing the wrong mix of skills, with too many graduates and too few technicians being educated in some STEM disciplines."[18]

Only about 65 percent of young people in the United Kingdom have a level 3 qualification, and most of them are academic A levels; by contrast, in most comparable European countries the figure is closer to 90 percent, and a good proportion are nonacademic qualifications. The section of society most let down by the underinvestment in decent nonacademic skill training does not have a loud voice: the parents of young people in low-level apprenticeships or taking unsatisfactory courses at further education (FE) colleges are not heard in the corridors of power, and those colleges themselves—often described as for "other peoples' children"—have none of the funding or lobbying power over public policy that the university vice-chancellors enjoy.

In 2017–18, despite high tuition fees paid by students, over £8 billion ($10.4 billion) in public funding was spent supporting 1.2 million UK undergraduates, compared with just £2.3 billion ($3 billion) of public funding for 2.2 million full- and part-time FE students. Thanks in part to this funding squeeze, the number of adult learners in FE—people retraining or trying to raise their skill levels—dropped from 4 million to below 2 million between 2005 and 2016. The *average* salary of an FE lecturer is £30,000 ($39,000) a year, which will soon be the starting salary of a primary and secondary school teacher.

Employers, for their part, have become part of the problem in the last twenty years in the United Kingdom (and similarly in the United States) with a sharp cut in training budgets[19] and increased dependence on immigrant labor, or "free" graduates, to deal with skill shortages. Since the 1980s much off-the-job training has been delivered not by employers themselves but by private training providers offering training in a bewildering range of functions and qualifications and certificates, several thousand in all.

Everything in the United Kingdom points to university by default, as one of the country's leading economic commentators, Paul Johnson, discovered for himself when his second son, Tom, decided after getting modest A level results that he didn't want to go to university:

> An apprenticeship look[ed] like a good option for son number two. The government is promoting this as an alternative route. So I spent a large part of the Christmas holidays helping him to apply for higher and degree level apprenticeships. It is staggeringly hard even to find the right opportunities . . . [J]ust 1,800 18-year-old school leavers started any form of higher apprenticeship in 2016 . . .

My son wants to be a computer programmer or software developer. Apparently this is a shortage occupation. You wouldn't know it from the scarcity of openings. By comparison there are hundreds of relevant degree courses, all clearly advertised . . .

Our education system is designed for students who go straight from A levels to university. Their route is clear. It's much tougher for the rest. The other routes are opaque.[20]

Johnson ended up making a BBC radio documentary about this experience with Tom, who did eventually get the software apprenticeship he was seeking. One of the most revealing moments in the program was when Johnson took some teachers from Tom's school to the local FE college, which they had never visited before and where they were surprised to see so many of their former pupils. Schools boast about the number of pupils they send to university but rarely mention those who have gone on to good apprenticeships or acquired useful vocational qualifications at FE colleges.

Too many people in Britain and America, and increasingly in France and Germany, too, are being sucked into higher education because of the prestige and the promise of professional security even when it is clearly not suitable.

A friend of mine has a nephew called Roger who studied physics at university. He did science A levels at a state school in Leeds, where the only option presented was university; indeed, the sixth form was given evidence of the higher earnings of graduates, and positive presentations were given by undergraduate ex-pupils.

Roger chose his university partly because of its great sports facilities, and he spent too much of his time playing sport. But he also complains that too much of the course involved memorizing equations, and there was no intellectual enjoyment in his studies. He failed his second-year exams and had to retake a year and then failed his final exams. So he owed four years of fees and living expenses and still had no degree.

Roger then did an unusual apprenticeship in fund-raising at a charity and now has a job, which he loves, working for a sports charity with young kids—a job that did not require a college degree in the first place.

Roger is just one case, but says he knows of many others who in retrospect realize they were pressured into going to university by their schools and parents and the wider culture when it was not the right choice. A 2017 YouGov poll in the United Kingdom found that 35 percent of recent graduates disagreed that the cost of university had been worth it in terms of career prospects.[21]

The result is not just many frustrated individuals but that glaring "missing middle" in the economy's skill base and the neglect of Hand that has left severe skill shortages in STEM-related areas, the skilled trades, and technician-level jobs, especially in construction, health, and information technology, from coders to web designers. UK employers in 2017 complained that they had trouble filling more than 40 percent of skilled-trade vacancies.[22] (Many Commonwealth countries, especially in Africa, that followed the United Kingdom down the path of university expansion are also now worrying about the weakness of their vocational skill base.)

The United States, France, and Germany

This failure is part of a bigger training and retraining failure, especially in the United Kingdom and the United States, in response to the exporting of large slices of manufacturing industry to lower-cost countries. Robert Reich, Bill Clinton's secretary of labor, argued in his book *The Work of Nations: Preparing Ourselves for 21st-Century Capitalism* (1991) that workers in rich countries should accept the great wealth-producing machine of globalization so long as responsible governments retrain them for the jobs of the future. Steelworkers would become IT technicians.

This retraining simply did not happen on any significant scale in either country. And according to Richard Reeves, prior to passage of the 2017 tax law, for every dollar the US government spent on trade adjustment assistance for workers, it spent almost $25 on tax subsidies for the endowments to elite colleges.[23]

At the zenith of American industrial power in the 1950s and 1960s, a significant proportion of young people did some Hand education at school and then served apprenticeships in local factories and offices, often rising to senior positions. But formal apprenticeships, combining work and off-the-job training, have always been relatively rare in the United States; in 1975 there were just 292,000 such apprenticeships, compared with 1.4 million in West Germany.

In 2018, 240,000 people began apprenticeships in the United States, and only 6 percent of young people are in formal technical or vocational training. According to official figures, there were just 15,000 apprenticeship places in 2018 for the whole of the manufacturing sector. Daniel Markovits, author of *The Meritocracy Trap: How America's Foundational Myth Feeds Inequality, Dismantles the Middle Class, and Devours the Elite*, says that the average US firm today spends less than 2 percent of its payroll budget on training.[24]

And since the 1970s the United States, like the United Kingdom, has seen schools downgrade their "shop" classes—metalworking, woodworking, and so on—as they came to be judged by how many pupils they sent to college. (See Chapter Seven.)

In recent years, and partly inspired by populist political alienation, there has been a recognition that governments need to think harder about the non-university 50 percent-plus of secondary-school graduates, and there is noisy political support for more investment in post-school vocational and technical education in the United States and the United Kingdom.

Governments have not been completely idle. The United Kingdom has a target of 3 million apprenticeships and introduced an apprenticeship levy on bigger employers in 2017. In the United States, too, there has been plenty of political speechmaking about vocational education, and President Trump passed an executive order in 2017 to expand apprenticeships, but the state of play is probably better summed up by President Obama's bid for a $12 billion boost to community colleges, which was whittled down by Congress to just $2 billion.

The ability of academic higher education to set the tone and priorities for the whole education system, especially in the United Kingdom and United States, remains undimmed. And one reason why the Anglo-American academic generalist approach has taken root is that it goes with the grain of modern school teaching methods.

A child-centered teaching style took hold in the 1970s and 1980s, especially in the United States and the United Kingdom, that downplayed drilling and practice and the acquisition of specific knowledge in favor of uncovering pupils' innate talent and creativity through learning general, analytical skills such as "decision-making" and "handling information critically." Those of middling or below-average ability have not in the main been helped by this shift in focus, and, according to a Sheffield University report of 2010, about 17 percent of pupils still leave secondary school in the United Kingdom functionally illiterate and innumerate. The figure in the United States is similar.

Supporters of the child-centered approach argue that we don't need to know particular things any longer because we can look it up on Google; what we need is a generic facility to acquire knowledge and think critically. By contrast, traditionalists insist that knowledge is cumulative: we have to build knowledge in order to think and be creative.

In the United Kingdom the popularity of generic skills also grew out of the particular deindustrializing circumstances of the 1980s. David Willetts, the British politician, again: "In my constituency in the 1970s you went to school and you knew that when you left you would do an apprenticeship in the Portsmouth dockyard. And the school had a reasonable sense of what you needed to know to work in the dockyard. But then the dockyard closes, the steel works closes, the car plant has just gone bust. We don't quite know what these 17 year olds are going to do but we are pretty sure it is not the old jobs in mass manufacturing. So they need some stuff that is broader and more flexible for a more flexible labour market."[25]

General skills came to be regarded by much of the educational and political establishment in the United Kingdom and the United States as the most relevant education and training for a complex modern world. As Matthew Crawford, the American author, puts it in his book *The Case for Working with Your Hands*, the manual trades are now given little honor in the US school system because of "the fear that acquiring a specific skill set means that one's life is *determined*. In college, by contrast, many students don't learn anything of particular application; college is the ticket to an *open* future. Craftsmanship entails learning to do one thing really well, while the ideal of the new economy is to be able to learn new things."[26]

Crawford argues that today's preferred role model is the management consultant, who swoops in and out and whose very pride lies in his lack of particular expertise. "Like the ideal consumer, the management consultant presents an image of soaring freedom, in light of which the manual trades appear cramped and paltry: the plumber with his butt crack, peering under the sink."[27]

In the United States, like the United Kingdom, a single route into the cognitive class via high SAT test scores and selective higher education has replaced the multiple routes of the recent past. In the United States before the Second World War, you could "read" law in a lawyer's office and take the bar examination without a law degree. By the end of the 1970s, in medicine, law, accounting and other professions, a college degree was increasingly necessary. Business was one of the main routes open to ambitious but nonacademic people.

The US story of rapid expansion of secondary and then higher education, as I described in Chapter Two, preceded the expansion story in Britain, although it has recently run out of steam, thanks partly to high costs and cuts to the federal funding of public universities. Both countries, as we have seen, have shown a somewhat similar neglect of vocational and technical education.

After the GI Bill surge, there was further expansion of higher education in the United States in the 1950s and especially the 1960s. Cold War competition and Soviet success in sending a man into space produced more public funding for higher education in the shape of scholarships and student loans, and by the 1970s, as noted, nearly half of young people were going into higher education of some kind.

The US system is more differentiated than Britain's. At the pinnacle are the Ivy League private universities and liberal arts colleges, which are highly selective and expensive, and then the somewhat less expensive state or public universities; both private and state schools usually offering four-year degree courses. Between tuition and residential fees, Ivy League colleges now cost over $70,000 a year, private four-year colleges about $50,000, public four-year colleges $38,000 (for those coming out of state), and around $22,000 for those from within the state.[28]

Entry to the elite colleges, as in most countries, is skewed toward those whose parents attended them, with the added bias in the United States of the "legacy admissions": students who are more likely to get a place at a top college because their family has been donating to the college. (Against that, many colleges are trying to become less dependent on SAT scores and give more weight to the social context of academic contributions.)

Lower down the chain are the community colleges: closer to Britain's FE colleges or former polytechnics, but counted as part of the higher education system. Nearly two-thirds of all undergraduates are currently studying in one of the 980 community colleges. Most of them are doing vocational two-year "associate degrees"; more than half part-time and often training for jobs in the health sector or public services, such as registered nurse or appointment manager at a health clinic.

Anyone can attend a community college if they have graduated from high school—nearly 6 million students were enrolled in 2016—and the colleges are far cheaper than four year state or private universities, with annual tuition fees averaging about $3,000 a year.[29] It is also possible to transfer after two years at community college for a final two years at a four-year university course.

Partly because so many people use community colleges as a way of making a four year liberal arts or humanities degree more affordable, there has been a drift away from more technical and vocational courses. So, in 2016–17, easily the largest category of community college graduate (386,658)—representing more than one third of all graduates—were studying "liberal arts and sciences, general studies and humanities." The next biggest group, numbering 186,299, was "health professions and related programs," and after that, at 108,353, came "business management, marketing and support services."[30]

In 1982 the average high school graduate graduated with 22.1 credits, rising to 26.6 in 2013. Academic credits have increased from 14.4 to 19.6, while vocational credits have declined from 4.6 to 3.4.[31]

The 60-plus percent of the US adult population who have only a high school education or less have seen their incomes stagnate since 1980, so it is no surprise that 90 percent of high school students want to go to college (the numbers are similar in the United Kingdom) and about 70 percent do now go to some kind of post-school education. But, to repeat, only 35 percent do a full four-year degree, and only 9 percent go to a highly selective college. About 13 percent of Americans have a postgraduate qualifications from one of the various "grad schools," which have long been more common in the United States than Europe, although Europe is catching up.

Overall, entry into higher education in the United States peaked in 2010 and is now in decline thanks to spiraling debt and a more brutal repayment scheme for the 45 million indebted students than in the United Kingdom, which has a lower cap on tuition fees and writes off more debt. It is little wonder that student debt is a big political issue in the United States, with all the Democrat candidates for president supporting some version of student loan forgiveness.

To some analysts it is the fact that America slipped back from being the leader in mass secondary and higher education that is the cause of its great income and status divergence since the 1970s. Claudia Goldin and Lawrence Katz argue that when college attendance no longer kept up with the pace of technological change, it started to sharply increase the demand for and pay of the most highly educated.[32] This surely downplays other factors, such as the disappearance of middle-income jobs thanks to trade openness, technology, and the decline of organized labor. Also, if there is such demand for graduates, why are so many working in nongraduate jobs?

American higher education, like British, also struggles to combine two functions—mass opportunity and elite selection—and both end up favoring the latter, perhaps because it is inherently simpler. Nicholas Lemann in *The Big Test*, his critique of the SAT, accuses it of being fundamentally un-American:

> The idea of educating everyone at public expense ranks with political democracy as one of the United States' great original social contributions. Both ideas rest on a belief that ordinary people are capable of more than the leaders of previous societies would have thought possible . . .
>
> Our apparatus of meritocracy is not part of this tradition. Rather, it belongs to an older, less distinctively American tradition of using tests and education to select a small governing elite.[33]

In Germany and France, at least until recently, the story has been a somewhat different one. In recent decades universities have carried less prestige partly because there have been attractive post-school alternatives: about 50 percent of German secondary-school graduates still go straight into an apprenticeship, and in France, while about 40 percent of secondary-school graduates achieve the academic *bac général*, another 15 percent achieve a *bac technologique* and 25 percent a lower-level *bac professionnel*, which lead to nonuniversity technical colleges of various kinds. Also, because universities are largely nonselective, once a student has achieved the graduation exam, the *Abitur* in Germany or *baccalauréat* in France, you have a right to attend university (although some courses have quota restrictions).[34]

About one-third of French high school graduates go on to the unselective university system, which is flanked by the highly selective *grandes écoles*, which take the top 3 to 4 percent of students but receive about 30 percent of state funding for higher education.[35] There are about 250 *écoles* overall—some general, such as the *écoles d'ingénieurs* or *écoles de commerce*; some much more specialized. After passing the *bac général*, students aiming for one of the *grandes écoles* undertake a grueling two-year preparatory course, known as the *prépa*, followed by a competitive national exam. Those who pass, about half, then have three to five years' study at a *grande école* before, in most cases, going on to staff the French political, administrative, academic, and business elite.

The École National d'Administration (ENA), established by General de Gaulle in 1945 as a symbol of meritocratic modernization, is the most notoriously exclusive of them all. The annual intake is just eighty, but it has produced four of the last eight presidents and eight of the last twenty-two prime ministers. It has now become a symbol of an ossified elite, and proposals to abolish it, most recently by Emmanuel Macron, are made from time to time.

The most prestigious *grandes écoles*—the École Polytechnique and the ENA—take about two-thirds of their entrants from the children of the highest professional and managerial class, and in 2015 only 1.3 percent and 4.4 percent, respectively, from working-class backgrounds. Looking more broadly at all those taking the *prépa*, the numbers from the highest social class fall back to about 50 percent.

Germany is unlike the United Kingdom, the United States, and France in having *no* elite higher-education institutions comparable to Oxbridge, the Ivy League, or the *grandes écoles*, although many elite children go abroad to study. Like France and the United States, Germany has a more differentiated higher education system than the United Kingdom, and has preserved the specialist technical colleges, known as the *Fachhochschulen*—again somewhat similar to the United

Kingdom's former polytechnics. There are about 210 *Fachhochschulen* (now classified as universities) educating about 22 percent of young people compared with 120 traditional universities educating 38 percent.[36] As in France, more than half of students go to a *local* college or university, although some may live in student halls of residence.

As the country that pioneered the modern research university, Germany remains deeply respectful of academic traditions but has managed to combine that with an appreciation of what one might call the practical intellect. Around half of secondary-school graduates, including nearly 20 percent of those who pass the *Abitur*, go into a traditional apprenticeship lasting between two and three and a half years.

This national "dual system" of apprenticeships, combining low-wage employment in a company with time in vocational schools, is embedded in all three levels of government (federal, state, and local) and in the social partnership system. It trains people in just 325 different occupational categories (compared to thousands in the United Kingdom) that are drawn up by employers, and every school child receives the *Beruf aktuell* (current professions handbook), giving details of the jobs the apprenticeships lead to and pay levels they might expect.[37]

Many of the longer apprenticeships include substantive theoretical content. A plasterer, for example, will have to do complex calculations on heat loss. Some apprenticeships are the equivalent of a level four or five in terms of the international education grading system. By comparison, the modern British apprenticeship is much more basic, generally lasts just one or two years, and the funding rules encourage training providers to focus on shorter, cheaper, lower level (level one and two) programs in subjects such as customer service and business administration.

The German apprenticeship system still has considerable prestige. I know middle-class professional German families in which it is still completely normal for a child to do an apprenticeship before moving on to do a further qualification. There is a sense in Germany that all qualifications are on the same spectrum, at least in status. Jens Spahn, the German health minister (at the time of this writing, March 2020) and one of the brightest sparks in Angela Merkel's government, did a bank clerk apprenticeship before going to technical college and then university. It is not an untypical story for political and business leaders.

The system is seen by some as too inflexible; it took seven years, for example, for the various parties to agree to the most recent addition to the apprenticeship job function, an e-commerce sales role. Some of the more traditional apprenticeships, and those that require anti-social hours, are increasingly hard to fill. And because of the tightness of the labor market, there is more poaching of recently trained staff than in the past.

But the biggest threat to the standing of the system is now the reformed university system. German university degrees used to last at least five years, and young graduates would often not start their careers until they were twenty-eight or even thirty. This is one reason why, according to the Organisation for Economic Co-operation and Development (OECD), only 31 percent of Germans age twenty-five to thirty-four had higher educational qualifications in 2017, compared with 52 percent in the United Kingdom, 48 percent in the United States, and 44 percent in France.

But recent reforms have copied the United Kingdom's three-year bachelor's degree (or four- to five-year year master's degree), and the government has been encouraging more people to go to university, with the participation level now rising to almost 50 percent (including the *Fachhochschulen*). It is also attracting more international students.

With the encouragement of the OECD, Germany is being pushed to swap its specific-skill–based system for a more Anglo-Saxon generic aptitude system based in higher education. But German employers, like those in the United Kingdom, complain that graduates' expectations make them poorly motivated employees. There is also a 35 percent dropout rate from degree courses with most people falling back on an apprenticeship.

Over the next few years, we will discover whether Germany can sustain an apprenticeship system that has succeeded in giving status to many middling- and even low-skill jobs or whether it will opt for UK-style mass higher education, with what seems to be its attendant squeeze on higher manual and technical skills.

Too Much Signaling?

Our societies would not work properly if people only had the education levels of the early nineteenth century. But that does not mean more academic education is always the answer to our ills. As Alison Wolf has demonstrated in *Does Education Matter?: Myths About Education and Economic Growth*, there is no clear link between education and economic growth except, perhaps, in the early stages of industrialization. Countries with similar levels of educational attainment can exhibit very different productivity and growth. Conversely, rich countries with very different numbers of graduates can produce very similar growth and productivity numbers. It is true that the United Kingdom saw a productivity surge in the 1980s and 1990s as graduate numbers were rising, but that was largely thanks to the elimination of the least productive companies and even whole sectors.

There is an extraordinary amount of magical thinking about the beneficial impact of higher education on productivity, economic growth, and social mobility; Alison Wolf compares it to the Soviet Union's irrational belief in capital goods.[38] In fact, all of these things have been stagnating in the years that university enrollments have been roaring ahead. (In 2017 an average of 44 percent of twenty-five- to thirty-four-year-olds in OECD countries had a higher education qualification.)*

---

* One high point of magical thinking was reached in 2002 when Estelle Morris, then United Kingdom secretary of state for education, wrote an article in the *Guardian* claiming that a 1 percentage point increase in the proportion of graduates in the workforce led to a 0.5 percent increase in GDP.

The American economist Robert J. Gordon, in his book *The Rise and Fall of American Growth*, even says that innovation has been nose-diving in the era when there has never been more investment in research universities. Productivity has been in particularly sharp decline in those parts of the economy that are graduate dominated. And some analysis even sees professional bureaucratization stemming from mass higher education as an active drag on productivity.[39]

Moreover, higher education has done nothing to reduce inequality, and, as Wolf suggests, its expansion in recent decades may actually be one cause of our political divides. Education, from an employment point of view, turns out, at least at higher levels, to be not so much about what you have actually learned but what your level or place of education will signal to a potential employer about your general academic aptitudes and your character and attitudes. It is a ranking system, and in the United Kingdom it is reinforced by the physical and social separation of the residential universities.

And the sorting hat of higher education creates credential inflation requiring ever more differentiation. When more than one-quarter of students in the United Kingdom receive a first-class degree, it encourages more people to differentiate themselves with a master's degree. Thus the number of adults with a postgraduate qualification rose from 4 percent to 11 percent between 1996 and 2013.[40]

A friend who is a senior psychologist, having done the necessary master's degree to enter the profession in the United Kingdom in the late 1980s, says that now it would be unthinkable for someone to rise to her level without a PhD. Indeed, most people at work address her as "Doctor" because they assume she must be one. And I know of a prestigious recruitment firm that, as a matter of principle, does not take people without master's degrees.

This also creates its own interests and demarcations much like the old trade union demarcation disputes. A former colleague of mine who runs a historic building in Scotland had an ugly dispute with his deputy, who has an MA in museum studies, when my former colleague wanted to recruit a very capable and experienced person who did *not* have that qualification.

But if academic education is partly a way of signaling the right aptitudes to employers, then—as Bryan Caplan argues in his book *The Case Against Education: Why the Education System Is a Waste of Time and Money*—there might be less time-consuming and costly methods of achieving the sorting than our current system of higher education.[41]

There is plenty of evidence that students forget much of what they have learned at college, and, as noted earlier, transferable skills like "critical thinking" are hard to measure. Indeed, there is an increasing body of research that finds that many students are learning almost nothing at college. Richard Arum and Josipa Roksa argue in *Academically Adrift: Limited Learning on College Campuses* on the basis of surveys and studying test results that a significant proportion of US college students demonstrate no improvement in a range of skills, including critical thinking, complex reasoning, and writing.[42]

And the hours that students devote to study has been in sharp decline in the United States. In the early 1960s students spent roughly forty hours per week on academic work (combining studying alone and class/lecture time), which has now fallen to twenty-seven hours per week, and studying alone has fallen to just thirteen hours. (A recent paper found that vocabulary among American adults had declined across all educational levels since the 1970s, with the largest declines among those with a bachelor's or graduate degree.)[43]

The situation in the United Kingdom is not very different. According to surveys conducted by the Higher Education Policy Institute, about 25 percent of students admit to working less than twenty hours per week. If it is still possible to be awarded a decent 2:1 degree by doing so little work, it cannot be a very demanding or rigorous course.[44]

The rapid expansion of higher education in the United Kingdom, combined with the incentive for universities to recruit as many fee-paying students as possible, has inevitably eroded degree class standards, especially in the humanities. Only 7 percent of students achieved a first (the top degree award) in 1994; the figure is now 29 percent, and 79 percent get a first or a 2:1 (the second-best degree award).

The grade inflation is also true of the A levels that students need for university entrance—although many universities are now offering "unconditional" offers because they are so desperate to fill places. According to professor of education Robert Coe, those who were receiving D and E grades in the late 1980s were being given Bs and Cs by the mid-2000s.[45]

In a 2016 OECD report on basic skill levels among recent graduates from twenty-three countries, England ranked in the bottom third despite the endless boosterism about "world-class" higher education.

And after all the huffing and puffing about the knowledge society and the importance of sending as many high school graduates as possible to university, it turns out that what many employers are looking for in graduates is not the little they have learned at college but rather "soft" social skills—application, concentration, the ability to cooperate with coworkers, and so on—learned primarily in the family, especially the middle-class one.

Some humanities graduates often have to *unlearn* the style and rhetoric they have painstakingly acquired in their essay writing years in order to be of any use to their employers. I vividly remember when a trainee journalist on the *York Evening Press* being put through the mill by an exasperated managing editor whose job it was to expel all the pompous circumlocutions from the new intake of graduate trainees. Writing in simple, direct prose and learning to put the most interesting facts first in a story can be surprisingly hard after three years of absorption in postmodern discourse!

It is true that people without decent levels of basic academic skills are at a permanent disadvantage in today's world. And society would not work without the higher academic skills of doctors, engineers, scientists, mathematicians, computer scientists, biotechnologists, and some of their counterparts in the humanities and social sciences. But, to repeat: education should increasingly be regarded as a "positional good"—one that gains much of its value from whether you have more than other people.

As we saw in Chapter Three, you have a much better chance of being a "top" or "near-the-top" sort of person if one or both of your parents graduated from a good university and you are also more likely to possess those relevant noncognitive skills that employers like. You are likely to progress, without fuss, into the cognitive class, as my own four children—three of whom have top degrees from Russell Group universities—have done.

Whereas in previous generations children from less privileged backgrounds would have been judged, and would have judged themselves, by different standards of capability, there is now—thanks to the expansion of academic higher education—something like a *single, common cognitive class*, with everyone measured by the same cognitive standard. In the past, the talented and ambitious were more randomly scattered about geographically and occupationally and were judged according to a wider range of aptitudes.

There is no longer a working-class intelligentsia thanks to the widening and democratization of society's *general* cognitive class. But, as Andrew Hindmoor, professor of politics at the University of Sheffield, has pointed out, this has the effect of skewing the geographical distribution of cognitive talent.[46]

Labour MP Angela Rayner gave an interview to the *Spectator* a few years ago and told the story of how a Tory MP had once approached her, saying: "You should be one of us, Ange! You've done well; you've climbed out!" She used this episode to explain why she could not be a Conservative but such views are just as common on the center-left, albeit using the language of upward mobility meritocracy rather than aspiration.[47]

As already observed, English working-class towns like Barnsley, Doncaster, and Wakefield each year suffer a brain drain, losing thousands of their academically brightest eighteen-year-olds to university towns and metropolitan centers like Leeds and Sheffield. Many of them never return to live permanently. Almost one quarter of all new graduates in the United Kingdom end up in London, at least initially, while big cities like Manchester, Birmingham, and Belfast retain about half of the students who studied there.[48]

According to a recent study drawing on the 450,000 people enrolled in the UK Biobank, this is now creating a "gene drain" in left-behind areas, with those who are healthier and brighter leaving for urban centers. "If these demographic processes continue, the biological inequalities we observe may grow larger each generation as like keeps marrying like," said David Hugh-Jones, the lead UK author.[49]

The same brain/gene drain occurs in the more depressed parts of the United States, Germany (especially eastern Germany), France—"*la France périphérique*," described by social geographer Christophe Guilluy—and elsewhere in Europe. In Britain the lack of prestigious local technical colleges, the dominance of residential universities, and the over-mighty London problem, makes the social and geographical imbalances even worse. The gap between richest and poorest regions in the United Kingdom is almost twice as large as in France and three-quarters larger than in Germany.[50]

With the single university-shaped funnel into the professional and business class and the increased dependence of employers on the signaling effect of a university degree, there has been a sharp falloff in promotion from below in recent decades. (See more in Chapter Five.) As noted earlier, as recently as 1991, only about half of senior people in professional and managerial positions had a university degree, and it was possible for ambitious people without extensive educational credentials to rise inside a company or professional organization.[51]

Flying the Nest, into the Middle Class

There is a final important point about the expansion of higher education: the social experience, particularly for *residential* students. Some people, like David Soskice, argue that this is the single most important thing about it. "The key element of the modern university are the social skills that people acquire often living away from home for the first time and mixing with people from different backgrounds," he says. "It's not so much the going to lectures but the ability to organize a meeting or work cooperatively with other people to achieve a social goal that matters."

This is a new version of the very old idea of joining a community of scholars and thereby becoming a better and different kind of person: more refined, more knowledgeable, closer to God. The modern case for the residential university experience might be seen, in part, as a more egalitarian way of spreading the magical confidence that is often thought to attach to young people emerging from elite private boarding schools (although the often-quoted "polish," charm, and soft skills associated with the privately educated are surely inculcated at least partly at home).

It is true that social skills are increasingly essential to many professional jobs as the more routine intellectual calculations and judgments are automated. It is assumed that three or four years away from home can breed confidence, self-reliance, and openness to different people and situations. That is no doubt the case for many students. And it is certainly the case that in increasingly multiethnic but often ethnically segregated societies, universities bring people from different ethnicities into close contact, often for the first time.

Set against that, the residential university experience also seems to be responsible for a sharp rise in mental stress among students. The *Guardian* in the United Kingdom reported in March 2019 on an online survey of nearly 40,000 students that found very high levels of anxiety and thoughts of self-harm, with fully one-third saying they had experienced a serious psychological issue for which they needed help.[52]

Every autumn 1.5 million British teenagers take part in a mass migration—leaving home to go to university—dividing the country into a residential university class of mobile, professional people and a more rooted nongraduate group. This has surely exacerbated the country's value and social divisions—and anti-London feeling—revealed in the Brexit vote.

Mass *residential* higher education remains a very British phenomenon, and even more so in England than in Scotland; it is less common in continental Europe and the United States, although the trend is for it to decrease somewhat in Britain—partly because of more students from less mobile low-income and ethnic minority backgrounds—and increase in the rest of the rich world. (If the Covid-19 crisis reduces mobility both within and between countries the growth of residential higher education may be checked.)

In the 2017–18 academic year around 80 percent of full-time British students left home for study. The most affluent and those going to the most elite universities generally travel farthest. Many poorer students either continue living at home or at least stay in their home regions.[53] But even if you just move the fifteen miles from Mansfield to university in Nottingham, you are still likely to adopt what one vice-chancellor described to me as the "leaving mentality."

In the United States, although the residential system was imported from Britain at the start of the twentieth century—at least for elite colleges—more than 40 percent of college students live at home and 77 percent attend college in their home states.

On the positive side of the balance sheet, the expansion of residential higher education in the past thirty years in England has played a big role in rejuvenating postindustrial cities like Manchester, Leeds, Sheffield, Newcastle, and Liverpool. Some of these cities are now primarily university towns. There is an element of unintended, redistributive regional policy too. A lot of relatively affluent and disproportionately southern English students move north for three years, bringing with them many tens of thousands of pounds to spend in tuition fees and living costs each year, and quite a few of them then stay permanently.

But these economic benefits have been bought at a price in social division. Anecdotally, graduates in the United Kingdom are far less likely to have close friends who are nongraduates compared with graduates in the United States and continental Europe.

To build an entire expensive edifice of residential academic higher education on the grounds that the extracurricular activities *might* have a positive effect on some students social skills seems like an irresponsible allocation of national resources, especially at a time of significant skill shortages in caring and middle-skill technical jobs. And both the US and German economies outperform the UK economy, at least in productivity growth, without such large numbers going into *residential* higher education.

Indeed, the Soskice argument overlaps with the Caplan (and Arum and Roksa) claim that many students effectively learn little specific of value at college, and employers are more concerned with both the signal of general academic ability sent by getting to university in the first place, followed by the acquisition of nonacademic aptitudes once there. However, Caplan draws the opposite conclusion from Soskice and argues that there is no case for public subsidy of higher education, and much of it—beyond technical and vocational specialisms like medicine and engineering—could be closed down or done in other institutions without any loss.

One might not want to go that far, but there are surely other ways, short of sending almost everyone to residential universities for three years, of enabling young people to develop social skills. It could be in a revised secondary school curriculum with more stress on social skills or in residential apprenticeships or forms of national service—a "gap year for all" volunteering on farms or in hospitals—that could replicate the horizon-raising and social-mixing experience of the residential university at its best, and help to provide some of those soft skills that not everyone gets at home.

Universities are, in the main, full of decent people. The institutions exist in part to challenge tradition and authority, and in recent years they have become overwhelmingly dominated by what French economist Thomas Piketty playfully calls the Brahmin left (as opposed to the merchant right), especially in the social sciences and humanities. The academics and administrators therefore find it hard to see themselves as part of the establishment, the gatekeepers of modern society's new class system.

Many people in the universities realize that they must do more than credentialize the new mass elite and build lots of shiny new buildings if they want to show that they are of use to the local people who do not attend them.

They might start by recognizing that university does not produce the best outcomes for everyone. It makes no sense for many young people from all social classes who do not flourish in the rigorous academic environment that a university *should* be. And it makes even less sense for an economy that requires a range of skills and aptitudes, many of which are better acquired in workplaces or other kinds of post-school educational institution.

And it is surely just narrow-minded to assume that the answer to the education-based status (and income) divides is to send ever more people to university. People from all backgrounds, especially less privileged ones, should be encouraged to go to elite universities *if they have the aptitude for it*, as spelled out by Lionel Robbins in his report. But in my experience too much of the case for mass higher education is based on an indiscriminate spirit of not wanting to kick away the ladder. It is a decent instinct but it can also be, as noted earlier, a kind of narcissism that says: Be like me, pass exams at school, go to a Russell Group University and enjoy a successful professional career. But there are strict limits on the number of people who can do that even if everyone in the society had exactly the same level of cognitive ability!

Isn't it better to widen the sources of achievement and try to raise the status of "not university" rather than send as many people as possible to university—in the process raising expectations of professional success that in many cases are likely to be disappointed—while starving the economy of the middling technical skills it needs? The

Covid-19 crisis may, in any case, prompt a period of retrenchment and rethinking on the part of higher education. In both the United Kingdom and the United States it is likely to cut the flow of international students—in the United Kingdom, more than 20 percent of the total—and force many universities to seek state support.

I would not advocate closing universities, although some, at least in the United Kingdom, would certainly benefit from rebranding themselves as technical or applied universities and offering something shorter and more vocational than the standard university degree course.

But, thanks to the imminent demographic bulge of eighteen-year-olds in the United Kingdom, the country would need another thirty to thirty-five universities over the next couple of decades—an extra 300,000 places—if we are to keep up the present proportion of secondary-school graduates going into higher education. So the simple answer is: Do *not* create these universities and let the proportion going into higher education fall back while investing in and raising the visibility and status of other forms of post-school education and training. This can help prevent academic standards falling further and provide a more socially useful balance between analytical and practical forms of knowledge—between Head and Hand.

Chapter Five

The Rise of the Knowledge Worker

There is a war for talent, and it will intensify.

Steven M. Hankin

At the age of eight most children want to be firemen or cooks, nurses or bus drivers or people who work in shops—obviously useful occupations that serve other people and make daily life possible, as we were reminded during the Covid-19 crisis. By the time they leave school, most children have been guided away to less hands-on, cognitive-based jobs.

The vast majority of British and American parents want their children to go to university, according to surveys that higher-education lobby groups take great pleasure in quoting. This is not surprising when everyone from politicians to schoolteachers to employers have been telling them for the past three decades that it is the only way to a secure, middleclass future for their offspring.

As we will see in Chapter Nine, this is actually ceasing to be the case, as the mass production of graduates has weakened the economic advantage of a degree, especially from less prestigious universities, and there is even some evidence of rising wages at the bottom and middle of the skill range, something postpandemic policy is likely to reinforce. Many of those parents would be better advised—at least from an economic point of view—to encourage their children to take a high-grade apprenticeship or train as a technician unless they are heading to one of the top universities.

Nevertheless, until very recently the assumption that academic qualification equals cognitive achievement and a respected, well-paid job has been hard to argue with, and is one of the factors driving the continuing "graduatization" of the labor market. To some extent this has always been true. What has happened in rich countries since the 1980s is that this logic, which for one hundred years applied to just a small, educated elite, started to apply to *everyone*.

That in turn was caused by the decline of the old industrial Hand economy and the shift to a more Head-based knowledge economy as a result of more open, global trade and new technologies, particularly computer technologies, that replaced a lot of middling administrative and secretarial positions and skilled manual jobs.

This "hollowing out" of the labor market that is often associated with periods of technological change saw the start of what some economists call the "great divergence"—a growing number of well-paid Head jobs for the highly qualified and Hand and Heart jobs—often with stagnant or declining wages—for the rest, especially in the United States.

Technological change does not have to result in this kind of divergence. The period from what is called the second industrial revolution at the end of the nineteenth century—associated with steel, chemicals, electricity, and automobiles—right up to the 1970s is often called, in the United States, the "great compression," because differentials between Head and Hand narrowed significantly.[1] In the United States in 1900 a university professor was paid four times more than an unskilled worker; by 1960 this had fallen to twice as much, although both were a lot richer. Overall inequality between blue- and white-collar Americans declined from 1900 to 1970.

In Britain the income share of the top 5 percent, which included all of the best educated people, fell from 40 percent at the end of the nineteenth century to 20 percent by the 1970s, writes Richard Baldwin in *The Globotics Upheaval: Globalization, Robotics, and the Future of Work*.[2] "The drop in inequality . . . reflects the fact that labor finally started getting scarce at the same time as the innovations started making labor especially productive. It is also surely important that this second phase corresponded, after World War I, with a rise in workers' negotiating and voting power," Baldwin adds.[3]

But there is now overwhelming agreement among economists that this relatively egalitarian period ended in the 1970s and 1980s and mutated into one of greater labor market polarization, with jobs "increasingly concentrated in high-education, high-wage occupations and low-education, low-wage occupations, at the expense of traditionally middle-skill career jobs," as the American economist David H. Autor puts it.[4]

In the United Kingdom the share of middle-skill occupations, measured by the share of all hours worked, fell from 58 percent to 40 percent between 1981 and 2008. Across the OECD as a whole middle-skill jobs fell as a share of total employment by 10 percentage points between 1995 and 2015.[5]

The hollowing-out story has been an even bigger one in the United States. In 1970, American jobs were more or less evenly divided between *low-skill* (manual and basic service occupations) at 31.4 percent of all hours worked, *middle-skill* (production, office and sales occupations) at 38.4 percent, and *high-skill* (professional, technical, and managerial occupations) at 30.2 percent. Over the next forty-five years the middle-skill hours fell steeply from 38.4 percent of hours to just 23.3 percent, with most of those hours switching from middle- to high-skill occupations, which grew from 30.2 percent to 46.2 percent of hours.[6]

So far, so good, one might think. And for those with a college degree that is broadly true, with around 60 percent in high-skill occupations. But for non-college workers it is a very different story. According to Autor in 1980 the employment of non-college workers was roughly split between low- and middle-skill jobs, with 42 percent in the former category and 43 percent in the latter. Over the next few decades the share of non-college employment in middle-skill jobs fell sharply by 14 percentage points from 43 to 29 percent and *almost all of this is explained by the movement of non-college workers from middle-skill into low-skill work.*[7]

This single statistic illustrates the stark reality of the declining status of so much nongraduate employment and the political reaction against it in recent years in the United States and elsewhere. It also illustrates how the relative wage stagnation at the bottom end of the labor market has worked. People have not generally been experiencing a cut in wages; rather they have lost a middle-skill/middle-pay job and can then only find a lower-skill/lower-pay job.

In his work on so-called deaths of despair in the United States—the sharp increase in suicide, and death by drug overdose and alcoholism—the economist Angus Deaton talks about the "the man who loses his decent $28 an hour job at General Motors and ends up working as a parking lot attendant," and in the process loses his health insurance and maybe his partner too.[8]

In broad terms the pay differentiation story has followed a similar pattern throughout the rich world. It is not just about the graduate premium, the higher incomes graduates receive relative to nongraduates—although that is most visible and most quoted in the academic literature; it goes all the way up and down the qualification range. And it is predicted by a branch of economics that has emerged to account for the higher returns to skill and education called human capital theory.

The theory—developed in the 1950s and 1960s at Chicago University by several economists, most notably Gary Becker—is that education directly increases an individual's stock of "human capital" and thus their productivity and earnings potential.[9] Other things being equal, additional units of education—years of study, qualifications gained—will be rewarded with increased earnings. The assumption is that employers respond to the increase in supply of high-skilled workers by altering production processes to take advantage of this new supply of skilled workers. In any case, at least until recently, the demand for skill has kept pace with the much greater supply, one of the factors behind the pay differentiation story (although this is now changing, as we will see in Chapter Nine).

It is not actually clear that higher pay for graduates is always the result of higher productivity as opposed to social convention and inherited differentials between blue collar and white collar work. Measuring everything by qualification can have perverse outcomes and leads to what one might call "cognitive creep." A job comes to be judged, and paid, by the qualifications you need to get it rather than how productive or demanding it is or how well or badly you do it. For example, many jobs in the care sector need few if any qualifications but great patience, skill, and emotional intelligence to do well. This is also the case with some driving jobs that appear from the outside to be basic. Consider this description of a London bus driver.

> In the space of a few seconds, the driver makes many decisions: whether to stop in the first place; if and when to open the front doors and how many passengers to allow on before closing them; whether to ask the man who's just got on at the back to get off again; and whether to move off when the bus is now so full that passengers obscure the view to the nearside mirror. The driver makes a series of difficult decisions at nearly every stop on the journey between Croydon and Brixton.
>
> In addition to these decisions, the driver has to make decisions to drive the bus! When to pull out, to overtake, to slow down, to stop or carry on at an amber light, to allow traffic to cross from a side road, to take special care of cyclists and pedestrians, some of whom dice with death as they weave in and out of the dense, slow-moving traffic. Driving a large vehicle with nearly a hundred people crammed tightly into it requires great skill; the responsibilities are onerous and the technical expertise is considerable.[10]

Since 1975 the hourly pay of bus and coach drivers in the United Kingdom has risen just 22 percent (in 2017 prices) compared with a

111 percent rise for advertising and public relations managers. In the United States, bus drivers have actually seen their average hourly pay *fall* by 20 percent in that period.[11]

In any case, fair or not fair, there is no escaping the broad trend on pay differentiation since the early 1980s. David Autor divides the recent history of pay in the United States into three phases: 1963 to 1972, when real wages rose robustly and evenly among all education groups; 1973 to 1979, when—following the first oil shock—real earnings stagnated for everyone; and finally the era of rising wage inequality from 1980 onward, when wages rose robustly among the most educated and fell in real terms among the least educated, most strikingly among men with less than a bachelor's degree.[12]

Again, it is worth remembering how recently the less well educated dominated developed societies. As late as the 1990 census in the United States, whites without a college degree were more than 60 percent of the adult population.

The divergence story has also been true of the United Kingdom and continental Europe, although less so in terms of pay because of high minimum wages and stronger unions: median pay in the United Kingdom has risen 78 percent since 1975, 63 percent in Germany, and 30 percent in France, while it has remained flat in the United States partly thanks to rising health costs for employers.[13, 14]

The increase in the high-skill wage bill has been steeper in the United States and the United Kingdom than in much of Europe between 1980 and 2004, reflecting sharper income dispersal. It rose by 13.9 percentage points in the United States and 16.5 points in the United Kingdom. Contrast this with rises of 6 to 8 percentage points for France and Germany.[15]

But in Europe as a whole there has been a similar growth in professional and associate professional occupations and a sharp decline in more routine "good jobs" in administrative-secretarial and skilled manual roles: Just think of the medium-size engineering company of the 1970s and 1980s with its small army of white-collar office workers and skilled manual workers who have marched off into history.

It is worth briefly recording the speed and scale of that march. Between June 1978 and September 2018 the proportion of UK jobs in manufacturing and mining fell from 26.4 percent to 7.9 percent.[16] The fall was slightly less sharp in Germany, which is down to 15 percent and France to 10 percent.[17] In the United States the fall was from about 22 percent to around 9 percent.[18]

These declines carry within them a story of the radical diminishment of working-class power and institutions. I was a witness to the dying days of that power as a labor reporter on the *Financial Times* in London in the early 1980s. I was one of five journalists who had a whole page of the broadsheet newspaper to fill every day with stories of pay deals, strikes, and trade union politics. We never had any trouble filling the page: there was still a last gasp of life in the unions and their centralized pay negotiation institutions.

But union membership in the private sector was in the process of collapsing, thanks in part to the closure of plants with high union density, and overall union membership fell in the United Kingdom from around half in 1983 to 23 percent in 2017, and most of the latter was public sector and professional workers.[19] Starting from a lower level, the decline in the United States was also sharp and now stands at just 10 percent of employees, mainly in the public sector. Government legislation in the United Kingdom and United States in the 1980s hastened the decline, as did suicidal strike action, particularly Arthur Scargill's yearlong miners' strike in the United Kingdom in 1984–85.

Union involvement in training and apprenticeship systems, management decisions, and pay bargaining gradually disappeared, at least outside the public sector and one or two niches in the private sector, and the era of the deregulated labor market, at least in the United Kingdom and the United States, was ushered in—with a corresponding rise of the knowledge worker and the graduate premium. The slice of income that workers had once laid a claim to through their collective power now seeped upward, to be claimed by the graduates with their cognitive qualifications in the offices.

The destruction of union power was mainly a British and American story; the social partnership system remained intact in Germany, and union power remained significant in key sectors in France, although some of the same trends in income distribution emerged in milder form.

But this is also in part a surprisingly happy story of more "lovely" than "lousy" jobs. Between 2001 and 2018 in the United Kingdom, jobs in the bottom three deciles of the earnings distribution have declined as a share of employment, while those in the top three have increased.[20] Many of the most unpleasant jobs have been exported to low-income countries, which is probably one reason why, despite the negative commentary, people tell opinion surveys that life at work has been improving. In 2015, 71 percent of British employees said they had a good job compared with just 57 percent in 1989, according to the British Social Attitudes survey.[21] In the United States, too, only 15 percent of employees say they are somewhat or very dissatisfied with their jobs, according to a recent Pew Research Center survey.

Meanwhile, the share of graduate level jobs has been expanding fast in the United Kingdom at a bit less than 1 percentage point a year since 1986 (although it has slowed since 2012) and is now estimated at almost 40 percent.[22] It is a similar story in other rich countries: in the United States, 47 percent of jobs are now classified as "managerial, professional, technical or associate professional."

As noted, the "great divergence" in pay in the United Kingdom and the rest of Europe has been less dramatic than in the United States, but real enough. The most recent pay data comparing hourly pay in 1975 and 2017 in the United Kingdom (in 2017 prices) finds a 137 percent increase for company financial managers and 86 percent for actuaries and statisticians, compared with 21 percent for welders and 9 percent for refuse collectors. In the United States the figures for the same period at the bottom end are *minus*: minus 12 percent for sheet-metal workers, minus 16 percent for truck drivers, minus 34 percent for butchers, and minus 42 percent for bakers.[23]

Numerous OECD reports have noted a sustained fall in relative wages of less educated workers from the 1980s onward. According to one of the most recent reports, in 2018, those who have attained only upper secondary education will on average earn 65 percent of what their graduate contemporaries earn across all OECD countries, although there is a great deal of variation across countries and course types.[24]

The basic "graduate premium" in earnings has been declining with the expansion of the graduate class but remains significant, at least from elite universities. In the United Kingdom, at the age of twenty-nine, the average man who attended university earns about 25 percent more than the average man with just five good General Certificates of Secondary Education (GCSEs). For women the gap is even more, at 50 percent, thanks to the relatively lower pay of women in nongraduate, often Heart jobs.[25] Even at the bottom end, those with A levels, GCSEs, and apprenticeships achieve significantly higher lifetime productivity and pay than those who without these credentials.[26]

The story is a similar one in the United States and France, and the graduate returns from higher education are even higher in Germany, partly because the expansion in numbers has been, until recently, less rapid than in the United Kingdom. According to the latest figures from the OECD, someone in Germany with a bachelor's or equivalent degree earns on average 63 percent more than someone with upper secondary education. With a master's, doctoral, or equivalent it is 83 percent. For France, the figures are 47 percent and 110 percent (reflecting the higher salaries of those who go through the *grandes écoles* system). And for the United States it's 64 percent and 131 percent.[27]

Permission to Think

This forward march of the knowledge worker and the income divergence associated with the knowledge economy is now a well-known story. But two aspects of the cognitive takeover story are less visible. First, the extent of the privileging of key cognitive employees that has been emerging in big multinational companies. Second, the extent of the spread of *graduate-only* jobs in recent years.

Higher returns on qualification have also been reinforced by other developments in modern economies, such as the so-called war for talent and winner-takes-all markets. Both are the product of technology and global openness. The war for talent was a phrase coined by Steven M. Hankin of the management consultancy McKinsey in 1997 to describe more intense competition among top companies for recruiting and retaining key knowledge workers.

The prediction that the modern market economy combined with certain new technologies would generate a new layer of superstars was made a few years ago by two American academics, Robert H. Frank and Philip J. Cook. In *The Winner-Take-All Society: Why the Few at the Top Get So Much More Than the Rest of Us* they describe how technology allows a few stars to corner a disproportionate level of earnings in a particular market.[28]

Frank and Cook quote Rabo Karabekian, the only moderately good painter in Kurt Vonnegut's 1987 novel *Bluebeard*: "Simply moderate giftedness has been made worthless by the printing press and radio and television and satellites and all that. A moderately gifted person who would have been a community treasure a thousand years ago has to give up, has to go into some other line of work, since modern communications has put him or her into daily competition with nothing but the world's champions. . . . The entire planet can get along nicely now with maybe a dozen champion performers in each area of human giftedness."

Now that most of the music we listen to is prerecorded, the world's best soprano can be everywhere at once. "And since it costs no more to stamp out compact discs from Kathleen Battle's master recording of the Mozart arias than from her understudy's, most of us listen to Battle. Millions of us are willing to pay a few cents extra to hear her rather than another singer who is only marginally less able; and this allows Battle to write her own ticket."[29]

The focus on the most talented people at the tops of organizations, combined, especially in Britain and America, with intense pressure to reduce costs and maximize shareholder returns, has also been reshaping the way that big corporations operate in what is sometimes called the "Future of Work" transformation.

Back in the 1980s what are sometimes called the global multinationals (GMNs) began introducing enterprise-wide IT systems and turned routine administrative work into specialist centralized "shared services centers" that supplied a standard service to all business units. As this work was classified as nonstrategic and non–value creating, it could even be outsourced and offshored to low-wage countries. GMNs reduced their head count and produced much better-looking labor productivity ratios.

This opening phase of the Future of Work established a sense of "core" work and work that could be contracted out to the "contingent" labor market. A friend of mine who designs remuneration systems for big companies, and therefore has to remain anonymous, described to me the next phase:

The next phase is driven by the GMNs' fear of the new wave of small, agile digital disruptors. Many of these new firms are well-funded start-ups who have no baggage to preserve and no patience. Many bright young people are choosing *not* to join the GMN graduate training schemes, preferring instead small organizations where everything is outsourced except the stimulating work of idea origination, design, IP protection, and marketing. They can try many things, fail fast, and follow what works. Digital start-ups can get products to market very quickly, even in something as traditional as razor blades.

By comparison, the GMNs look at themselves and see rigid job definitions, turf wars, [and] a command level that got there over time and is out of touch with the latest skills and technology. Their middle-rank employees are risk averse. Their career is built on long-term progress up a professional hierarchy rather than the success of the immediate mission.

The new business structure consists of three layers: elite core full-time employees; contingent professionals; and contingent service staff, cleaners, security, and so on, many in the gig economy.

> The core of the business is the elite talent who are trusted with the "secret sauce": the secret ingredients behind competitive advantage. The elite are considered exceptionally talented. The only ones clever enough to create new value. Logic suggests that these are the only people the firm needs to directly motivate and retain.
>
> Beneath that elite there will still be a lot of complex technical and professional work that requires human input but can be brought in at standard rates as needed from the external contingent labor market. Their role is seen as definable and standardized. This might include highly technical specialists such as project managers, scientists, engineers.

What my friend is describing overlaps with the work on digital Taylorism of Phil Brown and Hugh Lauder that will be explored in more detail in Chapter Nine.[30] Brown and Lauder break down service jobs into three categories, developers, demonstrators, and drones, with only developers—typically 10 to 15 percent of the workforce—given a degree of autonomy and cognitive judgment.

It is worth noting that this strict demarcation of those with "permission to think" and the functionaries providing contracted-out services seems to be a product of Western business schools and, paradoxically, has not been adopted by the more authoritarian-communitarian Asian business cultures. Several decades ago Japan surprised Western manufacturers by showing the value of asking all workers to think about process and quality in what was called "total quality management." The Future of Work strategy does not seem to have learned this lesson.

If You Can't Beat 'Em, Join 'Em

The relentless graduatization of the labor market is another trend that has been making it harder to achieve a wider spread of income and status. In the United Kingdom in 2017, 23 percent of jobs required no qualifications on entry, while around 38 percent of jobs needed at least higher-education qualifications.[31] There is widespread popular hostility to the graduatization of jobs like nursing, police officer, project manager, and even prison officer. And yet it continues inexorably with powerful professional lobbies pushing it. Most of the above jobs are not yet exclusively graduate entry in many rich countries, but the graduate entry channel is becoming more central to the ethos of the organizations involved, and nongraduate entry routes are increasingly seen as a permanent slow lane rather than an alternative route in.

But people seldom stop to ask whether the graduate pay premium actually reflects greater value produced by the graduate. Is it just the graduate class awarding itself a premium? If university education were abolished tomorrow, how many tasks would not be completed because people lacked the skills? Is the trend being driven by traditionally nongraduate jobs like nursing and policing just wanting some of the higher status associated with being a graduate profession?

Peter Cheese, head of the United Kingdom's Chartered Institute of Personnel and Development, the professional body for HR people, sees "high graduate supply creating its own employer demand," and so long as parents believe that going to university and getting a graduate job is the path to safety, and maybe even success, for their children, that supply will keep coming.

This also creates, according to Cheese, a "herd" effect: "If everyone else is only hiring graduates, then you assume that you should do that too."[32] But one of the issues in hiring too many young people who have exam-passing ability but little experience of life is that they may be weak on the noncognitive aspects that are actually required for most jobs: leadership, communication, judgment, and dealing with difficult people and situations.

Cheese says he has advised various different organizations with high levels of graduate entry but who need help providing people with a kind of remedial training in basic human skills. He thinks we need to find ways to embed more clearly in education at all levels the recognition of core "human" skills that are essential in the workplace.

Nevertheless, the case for graduatization is sometimes a strong one. As we will see, there is evidence that graduate nurses, for example, improve the overall quality and effectiveness of health care. Yet there is the balancing anxiety, just mentioned, of lack of real-life experience combined with unrealistic expectations and disdain for the more basic aspects of, say, nursing or policing.

As so often is the case in the cognitive takeover story, the graduatization of the labor market, even in the upper echelons, is a surprisingly recent thing. Managers, directors, and senior officials—the highest category in the United Kingdom's nine-level Standard Occupational Classification—have historically employed most graduates, but the proportion was just 53 percent in 1991, rising to 78 percent in 2014.[33]

In managerial, professional, and technical occupations—the second highest occupational class—there are now nearly as many graduates as nongraduates, while only about one in every six workers in these occupations was a graduate at the start of the 1990s.[34]

The official definition of a "graduate job" in the United Kingdom is anyone working in the top three occupational classes in that nine-class Standard Occupational Classification schema. However, many of these managerial, associate professional, and technical occupations have, historically, not required a degree and include jobs such as dancers and choreographers, fitness instructors, youth and community workers, and IT user support technicians.

The remaining occupations—those in Standard Occupational Categories four to nine—had a near insignificant share of graduates in 1991, but this share has increased to 21 percent for administrative occupations, 13 percent for both sales and personal service occupations, and 8 percent even for the lowest-skilled elementary occupations. Only the manual occupations, skilled trades, and semiskilled process operatives have seen less significant rises.[35]

The evolution of nursing into a graduate profession in the United Kingdom has crystallized the debate on the advantages and disadvantages of graduatization. The idea that the nurse should be "a professional among equals" and not a "handmaiden" to other professionals goes back many decades, but it was not until 2013 that nurses officially required a degree.

There have been some graduate nurses since the 1970s, but back in the 1980s it was decided that registered nurses should study for a diploma rather than a degree that left them as the poor relation of other health professionals who were mainly graduates. In 2009 the Nursing and Midwifery Council finally decided to establish all-graduate entry for registered nurses.

The 2012 Willis Commission did not find "any evidence that degree-level registration was damaging to patient care." But it did also say that there should be a diversity of entry points and career pathways into nursing.[36] A 2014 article in the *Lancet* that looked at hospital mortality in nine countries found growing evidence from across Europe and the US that a better-educated nursing workforce delivers better patient outcomes, in terms of morbidity and mortality.[37]

But the language used in much of the debate assumes that, without a degree level of training, people are somehow incompetent. When the decision was made in 2009 to establish an all-graduate nursing profession, Christine Beasley, then the chief nursing officer, said this: "We need to make sure that not only do nurses need to care and have compassion, but they also need to have real ability to think, to make critical decisions and have technical skills."[38]

The idea that before 2013 nurses were unable to think and make critical decisions is a bizarre one, especially coming from the chief nursing officer, which suggests that this is just as much an argument about the relative status and prestige of (mainly female) nurses relative to (mainly male, although now increasingly female) doctors.

The Willis Commission also reported that nurses with degrees are more likely to say that nursing did not live up to their career development expectations, compared with registered nurses without a degree. The Willis answer (in line with human capital theory) is that a clear postgraduate development pathway must be put in place.

The National Health Service (NHS) professional bodies and, of course, the universities that put on the degree courses are convinced of the benefits of graduatization, yet the public remains skeptical and the academics seldom find significantly higher levels of skill from the graduate route in general.

In 2018 the United Kingdom's Department for Education reported that only 57 percent of young graduates were in high-skilled employment, a decline over the decade since the 2008 crash of 4.3 percentage points.[39] The proportion of older graduates in high-skilled employment was only slightly higher at 65 percent. The Department speculates that this could reflect "the limited number of high-skilled employment opportunities available to younger individuals and the potential difficulties they face matching into relevant jobs early in their careers."

Graduatization, in other words, doesn't always mean new professional skills but can just be a way for employers to screen for more able candidates. Consider the graduatization of the UK police force. Around one-third of police officers are already graduates (up from just 1.6 percent in 1979),[40] but it was announced in 2015 by the College of Policing that all new officers in England and Wales will have to be educated to degree level by 2020.

Chief Constable Giles York, of the National Police Chiefs Council, said this would "improve our ability to attract and retain really good people."[41] York also said that it was "fair and right" that officers should receive the full respect they deserve as professionals. As with nursing, this reflects the deep cultural bias in favor of the academic along with a desire for *recognition*.

The better class of candidate that the College of Policing is seeking turns out to be someone with a different set of attitudes rather than professional skills as such. It says it wants improvements in both academic skills (such as critical thinking, reflection, communication, critical analysis, independent judgement and research skills) and "soft skills" "such as tolerance, willingness to embrace alternative perspectives, empathy, and moral and ethical reasoning."[42]

The College of Policing cites research that graduate officers are better at dealing with complexity, had a wider understanding of their role in society, used force more appropriately, and had wider belief systems. They also argued in their consultation that "many in the policing workforce already take decisions in complex and unpredictable settings, with limited information, meaning they tend to operate at the equivalent of . . . graduate level."[43]

But the graduate argument put like this is based on a logical fallacy. The fact that graduate officers are better at dealing with complexity does not mean it is *because* they went to university. The most intelligent police officers who deal best with complexity are likely to have been in the academic track at school and gone to university, but they might have dealt just as well with complexity without higher education. Higher education correlates with but does not necessarily cause higher performance.

Supporters of graduatization claim, with sometimes limited evidence, that it raises skill levels as well as the more obvious uplift to status. Critics say that concrete skills relating to research, organization, and information technology can be learned, and in some cases are already being learned, in settings other than universities. And to the extent that it is about soft skills, it represents a cultural shift that is not necessarily welcome and that can exclude too many potentially good recruits.

Moreover, for the capable nongraduate, graduatization can produce a double whammy: not only is promotion from below without a degree now much harder beyond a certain level in many organizations, but you are also likely to be pushed down by people who don't do your job as well as you.

An acquaintance who is a management consultant recalls helping to reorganize a government agency a few years ago. Part of the reorganization involved regrading and reclassifying jobs. He tells this dismaying story: "I remember a thirty-something guy who worked in accounts payable matching invoices to purchase orders. He was a long-term employee. He was fastidious and reliable in a repetitive clerical job. It was low grade, lowish pay, but he dressed in a suit and had a briefcase and looked for all the world like a manager. The job was due to be reclassified as a graduate position. A graduate would be bored and offended by the routine, errors would increase, turnover in the position would increase, a decent human being is discarded and degraded—for what? Satisfying a misguided theory about social mobility?"

This echoes the "missing middle" problem of the unsuitability of graduates for many middling jobs, described by Paul Lewis in the last chapter, as does a 2016 report for the UK think tank the Resolution Foundation on "the 'forgotten 40 per cent' of the workforce—mid-skilled workers . . . without a university degree."[44]

The foundation organized focus groups for members of that forgotten group who reported that the influx of graduates into their occupations had reduced their progression prospects. A woman in her forties explained: "I've got a friend who works at a company he started [at when] he left school at 16. Went straight in the back office at 16. He's my age, and he now recruits for his back office and won't take anyone who isn't a graduate."[45]

In some sectors a degree was viewed as essential in order to reach a management position. While sometimes this reflected the additional technical knowledge required, in the view of another focus group member it was more of a cultural decision as extensive training was provided. And for him it resulted in better people being overlooked for promotion: "In my industry, I've been held back by not having a degree. I've seen people who have a degree move on into better positions. They don't care what the degree is in, they just take them on and pass them through. They're absolutely useless at their job. Having a degree just opens the door, it doesn't matter what it's in. I've had to fight my corner and use [my] equivalent experience."[46]

Yet, in recent years, the idea that the "really good people" (in Chief Constable Giles York's phrase) who can turn their hands to almost anything are to be found graduating with good degrees from top universities has been reinforced by the success of organizations like Teach First.

Teach First, modeled on Teach For America in the United States, was designed to tempt top graduates of top universities back into the teaching profession, which they had largely deserted since the 1960s. It offered a short cut in training and demanded at least two years' commitment to work in usually challenging schools. It is regarded as a big success and continues to attract many talented and idealistic young people, a good proportion of whom stay in the teaching profession. (My eldest daughter is one of them.) In the United Kingdom it has also been copied in social work (Frontline) and in the prison service (Unlocked Graduates).

But we should be cautious about contributing to the cult of the elite university graduate. Clearly some of the value of Teach First has been in attracting more able young people with top degrees back into teaching, but wherever it has been tried it has usually been accompanied by other changes, such as breaking the monopoly of teacher training in education faculties and generally disrupting groupthink in public service professions.

A concluding observation: the knowledge worker is increasingly a female worker. The rise and rise of the knowledge worker in the last three decades is also, in part, about the rise and rise of the female professional.

Women in the United Kingdom have not only caught up with but overtaken men in jobs that require higher education. In 1997, 28 percent of men and 23 percent of women were in such jobs. In 2017 it was 36 percent for men and 40 percent for women.[47] Universities, law schools, and medical schools are now at least 50 percent female, and although few women are CEOs of top companies, roughly half of the jobs in the top managerial and professional class are now taken by women.[48]

The top end of the labor market has been almost completely gender desegregated, but the middle and bottom end remains highly segregated, with women overwhelmingly concentrated in caring sectors like primary education, nursing, and social care. This is one reason why the graduate premium is higher for women than men: because of the bigger earnings gulf between professional women and often part-time women workers in the lowest-paid corners of the economy. Men in low-skill jobs such as garbage collection and postal delivery tend to be better paid than women in low-skill jobs, partly because the jobs have historically been unionized.

Employment status is usually more connected to well-being in men than in women.[49] Women on average place a higher priority on home and children than men do, and household income is a stronger predictor of well-being among women. These changes have thus had a greater impact on status feelings of nongraduate men, as I will spell out in more detail in Chapter Seven. And because women have partly swapped work in the home for work in the public economy, the home has experienced higher income but higher stress, too, as we will see in Chapter Eight.

The rising status of women need not necessarily contribute to a corresponding decline in the subjective social status of men. Many men have welcomed such developments or at least not seen them as negatively impacting their own individual status. But many nongraduate men will be aware that a growing proportion of the people above them in the status order are women.

Over the last thirty years the female graduate has been one of the main winners, and the male skilled manual worker one of the main losers, from the rise of the knowledge economy—maybe something Hillary Clinton's campaign managers should have been more alert to. But, as we will see in Chapter Nine, the era of the ever-expanding knowledge worker class is now drawing to a close.

Chapter Six

The Diploma Democracy

*Comrades! . . . You do not imagine, I hope, that we pigs
are doing this in a spirit of selfishness and privilege? Many
of us actually dislike milk and apples . . . Our sole object
in taking these things is to preserve our health. Milk and
apples (this has been proved by Science, comrades) contain
substances absolutely necessary to the well-being of a pig.
We pigs are brainworkers. The whole management and
organisation of this farm depend on us. Day and night we
are watching over your welfare. It is for your sake that we
drink that milk and eat those apples.*

George Orwell, *Animal Farm*

John Adams, the American Republic's second president, thought
that the new American legislature should be "an exact portrait, in
miniature," of the population. The French revolutionary Mirabeau also
thought the French national assembly should represent the people as
accurately as "a map represents a landscape."[1]

In pre-democratic politics in Europe in the eighteenth and nineteenth centuries, politicians were mainly drawn from the landowning
or capital owning class that dominated the small enfranchised elite,
although their interests were often represented by lawyers who formed
a disproportionate slice of the political class.

One of the main demands of the labor movements and parties of
the left that emerged in the nineteenth century was that workingmen

should have the means to represent people like themselves and sit in parliaments and legislatures.

Should politicians resemble, and reflect the views of, the people they represent? Adams, Mirabeau, and early labor movement politicians have a formidable adversary in Plato, who argues in *The Republic* that the best government is one guided by philosopher kings who are able to rise above the atavistic demands and interests of ordinary people. One consequence of our pre-Covid political turbulence is that traces of Plato's views have been resurfacing among sections of today's cognitive class, some of whom are suspicious of mass democracy—particularly when it produces results that they dislike, such as Brexit and Trump—and would prefer more decisions to be taken by unaccountable experts.

An important strand of the democratic tradition going back to Athenian democracy has been the concept of "lay politics": the idea that anyone can be a politician and the political class should be a collection of ordinary and socially representative people—ordinary people doing an extraordinary thing.

In the early decades of mass democracy in the twentieth century, when socioeconomic cleavages dominated politics, this ideal was partly realized in the social composition of political parties and politicians; labor parties tended to be represented by working-class people with low levels of formal education, though allied with a large minority of middle class idealists, and, similarly, liberal and conservative parties tended to be represented by the affluent and better educated.

In recent decades, following the loosening of the class structure and a greater professionalization of politics, the idea that it is desirable for politicians to be *like* the people they represent has begun to weaken—at least for class, if not for race and gender. But the most recent wave of political alienation has returned this question to the center of the democratic conversation.

An exasperation with the existing political elites was a significant factor behind Brexit, the election of Donald Trump, and the national elections in France in 2017 and Italy in 2018. In almost all of these cases politicians were rewarded for their *lack* of political experience and, at least in some of those cases, for their "blokeish" lack of deference toward so-called politically correct speech: Consider the reluctance of Boris Johnson, Donald Trump, and Matteo Salvini to be constrained by the normal rules of official discourse.

But, of course, that list also underlines the fact that the idea of politicians being like ordinary people will always be a fantasy. "The uncomfortable truth is that all political systems are aristocracies . . . Democracies are only different in that the aristocracies are installed and removeable by popular vote," as the former British judge Jonathan Sumption put it in a 2019 lecture.[2] Leading politicians will always be different from the great mass of voters.

But *how* they differ from the great mass of voters matters. And in recent years one thing above all has distinguished the political class from at least two-thirds of voters: almost all of them are *highly educated*.

Mark Bovens and Anchrit Wille express it succinctly in their important book *Diploma Democracy*:

Most contemporary democracies in Western Europe are governed by a select group of well-educated citizens. They are diploma democracies—ruled by those with the highest formal qualifications. University graduates have come to dominate all relevant political institutions and arenas, from political parties, parliaments and cabinets, to organized interests, deliberative venues, and internet consultations.

. . . In the British House of Commons, after the 2015 elections, nine out of ten MPs were university graduates . . . In the 2013 Bundestag, 86 per cent of the MPs had attended an institute of higher education . . . After the 2012 elections, almost 97 per cent of the members of the Dutch Tweede Kamer had attended college or graduate school . . . In Denmark, Belgium and France, between 75 and 90 per cent of the MPs have the equivalent of a college or a graduate degree. This is not because everybody goes to college nowadays—over 70 per cent of the electorate in Western Europe is still only educated up to secondary level, at the highest.[3]

During President Obama's second term, 93 percent of House members and 99 percent of senators held at least bachelor's degrees compared to a national average of 32 percent. (And a large majority in both Houses have further degrees.)[4]

Cabinets and governments, as one might expect, tend to be even better educated than ordinary politicians. Of the fifteen ministers in Angela Merkel's third cabinet, fourteen held a master's degree, nine had a PhD, seven had worked at universities, and two had been professors. In David Cameron's two cabinets, in 2010 and 2015, 69 percent and 50 percent, respectively, were Oxbridge graduates.[5]

In France, most of the political, media, and business elite is still drawn overwhelmingly from the *grandes écoles*, which educate just 4 percent of all students. Between 1986 and 2012, 36 percent of members of the government had graduated from these top schools, above all the École Nationale d'Administration (ENA). At the time of this writing (June 2019) both the president and the prime minister are so-called *énarques*, as are the heads of the central bank, the finance ministry, the presidential office, the Republican party, the external intelligence service, the state railways, and several top private sector companies. Moreover, recruitment to ENA has become narrower, not wider, in recent years, with the share of graduates from blue-collar backgrounds down to around 6 percent.

ENA's annual intake is just eighty, but, as noted earlier, it has produced four of the last eight presidents and eight of the last twenty-two prime ministers. Eleven of the fifteen postwar British prime ministers graduated from Oxford (which takes 3,000 undergraduates a year) and six of thirteen postwar US presidents attended either Harvard or Yale (each takes around 2,000 undergraduates a year).

In many countries the takeover of politics by the cognitive class, like the rise of educational selection that we noted in Chapter Four and the increased economic returns to a large knowledge worker class described in Chapter Five, is a relatively recent phenomenon. In the United Kingdom's 1964 general election, graduates were still a minority in the British parliament, reflecting a country where most people still left school without qualifications.

In the nineteenth century and the early part of the twentieth century, political elites were based on class and property. They were usually better educated than the average citizen, but this was not the source of their power. As Bovens and Wille put it: "In the information society, however, knowledge and information are the most important social goods. Political power is concentrated not among the landed gentry, patricians, or manufacturers, but among the 'symbolic analysts', 'creative professionals', and all those other citizens with ample capacity to process information . . ."[6]

This cognitive class takeover of politics does not apply just to politicians but increasingly to *the whole apparatus of political parties and political activism*, and the voters themselves are increasingly divided along educational lines.

Bovens and Wille have produced a useful summary, drawing on many national and international surveys, of the political participation story in six European countries,[7] with the population subdivided into low-educated, middling educated, and high-educated.

Their political participation "pyramid" ranges from informal participation (reading about and discussing politics) to voting in elections, to conventional participation (lobbying an official) and protest participation (joining a demonstration), to party membership, and, finally, standing for political office. With the single exception of watching politics on television, the highly educated outscore the less well educated in all political activities, in all countries, in some activities significantly. The political activism gap is especially large in France and the United Kingdom.

As the authors point out: "For many highly educated people, writing letters or emails, engaging in debates, and running meetings are all in a day's work. Yet they can be intimidating for people for whom these are not regular activities."

Pathways into politics have changed, too, in recent decades, in ways that benefit the educated. Mass political parties, trade unions, churches, and traditional women's groups have all been in decline, while pressure groups, NGOs, advocacy groups, and Internet political forums of various kinds have expanded their membership. But whereas the former were usually rooted in particular communities, the latter tend to require a preexisting commitment or membership of a community of ideas. Barack Obama is a case in point: he moved from an elite university to becoming a community activist, unlike an elected trade union official of the old days. Community activists, you might say, appoint themselves to represent the communities they judge to be unable to represent themselves.

Mass political parties and trade unions, with membership and interest often passed down through family connections, provided basic political education to the less educated. The smaller "cadre" parties of today are often run by people who became involved in politics at university and then went on to a job with a political connection—working for a lobby group, or in the media, or a think tank/policy organization, or even as an aide to an MP—providing useful experience and networks. The number of Belgium MPs who had previously worked as a parliamentary aide rose from 10 percent in the early 1970s to 35 percent in 2010.

Modern forms of political participation, such as online discussion groups, public consultations, and e-petitions, show, according to the United Kingdom's Hansard Society, an even bigger divergence between those with high and low education than old-fashioned political activities such as attending party political meetings and demonstrations.

Why is the takeover of politics by an educated elite, the old Platonic dream, a problem? Does it not make sense to have the most intelligent or at least the best trained people running our political institutions?

Up to a point. But there are two big related problems with the cognitive class takeover of politics. First and most serious is that the cognitive class tends to pursue its own interests and intuitions even while believing sincerely that it represents the wider common good. Second, it turns out that a university degree is not necessarily the best training for a life in politics.

Of course, it is true that bright and ambitious people have always been drawn to politics, and many of those who went into politics before mass higher education would have had degrees today. Yet the cognitive class in general has become more homogeneous and parochial in recent decades through the shared experience of residential higher education, partnering together, and tending to live in the same places while often sharing the same interests and values. Americans seem to be dividing themselves into alarmingly homogenous residential communities reflecting their educational backgrounds and beliefs.[8] According to German sociologist Heike Wirth, there has also been an increase in the social distance between the high- and low-education groups.

There are many issues, of course, where the interests of the highly educated and less well educated overlap, above all in competent management of the economy and public services. And there is no inherent reason why the highly educated cannot represent the interests of the less well educated, particularly on traditional left-right socioeconomic issues on which there has been some convergence in recent years, as, broadly speaking, the middle class has become less right-wing and the working class less left-wing.

On sociocultural matters such as immigration, multiculturalism, globalization, national sovereignty, and European integration, it is a very different story, and we have seen a well-documented divergence between people with different levels of education in most rich countries. As noted earlier, about 75 percent of people with minimal educational qualifications voted for Brexit and about the same proportion with degrees or more voted to remain; a similar electoral divide was seen in the Trump vote in 2016.

The highly educated—who are usually more affluent and liberal than the average—also have a disproportionately loud voice in the political system and have used it to shape a society at least partly in their own interests. Martin Gilens, in his study of public policy and public preferences in the United States between 1964 and 2006, finds a fair amount of common ground across voter groups, but when preferences diverge, the affluent and educated almost always carry the day, on everything from free trade to social policy. Other studies in the United States, such as that by David Kimball, have found that the lobbying agenda does not reflect the policy priorities of the public.[9]

There has been a friendly, symbiotic relationship between modern liberal Anywhere values and the rise of a large class of cognitive Head workers, people who generally prioritize individual success, self-actualization, openness, novelty, autonomy, and mobility, and generally find social change comfortable. Economic openness has usually been the priority of the highly educated of the center-right, and social and cultural openness has been the priority of the center-left. The two often combined in recent decades in the default "double liberalism" of the new center represented by the New Democrats, New Labour, and others—against which modern populism is in revolt.

The "double liberalism" did win elections in both the United States and the United Kingdom, but with a fair economic wind behind it and when openness seemed to be producing more winners than losers, and even then the strongly liberal preferences of the cognitive class were not endorsed by a large minority, even a majority, of the population.

Today in the United Kingdom a bit less than half of the population support the death penalty.[10] Around two-thirds think that immigration has been too high or much too high in recent years.[11] Around half the population supported leaving the EU.[12] About 60 percent think that Britain "sometimes feels like a foreign country."[13] Fifty-eight percent of people think that newcomers are not integrating well.[14] Most British people broadly support gender equality, but only around one-third of women identify as feminists.[15]

Similarly, in the United States, more than half the population want stricter limits on legal immigration,[16] 54 percent support the death penalty for those convicted of murder,[17] a bit over one-third of women identify as feminists,[18] and nearly half of white working-class Americans agree that "things have changed so much that I often feel like a stranger in my own country."[19]

Yet most of the people who voted for Brexit and Trump are what I call "decent populists." They have accepted the great liberalization of recent decades on race, gender, and sexuality, even if those issues are not of primary concern. They are, in the main, social conservatives, not social authoritarians.

And yet, if you survey the political scene in the United Kingdom and the United States over the twenty-five years prior to the votes for Brexit and Trump, it is hard to find many policies that reflect these small-c conservative views. (The only political party represented in the UK Parliament to support leaving the EU was Northern Ireland's Democratic Unionist Party.)

On the other hand, it is easy to list half a dozen policy areas that have been at a sharp angle to the expressed preferences of many of the less well educated: openness to global trade and the deindustrialization it has led to; promotion of a knowledge economy and the 50 percent target for university attendance (in the United Kingdom) and relative neglect of vocational and technical training; openness to large-scale immigration and the embrace of multiculturalism, with its attendant ambivalence about majority identities; the social and geographical mobility that strips many communities of their most able people; a family policy that downplays the private realm of the family and gives priority to both parents working; and finally the embrace by the cognitive class of a more technocratic, global politics that has stressed international integration, climate change, human rights, and sex (and sexuality) equality, and downplayed national social contracts and national democratic sovereignty.

On global trade, as noted earlier, Robert Reich, Bill Clinton's secretary of labor, in the early to mid-1990s, argued in his influential book *The Work of Nations* that workers should not resist the wealth potential of globalization but should roll with it and an activist state would help them retrain. The factories closed in both the United States and United Kingdom, but the retraining barely happened at all. (It did happen to a greater degree in the Germanic and Scandinavian lands.)

A knowledge economy works, by definition, in the interests of the highly educated and requires a thriving higher-education sector. Yet in both the United Kingdom and the United States remarkably little thought has been given in recent decades to the reduced status of so much nongraduate employment or the vocational and technical training needs of former industrial areas. Politicians, who are almost all graduates and whose children mainly attend elite universities, have encouraged the school system to focus overwhelmingly on sending students to college, and, as we saw in Chapter Four, nonacademic post-school training has become a Cinderella sector. And, especially in the United Kingdom, with its 50 percent university target, cursory consideration has been devoted to the psychological impact on those not going to college or to the impact on the economic geography of the country of encouraging the geographical mobility of the most academically able.

The immigration story is also one of an openness-inclined cognitive class choosing to follow its own intuitions and essentially ignore the sentiments of more than half the population for more control and more modest inflows. Angela Merkel's decision in 2015 to allow more than 1 million refugees to settle in Germany is often seen as an act of great political courage but it deeply divided her country.

In the United States before Trump, there was only a debate about *illegal* immigration. But legal immigration running at more than 1 million a year is considered too high by more than 50 percent of Americans, a mainly less educated voice that was hardly ever heard.[20]

In the United Kingdom around two-thirds of the adult population has considered immigration too high or much too high for most of the last twenty years, since the number rose sharply after 1997 (although its level of salience to voters has shifted about and immigration anxiety has declined since the Brexit vote). Yet immigration levels have continued at historically unprecedented levels for two decades.

The most telling moment in the recent immigration story in the United Kingdom came in 2003 when a Labour government dominated by the highly educated decided to ignore the views of its less educated voters and allow people from the former communist countries immediate access to the British labor market when their countries joined the EU in 2004. In a speech in Poland in 2000, Tony Blair had talked about "popular but misplaced fears that freedom of movement means massive shifts of population."[21]

The United Kingdom was the only big EU economy not to use the seven-year transitional period allowed under EU rules. There were both geopolitical and economic reasons for the decision, but it remains a remarkable example of how center-left parties have come to reflect the priorities of liberal graduates rather than less well educated workers, many of whom have subsequently ceased voting for them.

The same is true of family policy that has favored the public realm of work over the private realm of the family itself. Policy has reflected the priorities of highly educated professional women concerned with competing on the most equal possible terms with men in their careers. At the middle and bottom end of the labor market most women with young children want to and need to work but would prefer to do so part-time or even not at all when their children are very young, yet the state provides little support to make it easier to stay at home.

As Alison Wolf has written: "Today's female workforce features a professional elite for whom a career is as central to personal identity as it is for elite men. It also features a female majority whose work patterns are very different. They do jobs. And they do jobs which fit with and around their family responsibilities and priorities. They are, therefore, very often part-time. Part-time work is both the norm and a preferred option for vast proportions of the female workforce. It is also the main reason for that notorious 'pay-gap.'"[22]

Social mobility, as I argued in Chapter One, is another idea and policy that has been relentlessly promoted, at least rhetorically, by cognitive class governments of center-left and center-right, especially in the United Kingdom and the United States, with little nuance or sense of its costs for those who are not upwardly mobile. For the politicians of the center-left, equality of opportunity is preferable to an unachievable and unpopular goal of equality of outcome, and for the center-right the stress on mobility helps to protect them from accusations of defending privilege.

Yet less well-educated people often hear speeches from highly educated and successful people about social mobility as exhortations to become more like them, especially as—in the United Kingdom, at least—getting on often means a ladder *out* and leaving your roots behind: you have to "leave to achieve." Some people do want to fly away, but others would prefer good, well-paid jobs in their localities that would allow them to lead successful, happy lives in settled communities close to relatives and friends.

More rooted individuals and communities have, in the past, been able to achieve status and recognition through work as *service* to their family and community. As the sociologist the late Geoff Dench put it: "It is the knowledge that they are being useful to their families and communities that assures ordinary people of the self-respect they need to carry on leading productive lives even when this does not result in great success and public recognition . . . Mobility does have a place for talented individuals and as an escape from a group experienced as oppressive. But when promoting mobility becomes a state objective, this seems likely to produce a profoundly discontented and unstable society."[23]

Technocratic Depoliticization

The argument over the more technocratic style of politics of the post–Cold War era also divides along educational lines. After the 2016 referendum, there was certainly a quiet undercurrent of sympathy on the part of more extreme Remainers for the idea of an epistocracy: the rule of the well educated. This is David Runciman in his book *How Democracy Ends*: "Living in Cambridge, England, a passionately pro-European town and home to an elite university, I heard echoes of that argument in the aftermath of the Brexit vote. It was usually uttered sotto voce—you have to be a brave person to come out as an epistocrat in a democratic society—but it was unquestionably there. Behind their hands, very intelligent people muttered to each other that this is what you get if you ask a question that ordinary people don't understand."[24]

Highly educated people often see the political preferences of the less well educated as morally wrong or irrational and contrast them with the rational deliberations of experts, who can see a question in all its complexity. And there is a widespread view that politicians are often swayed by short-term electoral cycle and pork-barrel motivations and that public policy is of a higher quality when it is conducted by clever technocrats, insulated from political influence.

These sentiments are not always wrong, and experts can usefully inform political debate in specialist areas of knowledge, such as how best to analyze and defeat a virus epidemic. But there is no expert who knows "objectively" whether you should be left-wing or right-wing, liberal or conservative, a risk-taker or a security lover.*

Moreover, there are two bigger problems with this approach to politics. First, it often assumes that highly educated people are more rational than less educated people. But the opposite is often the case

---

* There is some evidence that more intelligent people are on average more to the left politically. Ian Deary, a professor of psychology at Edinburgh University, has found that higher general intelligence at age ten is correlated with anti-traditional attitudes at thirty. His study confirms the general finding that people with higher intelligence tend to have less traditional moral values. But Noah Carl, another intelligence researcher, partly disagrees or rather argues that those with more open personalities are more likely to pursue careers in academia or a similar field, which *then* skews their views in a left-liberal direction.

in my observation, because educated people are more likely to have absorbed political ideologies into their personal identities and thus find it harder to look dispassionately at political options.

The political philosopher John Gray explored this issue in a recent BBC radio talk: "The ignorance of the learned can be a great deal more dangerous than the common or garden variety. Over time the errors of ordinary people can be corrected by their everyday experience. The ignorance of the learned, in contrast, tends to be invincible. They like to think they have a clearer view of the world; in fact they are often more easily taken in by mass delusions than the rest of human-kind. Those who have studied to degree level and beyond have often embraced ideas and projects that many less educated folk instinctively recognize were dangerously absurd. Something like this happened in Britain in the 1930s. Much of the intelligentsia was ready to junk democracy in Britain for a new order that they felt was coming into being somewhere else."[25]

Second, a drift toward *technocratic depoliticization*, with more and more aspects of life—from control of interest rates to immigration—being removed from the national democratic contest ends up contrib-uting to a populist reaction. And this is surely exactly what we have experienced in the past twenty-five years.

After the initial optimism about the spread of democracy at the end of the Cold War, some influential figures have been open about preferring the constitutional to the popular aspects of democracy. The writer and columnist Fareed Zakaria argues that the Western model is best symbolized not by elections but by the impartial judge and says that "what we need in politics today is not more democracy but less."[26] Similarly, Alan S. Blinder, then a senior official at the Federal Reserve Bank in the United States, published an influential article in *Foreign Affairs* in 1997 arguing that the independent central bank model should be extended to other areas of policy, including health and welfare, with decisions being removed from elected politicians and handed to independent experts.[27]

The late Peter Mair in his book *Ruling the Void: The Hollowing-Out of Western Democracy*, talked about the anti-politics politicians like Tony Blair, who once described New Labor as "the political wing of the British people" and set himself up as a leader above political partisanship.

This is one reason for the popularity of the European Union among the political classes of Europe. As Mair puts it, the EU has become "a protected sphere in which policy-making can evade the constraints imposed by representative democracy."[28]

Highly educated technocrats usually believe that national self-government is unable to solve many of today's most complex problems: the nation state is either too big for local problems or too small for global ones, as the cliché has it. They are happy to pool or transfer sovereignty to make markets and politics work better in a relatively interdependent world.

This does not just mean majority voting in the committees of the EU or WTO. It's also true of domestic politics: Think of independent central banks or a more activist judiciary striking down the decisions of politicians. All of these things that shrink the space of democratic accountability may be justified in their own terms, but it is invariably true that when policies are removed from the national democratic arena, they are decided according to the values and priorities of the cognitive class—namely, international openness, income maximization, individualism, diversity, and so on.

It is also the case that, on a personal level, many highly educated people are comfortable relinquishing sovereignty. They think they appreciate the trade-offs and benefits in GDP growth or in greater cooperation to combat climate change, and through their own friends and networks they may have connections to power. They also tend to have a high degree of agency in their own personal and professional lives, so they feel less directly diminished by the erosion of agency in the national political sphere. Most less-educated people have no political influence other than their votes.

In the recent book by Will Hutton and Andrew Adonis, *Saving Britain: How We Must Change to Prosper in Europe*, national sovereignty is described as merely "notional."[29] Technocratic politics, in other words, is experienced as expansive and empowering by cognitive elites and narrowing and disempowering by nonelites, whose response can mutate into populist rejection. As the former head of the UK representation to the EU, Ivan Rogers, has written: "If you evacuate many domains of public policy of any real element of choice at the citizen level . . . then the only way to voice opposition becomes to voice opposition to the *whole system* and to argue that it needs to be demolished rather than changed from within" (emphasis added).[30]

Those two decisions, both taken by Tony Blair's Labour government—the target of sending 50 percent of secondary-school graduates to university and the decision to accept immigration from the former communist countries of Central and Eastern Europe seven years before it was necessary—illustrate both a cognitive class lack of emotional intelligence and a social distance from less well-educated citizens. The same political instinct seems to have informed the extraordinary decision of Tony Blair, and many leading Blairites, to reject the referendum result and actively campaign for its reversal rather than lobby for the softest possible version of Brexit.

In the light of such decisions, it is not surprising that less well-educated voters have lacked confidence in contemporary politics. Many of them stopped voting at all, and withdrew from political participation more generally, on the grounds that from their perspective all the main parties appeared to pursue the same technocratic liberalism.

Robert D. Putnam's famous book *Bowling Alone: The Collapse and Revival of American Community*—on the breakdown of civic life in America—notes that voter turnout has declined by around 20 percentage points since the 1960s, while the likelihood of attending a public meeting about local affairs was down by one-third between 1973 and 1994.[31]

More recently, some voters have been prepared to support anti-system politicians like Donald Trump. Just as the 1960s and 1970s gave rise to a generational revolt and a new type of liberal and left-wing politics of the highly educated (green parties in Europe have the highest educational profile of any), so populist parties have emerged in the past generation as a kind of counterweight for the less well educated.

It is, however, as Bovens and Wille point out, one of the curiosities of the new political stratification that new political parties do not *explicitly* articulate the interests of lower- or higher-educated citizens—one reason why Donald Trump's famous phrase after victory in Nevada in the 2016 Republican primary, "I love the poorly educated," attracted so much attention. There is no Liberal Graduate party or Union for the Poorly Educated.[32] There would be too much stigma attached to the latter and egalitarian embarrassment attached to the former.

These cultural-educational divides did not exist until recently. In the United Kingdom, Labour's decision on Eastern European immigration would have been unthinkable in the 1980s, as would the Conservative decision to legislate for gay marriage. Both decisions were informed by a spirit of crusading progressivism while the concerns of less well-educated small-*c* conservatives were ignored.

If one goes back even further to the immediate postwar period, the current cleavages become even more unimaginable. The two front benches in the UK Parliament in the 1950s would have disagreed fundamentally about socioeconomic issues but would have held broadly similar views on race, nation, gender, and so on. Moreover, their views would have overlapped with the average man or woman on the street. Nations then were far more culturally homogeneous and conservative.

In the United States as recently as 1972, almost 80 percent of *Democratic Party* voters agreed marijuana should be illegal, against just 22 percent today; 78 percent agreed same-sex sexual relations were almost always wrong, against 28 percent today; and almost 40 percent opposed interracial marriage, a question that is no longer even asked today.[33]

In the past, the cognitive class was too small to have its own interests and divided along other lines, primarily socioeconomic. Now it has become large enough to have its own interests, which are expressed within the existing party political forms, taking a distinct center-left and center-right form.

One way of mitigating today's divides and retaining a sense of the broad church party is simply through a broader range of people being represented. Your own life experience really does matter when it comes to understanding the experiences of others.

This is Paul Johnson, whom we met in Chapter Four, struggling to find a decent apprenticeship for his second son, Tom, reflecting on how the experience had changed him:[34]

> Our failure to get enough young people into high quality, job-based training at 18 . . . creates our skills shortages, low wages and productivity problems. If there is a problem with our universities it occurs when students fall into low value courses by default because that's the easiest thing to do.
>
> I have known this for years. You can see it in the data . . . But it is not until it is part of your experience that you really feel it. Here's an admission. Having done well by the exam system myself, if I'd stopped at one son I would always have had that little voice at the back of my head telling me that if I could do it, and if he could do it, then everything is fine. Maybe everyone else should just buckle down and get on with it.
>
> . . . That little bit of extra experience [with my son Tom] has changed the way I think. That, by the way, is why I believed David Cameron's claim that the treatment received by his son Ivan brought home to him the value of the NHS in a way that mere theory never could.
>
> . . . This self-knowledge has also shaped my view about the importance of having people with a diversity of experience at the top of politics.

Perhaps it shouldn't matter if they have all been to public school and Oxbridge and are comfortably off. That doesn't make them worse people. They are perfectly capable of understanding the evidence and sifting the options. But human nature is such that different experiences will lead them to understand that evidence, and weigh those options, differently. Perhaps this is most true of education policy where we are all too much influenced by our own, dimly remembered, schooldays.

Many less educated voters do say they want people more like themselves in politics, although they seem to make an exception for people at the very top like Donald Trump or Boris Johnson who are allowed to be sui generis.

According to British political scientist Oliver Heath: "All else being equal, people with a given social characteristic prefer candidates or leaders who share that characteristic: women are more likely than men to vote for female candidates, and black people are more likely than white people to vote for black candidates."

Similarly, researchers Nicholas Allen and Katja Sarmiento-Mirwaldt find that "there is good evidence, from Britain and elsewhere, that citizens generally want representatives who are 'like them,' either in appearance or thought, who are local, and who have experienced what they have experienced."[35]

They are also more likely to want politicians to directly reflect the views of those they represent: a 2019 YouGov poll found that 80 percent of British MPs think they are elected to exercise their own personal judgment, while 63 percent of *voters* think that MPs should act according to their constituents' wishes, and just 7 percent think MPs should exercise their own judgment.[36]

The overall implication is that there are far too many graduates in the UK Parliament for the taste of a substantial section of the electorate. Political scientists Rosie Campbell and Philip Cowley were dismayed to find that in response to a questionnaire people preferred to vote for a sixteen-year-old school-leaver to someone with a PhD: "Perhaps because we spend our lives working in universities, the finding that respondents seemed noticeably to prefer a candidate who had *not* been to university surprised (and depressed) us somewhat."[37]

It is not, however, by any means obvious that people with a university education do make better political leaders. It is difficult to test this, and few political scientists have tried. But American political scientists Nicholas Carnes and Noam Lupu have attempted to check the claim by looking at economic performance of countries, performance of members of the US Congress (staying in office, passing more bills, and winning reelection), and levels of corruption of Brazilian mayors.

They conclude: "Politicians with college degrees do not tend to govern over more prosperous nations, are not more productive legislators, do not perform better at polls, and are no less likely to be corrupt."[38]

In my own observation of friends and colleagues from elite academic institutions who have gone into politics, it is clear that the knowledge they have acquired and their ability at abstract reasoning is only one part, and not always the most important part, of what is required to be a capable politician.

Charlotte Leslie is a high-flying Oxford graduate and was one of the youngest British Conservative MPs from 2010 to 2017. I spoke to her in Bude, Cornwall, where she used to work on the beaches as a lifeguard. She told me:

> Whilst many of my Balliol friends were doing internships in law firms, banks, and consultancies, I spent my holidays from Oxford working on the beach as a lifeguard in Bude. At the time I thought I was being a dropout and a bum. But I now know that what I learnt from working on the beach has been, without doubt, more valuable to me for a career in politics than what I learned at Balliol, or what I could have learnt in any London office.
>
> There I was, a privately educated, cosseted Oxford undergraduate, amongst a team of experienced Cornish and Australian

lifeguards on the dangerous Atlantic coast. It was tacitly understood that because I was "academic," I might be a bit back-of-the-class on the commonsense scale. And I was. But everyone was very kind and treated me as someone with a distinct educational disadvantage. If I did something a bit stupid, they would often laugh: "It's alright, Charlotte," they would say. "You're an academic!"

She remembers feeling at the bottom of a huge learning curve among the lifeguards and found her glittering academic career helped very little in many of the tests and exercises she had to undertake:

I was a former national-level competitive swimmer, and I was okay with the physical fitness requirements and the academic elements of the first aid. But I struggled with translating what I knew on paper into actual sand-spattered, rain-soaked, wind-buffeted action. Which knots to use, and when, I was pretty useless at. And the scenario tests—how would you rescue someone from a rock in these circumstances?—again, pretty poor. Being fairly proficient at analyzing Virgil's Augustan encomium poetry turns out to have very little to do with being practically useful in an emergency. I definitely wore the dunce's hat in that lifeguard hut.

Leslie believes that her lifeguard boss and mentor in Bude, Martin "Mini" Fry, was probably more important to her education in growing into the sort of person who could become a good MP than her university tutors: "Mini and my lifeguard friends have taught me so much. I am profoundly grateful for their influence in my life. Yes, MPs need a good analytical ability, but politics is more like fixing the boiler than writing an essay. I think academic people can easily forget that."

And her main lesson from that experience: "If you want an improvement done well, ask the people who do it for eight hours every day. Not the person wearing the suit."

Another example underlines the context dependency of ability and the limits of academic intelligence in the rough-and-tumble of politics. It concerns the former British cabinet minister Ed Balls. I used to know Balls when we were both working on the *Financial Times* in the early 1990s. He had just arrived from Harvard University to write editorials and was widely regarded as one of the brightest young economists in the country, which is why, in 1994, Gordon Brown plucked him from the *FT* to become one of his closest advisers for the next ten years.

But several years later in the runup to the 2005 election, Balls moved from being a government adviser to being a politician in his own right. And he was dreadful. I remember hearing him on the BBC Radio 4 *Any Questions?* show and cringing as he spoke. He was wooden and charmless and inarticulate. What it revealed to me was that being a politician and speaking well in public is a craft that you need to work at, and just being clever and well informed and probably in possession of a high IQ is not enough.

To be fair to Balls, he was able to learn from his early mistakes, which may have been exacerbated by a stutter, and over the years he worked at the craft of political rhetoric and became reasonably good at it before losing his seat in 2015.

It might seem obvious that academic ability alone is no qualification for political success. Yet the cultural bias toward higher cognitive aptitudes seems to have had some influence on the selection of front-rank politicians in recent decades, especially on the center-left of UK politics. Consider the elevation, and then rather limited success, of the academically luminous Miliband brothers, Ed Balls, and even Gordon Brown himself. They were all known for high ability but not the human touch.

A cabinet colleague of Alan Johnson, the former postman and home secretary, told me that Johnson would almost certainly have made a better and more popular prime minister than Gordon Brown but, surrounded by highly trained academic minds, he felt he wasn't up to it.

There are many explanations for the current wave of political alienation sweeping across Western societies. One way to think about it is that politics has a demand-and-supply problem. Voters are more demanding and less deferential to authority of all kinds. They have high expectations, and a click-button consumerist world has made people less patient of public realm inefficiency. They are also better educated and have the Internet and social media to help them challenge their leaders.

Yet, at the same time that the democratic demand has been rising, the democratic supply has been faltering. Globalization has increased inequality in the West while appearing to require a more technocratic, less national politics that makes many people feel less in control. The Iraq war debacle, the financial crisis and subsequent austerity, the inability to control immigration, the belief that life will not be better for our children, the increasing stratification by education—these have all reduced faith in the political class, stoked resentment, and encouraged people to vote for anti-system parties.

This period of relative political failure, compared with the immediate postwar period, has coincided with the entrenchment of cognitive class domination of Western politics. This is not to say that the former has been caused by the latter, but a rapid growth in the graduate share in the population in most countries, and the almost complete domination of politics by graduates and the interests of graduates, has not made our politics function more smoothly or rationally or, indeed, tolerantly. Instead it has become another source of popular resentment.

It was noticeable that a global survey tracking declining satisfaction with democracy published by the University of Cambridge's Centre for the Future of Democracy in January 2020 found that among countries bucking the trends were those—such as Poland and Hungary—that have self-consciously rejected the liberal graduate-centred politics of Western Europe.

The graduate-nongraduate divide is not a sharp one on all issues or political preferences, but according to YouGov Profiles data in the United

Kingdom there are significant differences in values and worldview. The Profiles contain some 330,000 questions across a very large panel of nearly 1 million Britons. This typically yields a sample of around 50,000 individuals per question, which ensures a strongly representative sample and high statistical power. Here are some of the traits where the two groups differ.[39]

While 71 percent of graduates agreed with the statement "I like to surround myself with a diverse range of cultures and ideas," just 51 percent of nongraduates did so. Nongraduates are more rooted than graduates, valuing locality and family more. Forty-three percent of nongraduates said they preferred to listen to local radio stations, compared to 29 percent of graduates. By a 73–62 margin, nongrads are more likely than graduates to agree that "family is everything." Indeed, when asked what they would like to be named after them—a theory, a grandchild, or a mountain—54 percent of nongraduates replied "grandchild" compared to just 33 percent of graduates.

Graduates identify heavily with their educational qualifications. Seventy-three percent of graduates said they "learned important things through my school education," while only 51 percent of nongraduates agreed. By a 73–44 margin, grads are more likely to say their education helped them get ahead in life. Nineteen percent of grads but only 6 percent of nongrads offer "well-educated" as one of their defining traits. In a three-choice question, 46 percent of graduates say their "head tends to rule the heart," and only 31 percent say the heart rules the head. For nongraduates the numbers are nearly reversed, with 42 percent opting for heart over head and 31 percent for head over heart. This spills over into the importance of work: 47 percent of graduates say they love their jobs, but only 34 percent of nongraduates agree.

Graduates are more achievement oriented and seek a more this-worldly sense of control over their lives. By a 36–20 margin, they're more likely to agree that "having goals" helps motivate them to get through the day. For having "a challenge" there's a similar gap. "Accomplishing," "learning," "challenging," and "adventure"—all associated with more open personalities—register 10–15 point premiums in favor of graduates. Nongrads are between 10 and 20 points less likely to exercise, say they are healthy, or emphasize physical appearance and weight loss. And while only 46 percent of graduates said they don't "plan too far into the future," 60 percent of nongraduates avoid long-term planning. This taps into a greater sense of fatalism among nongraduates. Witness the fact that 36 percent of them believe in fate or destiny compared to 22 percent of graduates. And nongrads are between 10 and 15 points more likely to believe in religious concepts such as reincarnation, life after death, and ghosts while being 10 points more likely than grads (72–62) to say the world is "getting worse."

I am not suggesting that a 50 percent nongraduate quota in the House of Commons or US Congress would necessarily improve the quality of national governance. But the lack of representation of the feelings and interests of the less well educated—and the gap that has opened up on many issues between the political class and around half the population— has bred political cynicism and created a space in which populist politics has thrived. The case for more cognitive and value diversity in national parliaments seems an overwhelming one.

Some people propose as an alternative a bigger role for citizen parliaments and consultations and deliberative forums of various kinds. They seemed to have worked well in Ireland's abortion referendum and elsewhere. It is easy enough to find a representative cross section of the public; it is harder to be truly neutral in the way that information is presented to such forums.

Bovens and Wille are skeptical about deliberative models, seeing them still heavily biased toward well-educated citizens: "An important assumption in this model is that citizens are knowledgeable about politics, understand their own interests as individuals and groups, develop thoughtful political opinions, and put these forward by means of political participation. They are expected to be able to read voluminous dossiers, attend lengthy meetings, and to intervene at the right moment and in the right tone of voice. It is only a mild exaggeration to say that at least a bachelor's degree in political science or public administration is needed to be able to live up to these expectations. Many political reforms are designed by political scientists for political scientists."[40]

But to the extent that such forums do give a voice to the normally voiceless, they are welcome. After all, why should the wisdom of the graduate-only crowd be better than the wisdom of the whole crowd?

Language, Value, and Design

One of the ways in which cognitive-class dominance impinges on mainstream culture is in the language we use and in the ethos of much art and architecture, the latter being the high art form that most directly effects everyday life.

Despite all the efforts of the movement for plain English, cognitive elites continue to use jargon, management-speak, and politically motivated euphemisms both consciously and unconsciously as a badge of distinction and a barrier for entry against the less well educated and more plainly spoken. Jargon and bureaucratic obfuscation are a form of professional power.

In higher education, too many academics, particularly in the humanities (and what Jordan Peterson has called "the activist disciplines") have for more than thirty years allowed their subjects to be rendered almost unintelligible by specialist language, while much of the text produced by public-sector organizations is often hopelessly convoluted and alienating.

Donald Trump understands the power of direct language, bypassing the Head to speak to the Heart. One of his campaign managers told BBC Radio 4 that the line that won the election for Trump was "It used to be that we made cars in Flint [Michigan] and you couldn't drink the water in Mexico. Now the cars are made in Mexico and you can't drink the water in Flint." This sort of imagery is very direct and concrete. It cuts through and speaks to how people feel.

An important source of the popularity of Boris Johnson is the belief that he is not afraid to describe things as they are—in his comments, for example, about how a woman in a burka looks like a mailbox—and offend against the new rules of discourse.

There is a danger that violent language used on the national stage can incite people to behave badly. But there is an equal and opposite danger that the gap between the way that people speak to each other in private and the official language of the society will grow too wide. One study of American political polarization found that 80 percent of people thought that "political correctness is a problem."[41]

An acquaintance of mine worked on a big regeneration project in Manchester a few years ago and recalls that they had to run classes for local residents to help them negotiate what they could or could not say in public meetings. "It was bizarre. It was their community, but we had to teach them the words they were allowed to use to talk about it in public," he says.

But this is a much bigger issue than so-called political correctness. The diversity of modern societies has had the unintended effect of smothering the language of virtue, and ultimately cooperation, for fear of offending those with different values. Jonathan Sacks, the United Kingdom's former chief rabbi, says that this is in part a confusion between judgmentalism (you are bad!) and judgment (not all ways are equally good). Sometimes it seems that we have conflated the two and thrown out *both*. This means that the most important questions about how to live a good life are relegated to the private sphere and too much of our public discussion focuses on technocratic process or economics and becomes dominated by an expert emptiness.

It also means that we lack the confidence to praise in the public sphere things that almost everyone values: self-control, self-sacrifice, working hard, being a good parent, strong marriages, responsibility. A senior civil servant friend of mine said she had to fight very hard to get some of this language into the relationships education curriculum, as people worried it was too judgmental and old-fashioned. If we cannot praise the successful mastery of the Heart, we shouldn't be surprised that it is less valued.

Charles Murray in *Coming Apart*, his book on the new class divides in the United States, blames the new American upper class for not preaching what it practices. The book describes, with a mass of survey evidence to back it up, the diverging way of life of the new upper-class America and working-class America. The new upper class continues to behave in a manner not that different from 1960s America in terms of marriage, work ethic, and religiosity, while all three of those things have partially collapsed in working-class America. According to Daniel Markovits, author of the *Meritocracy Trap*, this is because the new upper class is aware of the importance of these things in transmitting their educational advantages to their children. In 1963 white people age thirty to forty-nine were overwhelmingly married (94 percent of the college educated, 84 percent of those with just a high school education); in 2010 the figure was still 84 percent for the college educated but had slumped to just 48 percent for the high school educated.[42]

But the new upper class has a code of what Charles Murray calls "ecumenical niceness." Children are supposed to share their toys, not hit one another, take turns, and so on. But they are also taught that they should respect everyone else's way of doing things, regardless of gender, race, sexual preference, and cultural practices, which leads to the crucial weakness of ecumenical niceness. "The code of the dominant minority is supposed to set the standard for the society, but ecumenical niceness has a hold only on people whom the dominant minority is willing to judge—namely, one another," writes Murray. "... It has lost self-confidence in the rightness of its own customs and values, and preaches non-judgmentalism instead."[43]

The blanket of "ecumenical niceness" makes it harder for us to have the national conversations about value that we need. How we behave is not just a private matter. Surely it is possible to combine the freedom to pursue diverse goals and values while also having a robust public discussion about the best path to collective well-being and how that should be reflected in our laws and institutions.

David Lucas, the children's writer and illustrator whom I quoted earlier, has been thinking and writing about issues of language and value for many years. Lucas has a wry outsider's perspective on life and lights up when talking about the ideas that move him. I interviewed him about language and design at his home in Leytonstone, where he lives with his American wife and five-year-old daughter. (Some of the below arises from subsequent exchanges on email.)

He describes how he fell in love with words and writing: "I found my way into writing through an almost visual appreciation of words—seeing how the short, simple Anglo-Saxon monosyllables that are the core of English can be so vivid that it's almost as if the word itself is a picture."

One of the great treasure troves of modern English, along with Shakespeare, is the King James Bible, which drew heavily on the earlier translation by William Tyndale, who was burned at the stake for his trouble. Lucas lists a few of the vivid phrases that were carried over in the later Authorized Version of the Bible:

> twinkling of an eye
> a moment in time
> seek and ye shall find
> eat, drink, and be merry
> ask and it shall be given you
> judge not that you not be judged
> let there be light
> the salt of the earth
> a law unto themselves
> it came to pass
> gave up the ghost
> the signs of the times
> the powers that be
> fight the good fight

"The very familiarity of the phrases," says Lucas, "can make it hard to appreciate their beauty. It isn't easy to say things simply, much less to say them with style."

George Orwell, in his essay *Politics and the English Language*, translated a famous Biblical passage from Anglo-Saxon into Latinate English, to show how ugly and un-vivid long words can be. This is the original, a famous passage from Ecclesiastes:

> *I returned and saw under the sun, that the race is not to the swift,*
> *nor the battle to the strong, neither yet bread to the wise,*
> *nor yet riches to men of understanding, nor yet favour to men of skill;*
> *but time and chance happeneth to them all.*

And this was Orwell's translation into management-speak:

> *Objective considerations of contemporary phenomena compel the*
> *   conclusion*
> *that success or failure in competitive activities exhibits no tendency*
> *to be commensurate with innate capacity, but that a considerable*
> *   element*
> *of the unpredictable must invariably be taken into account.*[44]

Latinate words are emotionally distancing, which is why they are so favored by academics, or scientists, or for safety announcements, or when someone is telling you your train is delayed, and so on. They conceal blunt truths, they smooth over rough edges, and they sound fancy, as if whoever is speaking is in control.

Lucas sees both verbal storytelling and the visual storytelling of art and architecture as governed more by Heart than Head. He points to the influential British designer Richard Guyatt, who gave his inaugural lecture "Head, Heart and Hand" at the Royal Society of Art in 1950. In art and design, he said, the Head provides the "how" of something (that is, its function or utility); the Hand describes the "what" (its physical embodiment); and the Heart reflects the "why" (its value or meaning).

But the culture of high art and architecture has become overwhelmingly Head dominated. Anywhere architecture is usually faceless and devoid of the ornamentation that was a traditional form of visual storytelling.

As modernism gained momentum in the twentieth century, it came to focus mainly on How, on function. In architecture, it dispensed with decoration and narrative. Similarly, narrative was downplayed in fine art and highbrow literature. The late Roger Scruton has written about how often modern art is at war with ideas of home. Postmodernists have continued this hostility to belonging and meaning.

Lucas is an aesthetic traditionalist and goes back to Hogarth for inspiration: "In his book *The Analysis of Beauty*, Hogarth praised St. Paul's, a new building of his own time, saying its design displays 'the utmost variety without confusion, simplicity without nakedness, richness without tawdriness, distinctness without hardness and quantity without excess. Whence the eye is entertain'd throughout with the charming variety of its parts together . . .'

"He thought that a beautiful design, of any sort, is a battle between a host of opposing qualities. A good design sparkles with inner conflict; it is alive with inner tension."

This echoes the idea of the balance of Head, Hand and Heart. Beauty, in all the arts, is a tug of war between mighty forces. Stories work on the same principle: a good book unites all kinds of opposing themes, and a vivid character is alive with conflicting desires.

"There are other parallels between architecture and storytelling," according to Lucas. "All traditional architecture [across the globe] has these features in common:

1. Dramatic vertical asymmetry: i.e., the structure 'builds' to a dramatic climax.
2. Elaborate horizontal symmetries: like a story which replicates themes and images 'sideways' to create a rich, full world. Characters mirror each other, dilemmas, settings, motifs, etc., all echo one another.
3. Fractal pattern: so that small elements and details echo the whole.

"The driving force of all fiction, of all storytelling, is inner conflict: a good character is torn between what they want and what they need, the conflicting demands of the Heart and the Head. Jane Austen's Emma wants to be in control, not just of herself, but of others around her, but her Heart throws the plans of her Head into disarray. She becomes a more balanced individual as a result: she grows up.

"Like a good book, St. Paul's works on many levels at once, but for all its variety, it is one coherent story in a commonly understood language: in form and detail and materials, it tells the story of the tribe, reaching back to Christianity's origins in the classical world.

"Louis Sullivan, the inventor of the skyscraper in nineteenth century America, found another union of old and new. He pioneered steel-frame construction but loved rich ornament. Tradition was losing its grip, but Sullivan never sought to trash his cultural inheritance. He had fun with it, mixing up all kinds of languages of pattern—reflecting the mixed-up-ness of America itself—but underpinned by rigorous classical geometry, just as America was founded on classical ideals. His work is loved and 'the eye is entertain'd' because of that union of opposites in conflict. Sullivan coined the maxim 'Form follows function' but he understood that one of the primary functions of architecture is telling the story of the tribe.

"A big Victorian railway station like St Pancras in London is another neat halfway point between old and new: impressive engineering but still ornamented, with plenty of evidence of the work of the hand, and full of the symbolism of beginnings and endings, like a fabulous gateway.

"Europe imploded in the First World War, and in the catastrophe intellectuals declared a Year Zero. Modernism emerged in this value desert. Le Corbusier said that a house was just 'a machine for living in.'

"The Seagram Building in New York is a black brick, with no curves or diagonals to contrast with the grid of rectangles, with no hierarchy of form, no grand entrance, no sense of what each level might be for, no ornament. The exterior reveals nothing, gives nothing. It is one big 'No,' stripped of that energy that comes from 'the union of opposites in conflict,' and is impressive only because it is big and uses expensive materials. When you have no other values, those things do impress people. Hierarchy has been abolished in the name of progress, but with it difference and character and distinction.

"It is architecture of the Head, conceived as a snap-together kit of parts. I asked an architect friend to defend it and all he could do was praise its 'purity.' Purity is one-dimensional and inhuman.

"Similarly, the CCTV headquarters building in Beijing by Rem Koolhaas, is an eyeless, faceless monster: aggressively random and calculatedly incoherent. All that is left is a sort of desperate showiness, an empty 'Look at me!' The truly sad thing is that European civilization has exported its spiritual emptiness worldwide.

"A human architecture would not try to remake human nature or deny the stories and traditions and heritage that give people their identity. It could start by acknowledging that most people like buildings that have a face, buildings with symmetries that mirror the human body, buildings that greet you in welcome. It is human nature to anthropomorphize buildings. Buildings have personalities. They are loved if they are good company, hated if they are bullying monsters, tolerated (just about) if they are boring.

"And buildings are admired if they have the same qualities we admire in people: self-respect, generosity, authority, warmth, wit, poise, politeness, having something to say, being a bit different, but not being blank, or aloof, or grating, or attention-seeking for its own sake.

"The idea of beauty as a union-of-opposites-in-conflict goes back to Heraclitus. I see it as a universal truth: a work of art is beautiful in the same way that a good life is beautiful or someone's character is beautiful. An integrated person is a 'union of opposites in conflict.' So is a successful life. And a good design. If it was true for thousands of years, did it suddenly stop being true in the early twentieth century?"

Many of the big arguments of our time are over values and meaning. But what we tend to hear about in the media is the how, not the why. Brexit, to most Leave voters, was about values: sovereignty, belonging, identity, and so on.

David Lucas again: "Our working-class childminder said of the Remain campaign in 2016: 'Why do they think that all we care about is money?' She's an uneducated woman of forty who lives in a council house and had her first child at seventeen. She was a fount of common sense to us as first-time parents, and a real friend."

Many Remainers assume that Leave voters simply lacked the facts to make the right decision in the Brexit referendum. It is part of the widespread incredulity they feel that the people could have voted against what seem to be their own economic interests. This is despite the fact that well-paid members of the center-left branch of the cognitive class have supported parties of higher taxation for decades, a decision in which values are more important than their personal finances. In politics, the Heart usually trumps the Head.

PART THREE

HAND AND HEART

Chapter Seven

Whatever Happened to Hand?

What ordinary people once made, they buy; and what they once fixed for themselves, they replace entirely or hire an expert to repair

. . . While manufacturing jobs have certainly left our shores to a disturbing degree, the manual trades have not. If you need a deck built, or your car fixed, the Chinese are of no help. Because they are in China. And in fact there are chronic labour shortages in both construction and auto repair.

Matthew B. Crawford

When giving talks about my last book, *The Road to Somewhere*, about the value divides that have contributed to recent political upheavals, I would often declare that one of the reasons for the alienation felt by many voters is *the declining status of so much non-graduate employment.*

People in the audience would generally nod their heads in agreement. It sounds plausible, especially in the light of the evidence I have presented in earlier chapters of this book on declining relative pay for less well-qualified workers and the graduatization of so many of the most desirable jobs.

Yet status is a complex, slippery, and subjective notion. It is hard to rank people by status in the way that you can by income or social class, although the three do often overlap. Indeed, status is sometimes seen as the lifestyle aspect of class without being completely reducible to it. Where would you place a vicar? A minicab driver working on a PhD?

Status remains indelibly associated with notions of superiority and inferiority. In pre-democratic Europe, status or rank was often overt and expressed in the way an individual dressed or was addressed. In an era of more egalitarian citizenship, notions of superiority and inferiority may still be felt but are rarely expressed.

Wealth has always been, and remains, an important source of status, but older sources, such as land ownership, have declined, while new sources such as popular celebrity and educational achievement have emerged in their place.

In an interview from the 1970s in their classic work *The Hidden Injuries of Class*, Richard Sennett and Jonathan Cobb record a house painter saying: "Whenever I'm with educated people, you know, or people who aren't my own kind . . . I feel like I'm making a fool of myself if I just act natural, you know?"

Nearly fifty years on, J. D. Vance's bestselling memoir *Hillbilly Elegy: A Memoir of a Family and Culture in Crisis*, about his hometown in rust belt Kentucky and his own journey to Yale Law School, records many similar moments of feeling exposed before those of higher social and educational status.[1]

Judgments of status can be markedly different, depending on where you are standing. So when industrial working-class culture was at its height in the first sixty or seventy years of the twentieth century, manual workers often looked down on white-collar workers or even skilled professionals as people not doing real jobs.

In their 1957 study *Family and Kinship in East London*, Michael Young and Peter Willmott, found this: "A sizeable minority of men in Bethnal Green take a very different view from white-collar people about the status of manual work, placing jobs such as company director and chartered accountant towards the bottom of the scale and manual jobs, like agricultural labourer, coal miner, and bricklayer towards the top."[2]

At the same time working-class parents were often keen for their own children to escape working-class drudgery and, via a decent education, move up into Head rather than Hand work. A friend of mine, from a working-class background in eastern England, recalls his childhood just a few years after Young and Willmott's book appeared.

"As an infant before starting school, I remember playing with my toys while my mum, gran, and aunties were talking, and they all agreed they wanted their children to get an office job and not work with their hands. My dad was a builder and he was my hero so I was annoyed at this (and still am!). But they meant it. It was partly a gender divide. Male blue-collar culture despised people who worked in offices. My son still does!" he says.

There is no longer the same caste rigidity that was once the hallmark of the British class system, as Mike Savage's Great British Class Survey established in 2011.[3] The old three-class structure of upper class, middle class, and working class, which still had some meaning in the 1950s, has given way to a much bigger and more fluid middle grouping with a small and more meritocratic elite of around 6 percent of the population at the top and a larger precariously employed group of around 15 percent at the bottom.* Two-thirds of the 160,000 participants in the survey said they identified with no social class.

This greater fluidity used to be associated with "classless" America, although as we saw in Chapter Three there is some evidence of an emergent hereditary meritocracy in the United States. And in recent years more Americans have begun to identify as working-class instead of middle-class. In 2014 the National Opinion Research Center found that 47 percent of people identified as working-class and 42 percent middle-class.

---

* When the BBC published the Great British Class Survey, they provided a "class calculator" that 7 million people—more than 10 percent of the population—used to find out which class they belonged to. Mike Savage says this in itself was evidence of the fact that class membership was no longer obvious.

High educational achievement, which in both the United Kingdom and the United States increasingly means some kind of postgraduate qualification, is now a central source of status, and that working-class resistance of the 1950s on behalf of a useful, masculine Hand culture has largely disappeared. The nerd, once a figure of fun, has had the last laugh.

And this extends beyond Head achievement representing good employment prospects and secure future income, as Harry, the son of a former colleague of mine, has discovered. My ex-colleague has been professionally successful and sent Harry to a private school, where he did well at GCSE but lost interest when it came to A levels. After a year at university, he listened to his Heart and Hand. He dropped out and pursued his ambition to become a car mechanic.

He is now an experienced technician in the Volkswagen Group and earns more than many of his graduate contemporaries. "He earns £36K ($47K) a year, knocks off at five p.m., and loves his work and mates. But he is not a graduate and that makes him feel a bit of a second-class citizen," says his father.

Harry is a bright, articulate, and decent-looking young man who bought his own house and with income to spare, yet he finds that on dating websites being a car mechanic puts him at a significant disadvantage. He shares many interests and opinions with the people he grew up with. He still plays cricket, and he is at home in middle-class conversation, but he finds that his occupation acts as a filter in making contact with other young people, who are now graduates in junior professional jobs, sometimes earning half of what he does.

When he meets old school friends, he is disappointed when they dismiss people like his colleagues (and him), who work in complex, high-tech environments (you cannot service or repair a car these days without it being connected to a laptop) where they get their hands dirty. This is even visible at work, where smartly suited young service reception employees and technicians exist in an upside-down social pyramid of assumed superiority and income.

Some rare Hand workers—such as a surgeon or artist—are highly respected, but because their manual dexterity is usually combined with high levels of knowledge and cognitive ability, they are the exceptions that prove the rule. The cultural bias against ordinary manual occupations—even well-remunerated ones like Harry's that use diagnostic logic not unlike a medical professional's—seems to run deep, which helps to explain why it is so hard to fill many well-paid manual positions.

Yet this coexists with some nostalgia for the jobs of the manufacturing era, especially in the United States, even if people would prefer their own children not to be doing them. The American sociologist Mike Hout has found that the social standing of dozens of specific manufacturing jobs scored just as highly in 2012 as they had in 1989 and 1968.[4]

"Less cognitively demanding occupations are as esteemed as ever, though the number of people working in them is a fraction of what it once was. The guy who spent the first twenty years of his working life stressing and straining to manipulate heavy machinery in a factory manufacturing autos, appliances, or the steel to make them laments his current circumstances driving a forklift in a big-box store—if he is lucky enough to be doing that. A robot does his old job, maybe in the same factory but more likely in Mexico or Brazil. He'd still rather make stuff than move stuff around," says Hout.[5]

There is, of course, little point being nostalgic for the mass skilled manual labor of the industrial era. The millions of skilled jobs in mining, metal forming, printing, and so on are not going to return to rich countries. Nor are those middling secretarial and administrative jobs now done by computers.

But, equally, we shouldn't underestimate the psychological and political impact of the disappearance of decent Hand employment. There is persuasive survey and interview evidence that demonstrates this sense of loss, as I will show later in the chapter.

The middle income/middle status jobs represented by skilled manual employment provided social ballast. They also provided the people—mostly men—who performed them with a sense of being valued and useful. The work of a skilled lathe operator in an engineering factory required only moderate cognitive ability, but to do it well required several years' *experience*. This meant the worker's status was protected; this was part of the point of becoming a so-called time-served skilled worker. He could not easily be replaced by someone with superior academic qualifications.

One should be wary of romanticization, but some skilled jobs—especially skilled trades working with materials like leather, wood, stone, and brick—can also give people a deep sense of meaning and connectedness that goes beyond utility or economic value. Getting intimately involved in any physical process that requires skill, concentration, and a deep understanding of a particular material is a way of blurring subject and object, enlarging your sense of self by becoming what you are working with. Winston Churchill meditated by bricklaying. The ancient crafts of Japanese culture are performed as a meditation.

The story of the relative decline in *incomes* for middling and lower skilled jobs, thanks to more global openness and technological change, is a familiar one. The macro picture is captured by Branko Milanovic's famous elephant chart in which he shows the distribution of global income growth from 1988 to 2008.[6] He finds the world's poorest people, the new middle classes in poor countries, and the rich in rich countries all benefiting handsomely, while those occupying the 75th to 90th percentiles of world income distribution—essentially the West's working and lower-middle classes—have seen their incomes stagnate.

Typical of this story are the three hundred workers at the MG car plant in Oxford in the United Kingdom made redundant in 2005. Three academics interviewed them over a period of three years as they sought new jobs, mainly in the service sector, and in some cases retrained. About 90 percent got new jobs but very few of them achieved anything like the same earnings level as they had before. In fact they were earning on average about £6,000 ($7,800) less than they had been at MG Rover. And one-quarter of them admitted to living off their savings or being in financial difficulty.[7]

But this is a story about a whole Hand culture as well as income. In most developed countries there has been a dramatic decline in the manual and practical competence of the population.

It is true that new technologies have produced some new outlets for creativity and commerce—whether being a YouTuber or creating new kinds of games and music—but the overall direction of travel for many people has been away from Hand toward passivity. The disappearance of craft skills in the home, not just at work—playing a musical instrument, knitting, carpentry—has been a big and largely unrecorded story of the past fifty years. And the arrival of ever more sophisticated computers means that there are now many artists who cannot draw and musicians who cannot play an instrument.

A teacher friend reported to me this recent communication with a white working-class boy age twelve: "The boy wouldn't engage with my story-writing lesson. I asked him what he was interested in, what he did in his spare time, and all he could talk about was the computer game *Fortnite*. It's not his fault: it's the impoverishment of his culture, the passivity of being consumers, not producers."

Matthew Crawford, author of *The Case for Working with Your Hands*, has written about the sharp decline of shop classes in US schools in the 1980s and 1990s. These were high school programs teaching practical skills such as carpentry and metalworking.

Shop class in American schools is now increasingly rare. Writing in *Forbes* magazine in 2012, the American technologist Tara Tiger Brown lamented this decline:

> During my freshman year of high school I was required to take home economics and shop class where I learned basic skills in sewing, cooking, woodwork and metal work. Regrettably the cooking never made an impression, but I fondly remember learning along with a class full of boys and girls how to sew a pair of shorts, punch holes

into metal to create a hook to hang my bathrobe, cut and bend metal to make a box that still holds my pens to this day and use a rotary saw to make a hot plate that was used on the kitchen table at home.

Twenty years later I can still recall that sense of pride when I finished the blue metal box with only minimal guidance from my shop teacher. I remember him fondly, he wore a dark blue lab coat, coke bottle glasses and was missing the tip of one finger . . . I have continued to use those skills throughout my life both professionally and when needed around the house.

Shop classes are being eliminated from California schools due to the University of California/California State "a-g" requirements . . . Shop class is not included in the requirements, thereby not valued and schools consider the class a burden to support . . .

The UC/CA State system focuses on theory and not applied skills; a belief that learning how to swing a hammer or understand the difference between a good joint and a bad joint is part of a by-gone era, and as a society these skills are not something to strive for—something people resort to when they are out of options. Looking at shop class in this light is short-sighted and detrimental to America's future.[8]

Brown goes on to argue that it is often through learning practical skills that people can more easily grasp abstract scientific and mathematical ideas, learning *That* through learning *How*.

Paul Corby agrees with Brown that it is often the practical that is an avenue to grasping the theoretical. He is a lively and plain-speaking sixty-eight-year-old Englishman from Huddersfield, in Yorkshire, who rose to become a senior trade union leader and construction industry training official:

"Like most working-class children in the 1950s and 1960s I failed my eleven-plus and ended up at a lousy secondary modern that taught me very little, and I was completely unable to grasp algebra and geometry. Many of us were dismissed as thick, but most of us weren't. We often flourished in the world of work. I left school at fifteen and did a five-year construction apprenticeship with the Huddersfield company J Wimpenny. And I was soon using Pythagoras's theorem to work out my angles. In fact, eighteen months after I finished my apprenticeship, I was laying the foundations of multimillion pound buildings using Pythagoras."[9]

Knowing *How* and knowing *That* turn out to be complementary. There's an old story about the Medieval scholastic who tried to learn how to swim by reading a book on swimming technique. A friend who is training to be a teacher said this story came to mind when he saw trainee teachers in college grappling with issues of lesson planning and behavior management in theory. He and some other teacher colleagues had been thrown straight into school and knew about these things from direct experience, and their one day a week in college with the full-time students learning about "synthetic eclecticism" seemed comically irrelevant.

Decline of the Skilled Trades

Some of the neglect of skill training in manual-technical occupations in the United Kingdom and the United States was described in Chapter Four. Skill shortages have been especially acute in the construction industry in the United Kingdom. Over 2 million people work in construction and it is still easily the largest employer of young men.[10] But with more than 90 percent of enterprises with less than thirteen employees, and nearly half of all employees self-employed,[11] most are not in a position to offer much training. And the cyclicality of the work also tends to discourage both employers and workers from investing in skills that may then not be used for several months of the year.

Nevertheless, the number of construction apprenticeships in the United Kingdom has been in free fall. It fell from nearly 17,000 to just over 8,000 between 2009 and 2017,[12] and most of those apprenticeships were less than two years.

According to the Construction Industry Training Board, the numbers entering full-time college-based training also fell from 47,000 to 16,000 between 2005 and 2017.[13] Moreover, most construction qualifications are now just level 2, the equivalent of GCSEs, compared with construction apprenticeships in Germany, which are at least level 3 and sometimes level 4 or 5. The construction industry workforce has always been a mobile one, but it is no wonder that more than one-third of people working in construction in London are foreign-born.[14]

More than one third of vacancies in the UK construction sector were described as "skill shortage" vacancies in the 2017 Employer Skills Survey.[15] Skill shortages in rich countries today are at least as concentrated in the middle and bottom end of the job market as in higher cognitive domains, where the shortages of, say, engineers, computer scientists, and web designers tend to be in very specialist fields.[16]

The UK Employer Skills Survey also found that two in every five skilled trades vacancies—chefs, electricians, car mechanics—were proving hard to fill for skill shortage reasons.[17] A CBI/Pearson Education and Skills Survey in 2018 found that only 54 percent of companies were confident of filling low-skill roles in the future, and only 42 percent were confident of filling middle-skill roles.[18]

In the United States a combination of low investment in training and baby boomer generation retirement has increased skill shortage pressure, one of the reasons employers tend to be pro-immigration. In recent years employers have found it harder to fill blue-collar positions than college graduate jobs. Jobs with the highest vacancy levels in 2018 were health care aides and hotel staff.[19] There is an acute shortage of truck drivers in both the United States and United Kingdom.[20]

France has a similar deficit of skilled-trade workers, and according to INSEE, the National Institute of Statistics and Economic Studies, the hardest to fill jobs are carpenters, manufacturing technicians, roofers, and metalworkers.[21] Thanks to its apprenticeship system, the German economy is not suffering the same lack of skilled-trade workers as many other rich countries, but even Germany is struggling to fill some of the more traditional trades or those that require antisocial hours, like a trainee baker.

Why is it that skilled manual work has become so unpopular? It is partly the lure of higher education and graduate jobs for those who are even semi-successful at school. But it is also a sense that these occupations, with the partial exception of jobs like coding (which is also suffering shortages), belong to the past, not the future, and do not offer long-term security. It is true that overall demand for the skilled trades has been falling and will probably continue to fall. The jobs are either being made completely redundant by technological change or are being de-skilled; consider the switch from the old London black cab driver who has memorized the "knowledge" to the Uber driver who just follows directions from his phone.

Skilled-trade jobs fell by almost 30 percent in the United Kingdom between 1990 and 2018, falling from 4.7 million to 3.2 million, despite an increase in the UK population of around 15 percent in that period. And a lot of skilled-trade people from Central and Eastern Europe have been attracted to work in the United Kingdom thanks to the declining interest in the skilled trades on the part of young British people combined with the openness of the UK labor market. So it is estimated that about 14 percent of the 3.2 million working in the UK skilled trades are foreign-born.[22]

The skilled trades have seen similar declines in other rich countries: in the United Kingdom, France, and the United States the proportion of people working in this area has fallen to between 8 and 9 percent from around 12 percent in the 1990s. Germany is an outlier, with more than 12 percent still working in skilled trades.

Moreover, pay in the skilled trades has not kept up with the increase in median UK pay since 1975 (78 percent), but it has risen on average by 41 percent for electricians, 52 percent for plumbers, 39 percent for cooks and chefs, 38 percent for truck drivers, and 27 percent for bricklayers, although some individuals with specialist skills can often earn very much more than those figures imply. (In the United States, where median pay has been static since the mid-1970s, the pay for most skilled-trade jobs are in the minus range for that period: electricians, minus 8 percent; plumbers and plasterers, minus 9 percent.)

Thanks to the skill shortages described above, the next few years are likely to see a sharp uplift in pay in many of these skilled trades, which will, in turn, attract more people into the jobs so long as there are still the colleges and courses and teachers to train them.

In big cities like London the culture of the skilled trades has also changed, generally for the worse. I have a nephew, Sam Kershaw, who, rather unusually for someone privately educated from an upper-class background, became a plumber in west London—the plummy plumber!—who describes a bleak world of careless, transactional relationships.

Sam, who is dyslexic and did not flourish academically at school, did a two-year apprenticeship with the small plumbing company, Staunch and Flow, in west London, including one day a week at College of North West London in Willesden.

He says that it took him at least another two or three years after the apprenticeship before he became a competent plumber. By that time the five employees had bought the company and changed the business model to escape the misery and pressure of London plumbing life.

"All the incentives push you into doing the most basic, slapdash work and then move on in the knowledge that no one will hold you to account and in the anonymity of the big city you will avoid reputational damage. From what I know it is different, and better, in smaller towns and the countryside because there word of mouth counts for more."

Sam says Staunch and Flow has now turned itself into a complete building company, including plumbing, because in renovating houses or helping to build new ones you have much happier customers and you are more in control of the work. But the company no longer takes on apprentices. The pride and prestige once associated with acquiring a skilled trade has drained away as academic qualifications and professional office work has become the main route to secure and prestigious employment.

"The expectations of apprentices were far too high: they expected to be paid full whack as soon as they were qualified. And some of them behaved very poorly, dragging dog shit into houses, speaking disrespectfully to customers, and so on. You need soft skills even as a plumber."

The company now has twenty staff, about half of them from abroad. It wants to employ more, but potential staff usually fail to turn up for interviews and even for the first day on the job. But, says Sam, good people can earn £80,000 to £100,000 ($100,000 to $130,000) a year. "We have one guy who earns so well, he works one month on and then takes one month holiday through the year."

The related story of the decline of the work ethic in Hand work, especially in parts of the United Kingdom and the United States, is a constant refrain of exasperated employers. Toby Baxendale, who built the United Kingdom's largest fresh-fish processor, Direct Seafoods, with an annual turnover of £100 million ($130 million), said that by the late 1990s half of the skilled staff he needed, especially butchers for his meat subsidiary, were from abroad. Butchering skills were simply dying out in Britain, so he was increasingly employing either Australians or Eastern Europeans.

But it is not just about some traditional skills dying out. "I and my core staff found ourselves discriminating against young Brits who would apply for jobs. Why? Their attitude of entitlement, their complete lack of dependability or work ethic—and if we did employ them, they usually didn't stick beyond the first week," said Baxendale.

The overall standing of the skilled trades has also been diminished by the replacement of the old "patch-and-mend" culture with a "Chuck it out and buy a new one" culture. A friend told me a sad story about her washing machine fixer:

It must have been about 2011 when a washing machine repairman came to the house. He had come maybe once or twice before over the previous twenty years, and each time we had had a conversation. He lived in Essex, had set up a business repairing and reconditioning washing machines.

He was probably in his mid-fifties; he was very knowledgeable and saved me hundreds of pounds with various bits of advice about what machines to get, and sold us one of his reconditioned machines for a fraction of the price of a new one. It lasted a ridiculously long time . . . twelve years or so . . . and then we bought another one, which also lasted really well. On his last visit, he said he was finding it really hard to keep the business going . . . First, new machines were so cheap, it was hard to compete. Second, machines were now so flimsy that they broke easily and were far harder to recondition.

He was very bitter, all those flimsy machines filling up landfill every two or three years. He was probably not much of an environmentalist type, but even he could see it was insane. And of course the system had made all his skill and knowledge pointless. He didn't think the business would last him through to retirement. He was angry. And I felt embarrassed standing on the doorstep . . . [H]is hand skill was irrelevant but it shouldn't have been.

This last story is not just about nostalgia for the past; it is about the alienation that too many people, especially older people raised in a more Hand-friendly era, feel about the fact that there seems to be no place for them in a society focused on academic qualifications and digital technologies.

These are the people who often live in second- or third-tier towns in Europe or the United States without degrees and, in the United Kingdom, are likely to be among the 68 percent of working-class voters who say that Britain has changed for the worse in the past twenty to thirty years or the 62 percent who think that their children will not be better off than they are. The numbers are similar in the United States.

In most societies, the hardest jobs to fill are the menial but often vital positions toward the bottom of the occupational hierarchy, many of them the key worker jobs like supermarket worker and delivery driver that became more visible at the height of the Covid-19 crisis. Because of the educational and social trends described in this book, it's very hard in a country like Britain to motivate people, especially young men, to take work at the lower end of the jobs hierarchy, or even, as we have noted, middling work. Why perform work that is not valued and can be done by "failures and foreigners"—especially if you can earn similar amounts on the fringes of the black economy? Moreover, cognitive work is not only more prestigious and better paid; it usually involves more comfortable circumstances and greater autonomy and control over working time.

What the celebration of education and mobility actually means to a significant proportion of the population is that those who don't have decent academic qualifications and feel corralled into the bottom half of the labor market must submit to those who do. Many young people would prefer to opt out of the system completely than accept that fate. It is possible that this trend could be partially reversed in the wake of the Covid-19 crisis, which, at least temporarily, has generated a new respect for people doing basic but vital jobs in the food, pharmaceutical, and other supply chains.

Measuring Status

In the last two decades it sometimes feels as if an enormous social vacuum cleaner has sucked up status from manual occupations, even skilled ones, and reallocated it to the middling and higher cognitive professions and the prosperous metropolitan centers and university towns.

Yet, as I said at the start of this chapter, status is a fuzzy and contested concept. It is usually focused on occupations and includes both objective and subjective elements. "Objective status" means a kind of ranking that everyone can agree on: a surgeon or an architect has higher status than a plumber (and note this is not necessarily about pay: a successful plumber may be paid more than an architect). Conversely, "subjective status," as Noam Gidron and Peter Hall define it in their paper in the *British Journal of Sociology* on the politics of social status, "reflects people's own feelings about the levels of respect or recognition they receive relative to others in society."[23]

And the evidence for declining subjective status turns out to be elusive. With one or two notable exceptions (the Gidron and Hall paper being one), social scientists have not been digging into how people in rich countries feel about their relative status over recent decades in the light of the new education-based stratifications and the disappearance of so many middling-skill, middling-status jobs.

Or rather social scientists have produced relatively little mass survey evidence, but there is a library of so-called ethnographic research—meaning accounts based on structured individual interviews—on the feelings of the "left-behind" people, the losers as a result of globalization, especially in the United States. Not surprisingly, these accounts, mainly linked to an analysis of support for populist politics, describe feelings of loss and what Michèle Lamont, the American sociologist, has called a "recognition gap."

In her book *The Dignity of Working Men: Moralities and Boundaries of Race, Class, and Immigration*, in which she interviews 150 blue-collar workers in the United States and France, Lamont focuses on "boundary maintenance" as a source of esteem and how people come to feel like losers when it is no longer enough to be a hard worker to be successful. Some of this analysis is partly focused on race and the perceived lost "cultural privileges" of white working-class Americans as they have seen other groups rising above them economically or attracting more elite attention.[24]

Lamont finds the same in France: "The workers' feelings of isolation and powerlessness are accentuated by the fact that in their environment the cultural and religious institutions of immigrants are gaining in visibility . . . [T]hese feelings of loss are also accentuated by the perception that France is going downhill, due largely to the presence of immigrants . . .

"French workers deeply resent this perceived loss of national status, given that their nationality is one of their rare high-status characteristics."[25]

And Justin Gest, in *The New Minority: White Working Class Politics in an Age of Immigration and Inequality*, somewhat sweepingly detects similar sentiments right across the West: "Across the post-industrial regions of Western Europe and North America . . . white working class people sense that they have been demoted from the center of their country's consciousness to its fringe . . . [M]any white working class people feel like victims of discrimination . . . Their politics motivated and pervaded by a nostalgia that reveres, and seeks to reinstate, a bygone era." He quotes a white Londoner called Nancy Pemberton saying: "It's a fact that we are the minority . . . I won't allow myself to feel on the outside of my society. But a lot of other people are scared."[26]

Gest has created a measure of deprivation that measures feelings of economic, social, and political "centrality." He finds that patterns are similar across the United States and the United Kingdom, although the British tend to feel less central socially and the Americans less central economically.

Arlie Russell Hochschild, in her book *Strangers in Their Own Land: Anger and Mourning on the American Right*, ventured into the heart of red state America in Louisiana and over the course of five years befriended pipefitters, plant operators, truck drivers, telephone repairmen, postal workers, and so on, most of whom could no longer take pride in their work.[27]

She talked to one man who said that the more you stand on your own two feet and the less you depend on the government, the higher your status, echoing the observation of nineteenth-century sociologist Thorstein Veblen, who observed (in her words) that our distance from necessity tends to confer honor.

Hochschild writes: "You are a stranger in your own land. You do not recognize yourself in how others see you. It is a struggle to feel seen and honored . . . [T]hrough no fault of your own, and in ways that are hidden, you are slipping backward.

". . . Most people I talked to loved the South, loved Louisiana, loved their town or bayou. But they were sadly aware of its low status, 'Oh we're the flyover state', one Tea Party teacher told me. 'We're seen as backward and poor', another complained."

This ethnographic work is of some value, but it is easy for researchers to find what they are looking for and it is not clear how representative the interview subjects of depressed American and British towns are of the wider society.

But alongside the ethnographic work there is what one might call the physical evidence of the toll of low status in depression, alcoholism, drug addiction, and suicide. The increase in the United States, and to a lesser extent the United Kingdom, in deaths from suicide, drug overdoses, and alcohol-related liver disease among middle-aged people—the so-called deaths of despair, referred to already several times—is concentrated heavily among the lower-educated population.

US whites had much lower mortality rates from deaths of despair than France, Germany, or Sweden in 1990, but while those other countries have now converged on a level of 40 such deaths per 100,000 of the population, white Americans have risen to 80 per 100,000. The United Kingdom had an unusually low rate of such deaths in the early 1990s, but it has risen sharply to around 40 deaths per 100,000, the European norm today, with women increasing from 15 to 26 per 100,000 and men from 30 to 60 per 100,000.

According to Angus Deaton and Anne Case, this rise in deaths of despair since the turn of the century, especially for 45–55 year old whites, has been causing life expectancy for Americans as a whole to decline for the first time since records began. If death rates had continued on the downward trend of the twentieth century, 600,000 fewer people would have died over the past twenty years.

Deaton and Case suggest that the deaths are linked to a process of cumulative disadvantage for less-educated people along with the weakening of traditional social structures like church and family. White Americans with no college degree have gone from having mortality rates 30 percent lower than African-Americans in 1999 to 30 percent higher.

There is also the work of British social scientist Michael Marmot on the so-called social gradient, the idea that, as socioeconomic status rises, so do health prospects and life expectancy. He pioneered this understanding with his studies of Whitehall civil servants, in which he discovered a steadily rising gradient in the risk of heart disease as you go down the hierarchy.

Men at the bottom were four times more likely to die, and only a little less than a third of the gradient disappeared when factors such as smoking and cholesterol were factored out. This finding, which was also found to hold outside Whitehall, is based on the idea that low status in a hierarchy produces constant stress and anxiety—especially for men, who derive more status from work than women—and this produces higher levels of cortisol, which damages the immune system. This could be part of the explanation for why at the height of the pandemic men in low-skill jobs were twice as likely to die from Covid-19 as in the wider working population, at least in the United Kingdom.

Although there is a commonsense connection between poverty, poorer health, and longevity, Marmot's work has been criticized for its assumptions about status and stress. Many people go to work just to earn a living and derive their status from things outside work; moreover, high stress is also associated with high-status individuals with large responsibilities.

In any case, I am interested in the wider phenomenon of how the relatively rapid emergence of educational stratification in recent decades and the growth of a large cognitive class has impinged upon those who have not gained entrance to the class, or even to its higher levels, and whether this has more generally disturbed the status balance in society.

I therefore wanted to find broader, more objective empirical evidence of feelings of status decline, especially among nongraduates. I believe I have found a decent amount of evidence for this trend, as I will describe below.

But the evidence for status loss needs to be set in a broader and rather contradictory picture of occupational and labor market change in rich countries, much of which points to *high levels of work satisfaction* even for Hand workers, already mentioned in Chapter Five.

Many ideas about the job market—how insecure employment is for many people, especially young people, and how middle-income jobs are disappearing—turn out on closer inspection to be rather exaggerated, at least prior to the pandemic.

The proportion of people in conventional full-time employment at 63 percent has hardly budged at all in the past twenty years in the United Kingdom[28] despite a big rise in self-employment, and average job tenure remains around nine years, where it has been for several decades.[29] And the numbers in nonstandard, nonpermanent employment have also held steady: only 2.4 percent of the workforce in the United Kingdom in 2018 were on zero-hours contracts, and most of them were content with the arrangement.[30] In the United States the so-called gig economy, in which short-term freelance work is accessed through online marketplaces, is only about 1 percent of total employment.[31]

In 2018 the employment rate was at record highs in Britain and Germany and twenty-two other OECD countries.[32] And the Internet has made job "matching" easier and cheaper for both employers and employees. High minimum wages in many European countries, which have partly replaced the power of organized labor, are also reducing the number of low-paid workers in some European countries; in the United Kingdom the proportion has fallen from 21 to 17 percent since 2015.[33]

Here is Francis Green, a leading British labor market economist: "In the affluent economies of the industrialized world, life at work in the early twenty-first century has evolved in a curious and intriguing way. Workers have, with significant exceptions, been taking home increasing wages, exercising more acute mental skills, enjoying safer and more pleasant conditions at work, and spending less time there. Yet they have also been working much more intensely, experiencing greater mental strain . . . In many cases, work has come under increased and unwelcome control from above, leaving individual employees with less influence over their daily work lives and a correspondingly less fulfilling experience than before."[34]

It is true, as described earlier in the chapter, that many of the middle-skilled manual jobs of the industrial era that have been exposed to global competition or technological change, from lathe operators to secretaries, have either disappeared completely or been faced with relatively stagnant incomes. But they have been replaced with a "new middle" in terms of income, though not necessarily skill.

A report by the UK human resources think tank CIPD explains: "The share of low-paid jobs measured by OECD definitions of hourly full-time earnings has fallen from 22% in 1997 to just under 18% in 2018. The share of high-paid jobs also using OECD definitions has not significantly changed since 1997, at just over 25% of all jobs. It must therefore follow that on these measures the share of 'middle wage' jobs has not fallen over this period . . . [T]he middle has not contracted in terms of the wage distribution because the 'old' middle of skilled trades and administrative jobs has been replaced by a 'new middle' which includes managers in low-pay industries [such as catering] and some professional associate and technical jobs."[35]

And most of the net employment increase in the United Kingdom over the past decade has been in relatively higher-paid work: an increase of over 1.2 million professional jobs, over 600,000 associate professional roles and over half a million managerial roles.[36] It is a similar story in the United States with around half of the 10 million new jobs created between 2008 and 2018 described as professional, and an even higher proportion in the EU.[37]

Another challenge to the idea of a dramatic polarization between good, mainly Head jobs, and lousy ones, mainly Hand and Heart, comes from the British Social Attitudes survey of 2015, which had a special focus on work and jobs. It asked people whether they thought they had a "good job" based on seven factors—security, income, opportunity for advancement, interest, autonomy, opportunity to help others, use to society—and the proportion who thought they did *rose* to 71 percent from just 57 percent in 1989.[38]

It is a similar story in the United States. About half of American workers say they are very satisfied with their current job, 30 percent are somewhat satisfied, and the remainder say they are somewhat dissatisfied (9 percent) or very dissatisfied (6 percent). Highly educated workers are the most satisfied and the least educated the least satisfied.[39]

The same more positive story can be found in general indicators of well-being that have been holding steady or even rising in many rich countries, including the United Kingdom and the United States, although the highest measures of well-being do tend to be correlated with high levels of education and with professional careers.*

These benign trends probably have something to do with the decline in the number of routine manual occupations and manufacturing operations in Britain and other rich countries. For all the nostalgia about industrial jobs, for most people, working in a call center is preferable to working on a production line.

But the same BSA survey and other workplace data points to less benign data, too, about the rise in stress levels and reductions in autonomy. In 2015, 37 percent said they found work stressful either always or often, up from 28 percent in 1989, with a slightly higher proportion saying this in professional and managerial jobs.[40]

But Hand and Heart workers have been hit hardest on the loss of autonomy in recent years. While autonomy rose on most counts for

---

* The Office of National Statistics (ONS), UK statistical authority, has been collecting well-being data since 2012, and the indicators have generally been on the rise, at least until the Covid-19 crisis. See https://www.ons.gov.uk/peoplepopulationandcommunity /wellbeing.

professional and managerial staff, the proportion of people in routine and semi-routine jobs who said they were not free to decide how their daily work was organized rose from 42 percent to 57 percent between 2005 and 2015.[41]

This is Marx's theory of alienation in modern form. For many people, work has had all forms of self-expression and self-determination removed. And as Daniel Bell predicted in his writing about postindustrial society, the rising status of Head workers has gone hand in hand with routinization and loss of autonomy lower down the occupational hierarchy.

The loss of autonomy also informs the concept of "precariat," a new insecure stratum of the workforce whose long-term job prospects are unclear and are therefore unable to develop a consistent work identity. Although analysts of the precariat tend to exaggerate the degree of employment insecurity in rich countries, they are describing the status of those who are unable to move from job to career.

So, even if one accepts that working life in general has been improving for the average employee in many rich countries, this is still compatible with relative status decline for those in non-Head jobs, and especially if one takes account of the wider cultural factors surrounding work.

One such factor is that until recently most people went to work for *similar reasons*, whether they were a bank manager or a refuse collector. They went out of duty and to support themselves and serve their families. But increasingly since the 1970s, as Head jobs have grown, the world of work has diverged between a large minority with *careers*—something that used to be the preserve of a small elite—and those who still just have *jobs*.

And, according to the "post-materialism" theories of Ronald Inglehart, those with careers increasingly see work as a form of self-expression or self-actualization in the way that a craftsman once did. Inglehart estimates that in most of Europe and the United States this idea of work spread to about half the workforce between 1970 and 2006.[42]

On the other hand, according to the 2015 British Social Attitudes survey, a tenacious 40-plus percent of British employees continue to say that a job is just a way to earn money and nothing more, as they have done now since the 1980s.[43] The so-called work instrumentalists are to be found in almost equal number in the United States, where the Pew Research Center finds that 51 percent of employed Americans says they get a sense of identity from their job and 47 percent say their job is just what they do for a living.[44]

This divide is unlikely to precisely follow the distinction between Head on the one hand and Hand and Heart on the other, not even between graduate and nongraduate, but it is just common sense to assume that the majority of graduate Head jobs are careers that provide an important aspect of meaning and identity to those who hold them.

And indeed the Pew data from the United States does find that 77 percent of people with a postgraduate degree are the most likely to say their job gives them a sense of identity, 60 percent with a bachelor's degree do so, and 48 percent of those with some college education and about 4 in 10 (38 percent) with a school diploma or less say the same.[45] Similarly, employed adults with a bachelor's degree or more are nearly twice as likely as those with less education to say their job is a career.[46]

Meaning in work may also be harder to achieve in some of the "new middle" of routinized white-collar work compared with either upper professional careers or being a welder in a shipyard, where the purpose and value of your work is obvious. One-third of British workers told YouGov in 2015 that their jobs made no meaningful contribution to the world.[47]

So, with declining relative pay, less meaning and autonomy at work, and the realization that as a nongraduate you are denied access to the higher-income, more prestigious jobs above you, the declining status of nongraduate employment is surely a major social fact.

One big international social survey does indeed find that the relative social status of non-college–educated men is lower, in some cases sharply lower, than it was twenty-five years ago. The International Social Survey Programme (ISSP), which covers twenty developed countries, with sample sizes averaging 1,500 to 2,000, asks respondents to place themselves on a 10-point social ladder reflecting their position in society.

The sharpest declines in status between 1990 and 2014 among non-college–educated men are found in the United Kingdom, Switzerland, Australia, Sweden, and Poland, with less sharp declines in Germany, Austria, the United States, and Norway. Two countries, Hungary and Slovenia, recorded small rises in status. The combination of economic disadvantage and shifting cultural norms have pushed lower-status men toward support for populist parties, argue the authors of the paper.[48]

There is another set of questions in the ISSP that provide further support for the status decline thesis, this time asking working-class and professional class respondents in France, Germany, the United Kingdom, and the United States whether their status is higher or lower than their fathers'. In almost all cases well over half of professional people say their status is higher than their fathers' and well below half of working class people say the same. In the working-class United States the fall was from 57 percent in 1992 to 46 percent in 2009, in the working class United Kingdom from 35 percent in 1999 to 30 percent in 2009.[49]

There is a gender aspect to this, too, as we saw in Chapter Five. Hand work outside the home has traditionally been male dominated and continues to be so. But as women have moved into the workforce in much greater numbers, both at the top and the bottom, some men have been pushed down the occupational ladder and have lost relative status. The ISSP data finds that over the past twenty-five years the average social status reported by women has risen relative to that reported by men in nine out of the twelve countries for which research-ers have data.[50]

So there is certainly some hard evidence for status decline for those in nongraduate jobs in recent years. Status rather than class issues also appears to be relevant in support for Brexit and similar antiestablishment political preferences.[51]

But given how relatively little data there is on the status question, I also commissioned some original polling on the question for this book. YouGov undertook two nationwide surveys, one in the United Kingdom and one in the United States. The results confirm the public perception of status decline for nongraduates in those countries.

When asked "Do people who have not been to university find it harder or easier to get good jobs than a generation ago, or is it about the same," 53 percent of British respondents who had a view on the matter said it was harder, and 57 percent of Americans agreed.

Shifting to questions around status, as indicated by the term "respect," shows similar results. The question was "Do you think that people doing ordinary jobs—like driving a truck or working in a shop—are given more respect in society, less respect or about the same level of respect as 25 years ago?" The response: 53 percent of Britons and 51 percent of Americans agreed that they received less respect. Moving to respect for those without degrees, YouGov found that 39 percent of British respondents and 49 percent of Americans thought nongraduates had lost respect in society.

Few respondents actively *disagreed* with the assumption that non-graduates had less good job opportunities and received less respect, ranging from just 12 percent to 17 percent. And there were few partisan differences except on the theme of it being harder for nongraduates to get good jobs. Here left-leaning voters tended to identify this as somewhat more of a problem. Conservatives in Britain were less likely to think that manual workers had lost respect over the past twenty-five years.

This degree of agreement across demographic and political groups suggests that a politics of the Head-Hand-Heart triumvirate could establish deep roots. In the United States even the partisan gap between Clinton and Trump voters was negligible. The table below shows the unusual demographic and political consensus that nongraduates and manual workers have lost status and opportunity in the last generation.

Is this status loss an economic or cultural phenomenon? It is evidently a combination of the two. There has been a shift to Head and away from Hand both in what society rewards in hard cash and, as this chapter has illustrated, in the less tangible and quantifiable matters of respect and status.

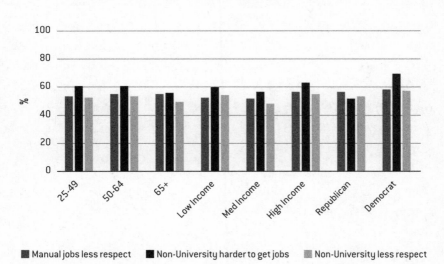

The Declining Status of Nongraduate Work (US)

Chapter Eight

Whatever Happened to Heart?

Modern liberalism is about choice and autonomy. But care is at an angle to both because it is often about responding to dependence, human beings after all spend a lot of time at both ends of their life-span dependent.

Madeleine Bunting

Looking at the economic balance sheets of rich countries over the past few decades it would be hard to claim that society's Heart—meaning, in this context, the caring functions once done in the home and now often done in the public care economy—has been neglected.

In most of those countries, health and social spending continues to rise as a proportion of total spending and of GDP, and many more people, still overwhelmingly women, are employed as caregivers, nurses, and early-years teachers than was the case fifty years ago even allowing for the growth in population. The warfare economy of the 1950s has given way to the welfare economy of today, especially in Europe. The Covid-19 crisis, and fear of a repeat, is likely to push up health and social spending even higher.

And pay in the welfare economy is not as low as is often assumed, at least in the United Kingdom. The daughter of a friend of mine is earning £41,000 ($53,000) as a teacher after just five years in the profession, and the daughter of another friend is earning £36,000 ($47,000) as a National Health Service (NHS) nurse with just three years' experience. (The latter includes some hefty night shift bonuses and both include London allowances.)

Overall the pay of jobs in the broadly defined care sector has been a mixed bag in recent decades, following the general pattern of higher returns to the more skilled and lower to the less skilled. Since 1975 median pay (adjusted for inflation) has risen 78 percent in the United Kingdom, nurses' pay has risen by exactly the same amount, with a 91 percent rise for midwives and a 79 percent rise for social workers. The picture is much less favorable for primary school teachers, who have had just a 19 percent rise, day care and nursery staff 13 percent, and ambulance staff a miserly 6 percent. It is a similarly mixed picture in the United States, with nurses seeing a 96 percent rise since 1975 but secondary school teachers with only a 26 percent rise.[1]

The pay of most people working in adult social care in the United Kingdom has risen by only around 20 percent in that period—it is particularly low for workers who care for people living in their own homes—and over the past twenty years the United Kingdom has repeatedly failed to follow Germany, Japan, and many other rich countries by investing properly in care for the elderly, which suggests that Heart has limited political leverage.

The Private Realm and the Crisis of Meaning

But this is to take a Head view of Heart. There is another way of looking at modern life in rich countries and seeing an emerging crisis of values and meaning, *a crisis of Heart*. The historian and futurist Yuval Noah Harari has characterized liberal modernity as a Faustian exchange in which meaning (the Heart) has been exchanged for power (the Head). "Modernity is a deal," Harari writes. "The entire contract can be summarised in a single phrase: humans agree to give up meaning in exchange for power."[2]

That power over the environment means that in many ways there has never been a better time to be alive both in rich and poor countries, notwithstanding the ecological damage to the planet and now perhaps the hovering pandemic threat. Over the past two hundred years, in rich countries, each generation has been around 50 percent better off economically than its predecessor, life spans have doubled, and recently global poverty has been plummeting too.

There is, however, a price to be paid for this power, and the price is disenchantment. Harari predicts that the moral and cosmic certainties of religion will be replaced by "Dataism," a universal faith in the power of algorithms.

The United States, which for some decades defied the general secularization trends of other rich countries, is now catching up, and the European caricature of the Bible-thumping, working-class American is wide of the mark. In 1976, 81 percent of the US population identified as white Christian, and that is now down to 43 percent, with only 17 percent identifying as white evangelical Protestants and poorer white Americans less likely to be observant Christians than richer ones.[3] Overall, 70 percent of Americans still self-identify as Christian,[4] but that number has fallen sharply in recent years, and only 56 percent believe in the God described by the Bible.[5]

Europe is still more secular. The 2018 British Social Attitudes survey found that 52 percent of adults did not have any religious affiliation.[6] But that may have been an outlier: other recent surveys have found 55 percent describing themselves as nonpracticing Christians, slightly higher than 49 percent of Germans and 46 percent of the French. The same survey found the actively nonreligious highest in France at 28 percent, with Germany at 24 percent and the United Kingdom at 23 percent, though France and Germany also had a higher number of active believers.[7]

This European secularization will be slowed, but is unlikely to be reversed, by the higher religiosity of growing ethnic minority populations and by the revival of religion in some Eastern European countries after the end of communism.

Harari predicts a secular future of extreme inequality in which extra longevity and superhuman qualities are likely to be the preserve of the techno-superrich, the masters of the data universe.

What about everyone else? Harari writes: "The Russian, Chinese, and Cuban revolutions were made by people who were vital to the economy but who lacked political power; in 2016, Trump and Brexit were supported by many people who still enjoyed political power but feared they were losing their economic worth. Perhaps in the 21st century, populist revolts will be staged not against an economic elite that exploits people but against an economic elite that does not need them anymore. This may well be a losing battle. It is much harder to struggle against irrelevance than against exploitation."[8]

Are those deaths of despair in the United States not mainly found among people who have become socially, economically, and personally irrelevant? As noted earlier, Angus Deaton, who along with Anne Case has led the research on the epidemic of deaths of despair, says: "There is a rising sea of pain and poor mental health in the US among whites with less than a college degree . . . And what surprised us is how *little* material deprivation seems to matter with this story."[9]

Similarly, the new discipline of happiness research finds relationships, work, and community hugely more important than income in promoting well-being.[10]

Family breakdown is, according to Deaton, one of the key causes of the deaths of despair in America. The median nongraduate white woman has at least one child out of marriage in the United States and cohabitation tends to be more short-term than in Europe. Many men at the bottom of the pile do not know their children and lack the family support structures that previous generations took for granted. As noted in Chapter Six, in the United States in the mid-1960s, among white people aged thirty to forty-nine, almost everyone was married; in 2010 the figure was still 84 percent for the college educated but had slumped to just 48 percent for the high school educated. Similarly, in 2005, 85 percent of children born to upper-middle-class families were living with both biological parents when the mother was forty; among working-class parents the figure was only 40 percent.[11]

There has also been that big decline in religious observance in America among the less well educated, and two-thirds of them are utterly cynical about the public realm, believing that elections are rigged by the rich and large corporations.[12]

There is a surprising consensus about the importance of these eroding social norms in the United States among both conservative analysts like Charles Murray and liberals like Robert D. Putnam. Putnam describes the country as being beset by "purple problems," meaning a combination of blue state concerns over economic opportunity and inequality of all kinds and red state concerns over status, order, and tradition.

Many of today's most pressing social problems in Europe—from the lack of affordable housing to the state of elderly care, mental stress, and loneliness—can also be traced back, at least in part, to the weakening of family ties. In Britain today, almost 40 percent of all fifteen-year-olds do not live with both their natural parents—the number has been falling slightly in recent years[13]—and family breakdown doubles the likelihood of children failing at school.[14]

Statistics about mental illness are somewhat unreliable, as they are often based on self-assessment surveys and are not adjusted for changing attitudes and destigmatization. An official ONS/NHS health survey in the United Kingdom in 2016 indicated that 19 percent of adults had a degree of mental ill health, and it was markedly higher among those in the lowest income quartile.[15] The dispensing of anti-depressants has doubled between 2006 and 2016.[16]

The data relating to actual contact with health services has been rising only gently in the United Kingdom: in 2017 around 2.5 million people, about 4.5 percent of the population, had contact with the NHS over learning disabilities, autism, or so-called secondary mental health issues (meaning more serious psychiatric disorders, like anxiety disorder, severe depression, or psychosis).[17]

Simon Wessely, one of Britain's leading psychiatrists, is critical of some of the alarmist analyses about an "epidemic" of mental illness but does point to the Adult Psychiatric Morbidity Survey, a large survey conducted every seven years, which found so-called common mental disorders—depression, anxiety, panic attacks—to have increased sharply for one group in recent years from 19 percent to 26 percent. That group is young women aged eighteen to twenty-four.[18]

In the United States, mental illness is now the second most common cause of a disability claim on the Social Security system after musculoskeletal disorders,[19] and the Mental Health America report, *The State of Mental Health in America*, found 18 percent of adults to have some kind of mental health condition.[20] Stephen Ilardi a clinical psychologist at Kansas University, says that 23 percent of Americans will experience a bout of depressive illness before the age of seventy-five and the incidence is rising among younger cohorts. He also says that one in nine Americans over the age of twelve are currently taking some form of antidepressant.[21] And, as we saw in the last chapter, thanks to the sharp increase in those deaths of despair among the middle-aged—an extreme form of mental stress—life expectancy in the United States is now falling.

Loneliness is a significant issue in the United States, especially among the baby boomer generation, one in six of whom live on their own. According to the US's General Social Survey, American social networks shrank by one-third between 1985 and 2009 judging by the number of close confidants people say they have.[22]

Loneliness levels are somewhat lower in Europe, according to a NORC (National Opinion Research Center)/University of Chicago study, presumably because family life remains stronger: just 8 percent of people in Germany and the Netherlands admit to being lonely most or all of the time, and 10 percent in Sweden—although, surprisingly, the number was higher in less individualistic, more family-orientated Southern Europe. The US figure was 16 percent, although other surveys have put the figure much higher.[23] A British Red Cross survey in 2016 found that 18 percent of adults in the United Kingdom felt lonely always or often.[24]

One should be wary of "golden-ageism" about the family, and it is certainly true that there is no tradition of elderly people living with their adult children in northern Europe or America as there is Japan and India. Nevertheless, with the number of intact couples in decline, especially in the United States and the United Kingdom, the private networks for delivering care to the young and the old have become weaker, particularly at the lower end of the income spectrum, and big majorities in opinion surveys regret this development: 72 percent in a recent one in the United Kingdom said they felt family breakdown was a serious problem.[25] (There is some evidence in the United States of a return of the multigenerational extended family especially among poorer and nonconventional families who cannot afford to buy in extended family services in the manner of affluent families.)[26]

Married or cohabiting couples with children will not, of course, be persuaded to stay together if a relationship has irrevocably broken down; people can make mistakes when choosing a partner. But family charities argue that plenty of breakdowns could be avoided, or at least delayed until children are older, if there were less economic stress on young couples: half of family breakdown in the United Kingdom happens before a child is three, with less committed, unmarried couples counting for the lion's share.[27]

Big families are increasingly rare, and the singleton life is increasingly the norm throughout the West. More than one-third of households in some countries now consist of someone living alone; in some Nordic countries it is closer to 40 percent.[28]

The cognitive class worldview in Europe and North America, especially what one might call the "creative class" wing, leans toward the secular, open, mobile, autonomous, and novel; it is often suspicious of national and group attachments, tends toward the androgynous in male-female relations, and while community and belonging are recognized as important, the dominant cultural narrative is that of the unencumbered individual breaking free of tradition and authority.*

Societies that place a high value on freedom and individual achievement are bound to value less the constraints of long-term partnership, family commitments, and community; this is one of the central tensions of liberal modernity. And an inevitable consequence of the rise of this creative class worldview is the weakening of the care economy and the family—the private domain of obligation, unconditional recognition, and submitting to the needs of others. The art and habit of caring is in danger of being lost as more of us put our own interests above everything else.

Every day, even in rich countries, there are still more hours spent caring, in its many forms, than in any other activity. Caregivers UK estimates that 9 million people care for others part- or full-time; it is roughly the same proportion in the United States. And caring work—in both the private realm of the family and the public economy—is some of the most emotionally, physically, and intellectually demanding labor of all.

Yet most economists disregard child-rearing or elderly care work done in the private realm because it is unpaid and so doesn't directly contribute to the GDP; some feminists characterize it as a place of entrapment and oppressive burdens for women, while for promoters of the achievement society it's often seen as a place of wasted cognitive ability. Traditional roles such as male breadwinner and female homemaker have been partially delegitimized and replaced with a far more fluid ideal of family relations.

Freer societies have unavoidably weakened many of the cultural

---

* The size, influence, and definition of the creative class is contested, but the connection with both liberal attitudes and economic inequality is not. Here is Richard Florida, the author of the concept, himself: "Across the United States, inequality is not just a little higher, but substantially higher, in liberal areas than in more conservative ones. All of the twenty-five congressional districts with the highest levels of income inequality were represented by Democrats, according to a 2014 analysis."

forces that historically legitimized and honored care and service to others: large families with many economic and social functions performed in the private realm, usually managed by women; religious observance and the idea of acting in the eyes of God; the traditional notion of women as naturally nurturing and altruistic; stable societies with clear gender roles and strong mutual obligations. Liberal modernity has not, in the main, looked kindly on such notions.

Care now faces a crisis of identity in achievement societies that are utilitarian, problem-solving, and goal oriented. The writer Madeleine Bunting, author of *Labours of Love: The Crisis of Care*,[29] sees care in tension with modern liberalism's twin priorities of choice and autonomy. "And good care is about what one might call self-effacement, which is not a virtue that is celebrated in modern culture. It is also *embodied* work in a culture dominated by the abstract and analytical."[30]

The result of this cultural undervaluing of Heart is plain to see. Most rich countries with aging populations will see a big increase in demand for face-to-face caring jobs, and caring remains partly immunized from automation, yet there is a long-standing crisis of recruitment in these sectors and few signs that the status or rewards associated with them are rising in response.

There are currently 41,000 nursing vacancies in the United Kingdom's NHS out of a total nursing workforce of around 300,000, and 24 percent of trainee nurses failed to complete their three-year-degree courses in 2017, probably after discovering how demanding it is, especially on clinical placements. In adult social care the situation is even worse, with 110,000 vacancies out of a total workforce of 1.4 million.[31] And almost *one-third* of the workforce leave every year for better-paying and less demanding work; that can sometimes mean working as a shop assistant.[32] According to the US Bureau of Labor Statistics, America needs an extra half a million nurses by 2026. Germany needs to double its social care workforce in the next twenty years yet is already facing recruitment difficulties.[33] It is a similar story in most rich countries.

Women and Care

There is one benign reason for the crisis of recruitment in care jobs, especially nursing: women have many more career options today than they did fifty years ago and, on average, are better educated. Nurse recruitment has undoubtedly suffered from the breaking of glass ceilings. In the decades after the Second World War, some of the most capable women in rich countries were working as ward sisters or primary school heads. Their daughters are partners in city law firms, management consultants, or, indeed, medical consultants. Society as a whole has benefited from this greater freedom for women, but many parts of the care economy, including teaching, have suffered.

My late mother-in-law, Deborah Kellaway, illustrates the generational shift. She had two degrees, including one from Oxford, but partly because of her family commitments chose to become a secondary school teacher when her three children were of school age. She was an inspirational English teacher at a North London grammar school, but her own children all chose better-paid and more glamorous careers in journalism and financial services.

Hardly anybody wants to return to the family norms of the 1950s*— to overwhelming female dependence on male earnings, high levels of domestic abuse, and the stigmatization of single parenthood. But surely it is possible to find ways of valuing care work more in the family and the public economy, both by women *and* men, without abandoning the greater choice and freedom that have been achieved by recent generations of women.

Yet it now often feels as if we have reached an unsatisfactory compromise, especially in the United Kingdom and United States. The

---

* According to the 2012 British Social Attitudes survey, only 13 percent of people agree that "a man's job is to earn money; a woman's job is to look after home and family," with little difference between the genders. In the mid-1980s the figure was 49 percent. Surveys in the United States show somewhat more traditional attitudes.

obligations of the private realm are seen as a constraint on freedom, especially for women, and the state does little to support the family, pushing mothers back into the labor market as soon as possible. Yet women, often by choice, still carry most responsibility for that private realm, leaving many struggling to compete fairly with men in the public realm—thanks in part to the "double shift."

The proportion of working age mothers in work in the United Kingdom has increased from 50 percent in 1975 to 72 percent in 2017,[34] and while men have on average increased their share of domestic work in the home to sixteen hours a week, women still do twenty-six hours.[35]

Although many of the professions are now more or less evenly split between men and women, the middle and lower ends of the job market remain highly gender segregated. The proportion of male registered nurses in the United Kingdom is about 12 percent, an increase of only 1 percentage point from the turn of the century. (It is much higher in mental health nursing, which has different historical origins.) In the United States it is even lower.

"Many women today are less socialised into caring roles and some women have just given up on care but men have not, in general, taken up the slack," says Bunting.[36] Men are, in fact, doing a larger share of domestic labor than in previous generations, and elderly care is shared more equally than child care. But, says Bunting, many women are still doing more care than ever, especially in that corridor from mid-forties to early-sixties when, thanks to children spending a longer time in education and the greater longevity of older people, women some-times have primary responsibility for looking after teenage children still living at home *and* their parents.

Joanna Williams, a former colleague of mine who was raised in a working-class home in Middlesbrough, has an interesting perspective on changing attitudes to care and the family. Her own mother was a caregiver who later qualified as a social worker, and as the oldest child Joanna had to spend a lot of her childhood looking after her siblings. (Her father did an unusual amount of domestic work for a man of his generation but always made sure that the neighbors could not see him when he was hanging up the washing.)

"I rebelled against the idea of care as destiny for a woman and when I had my first child [when I was] aged twenty-four, I was back at work as a teacher within three months. Me and my husband split most of the domestic work fifty-fifty."

She had a second child at twenty-six, partly to escape a job that she had come to dislike, and took two years out as a full-time mother. She found that didn't suit her, either. "I was a very controlling mother and needed another outlet for my energy."

Williams is a successful writer and academic who has not wanted to follow the path of more family-focused women, but she thinks that their choices should be respected too. "Whether it is nature or nurture, who knows? But lots of young women want to work with children or look after their own, and they derive pride and status from that," says Williams.

She thinks that some feminists are ambivalent about the idea of raising the status of care, in the family or public economy. "They just don't consider caring to be the big issue. In part this is because feminism is such a middle-class preoccupation—concerned with the proportion of women in Parliament or on company boards. Yet survey after survey suggests only a minority of women identify as feminists in that sense.

"Ironically, it is the education revolution that has brought about this class-gender divide in relation to the experiences of women. Back in the sixties/early seventies, when feminism first took off, there was a common experience of being a woman—motherhood, domestic work, limited opportunities in the labor market—that women shared irrespective of class background. When more women gained entry to higher education and entry to the professions, that shared gendered experience disappeared and class differences were reinforced."

Some feminists seem to fear that even in a world that values care more highly, women will continue doing most of it—that the woman-equals-caregiver equation will be reinforced, even if it is with a higher level of pay and respect—and the goal of a more gender neutral society will be pushed back.

The evidence in countries like Sweden lends some support to this view: women's status in Sweden is high and the care economy has higher levels of status and pay than almost anywhere else in the world, and yet occupational gender segregation is higher, not lower, with women overwhelmingly concentrated in the care economy and the public sector.[37]

The preferred alternative of many feminist writers is for more men to take up traditionally female caring roles both in the private realm and the public economy, and this is happening to some extent but rather slowly, as I have just noted.

But if women *are* going to continue doing most care in both the home and the public economy, then surely raising its pay and status— and, in the case of England, finally sorting out the funding of adult social care—ought to be a central concern of all mainstream politicians, but especially for those who prioritize women's issues. The fact that it is not such a central concern seems to reinforce the analysis of Alison Wolf, Joanna Williams, and others who argue that family and gender politics have been captured by the cognitive class, professional women whose interests are not always the same as those of other women.

Ever since the failure of the Wages for Housework movement in the 1970s, the main concern of women's politics has been equality at work *outside* the home and, in more recent decades, above all equality with professional men in the world of careers. This goal has been substantially achieved, according to Wolf, with women, as already noted, now accounting for half of all members of the top—professional and managerial—social class in the United Kingdom, even if they are still largely absent from the very pinnacle of the professional and business tree. There is only a very small *gender* pay gap, as such; rather there remains a *motherhood* penalty caused by women with children working part-time or not at all, breaking their careers and so losing out on top positions.

Much policy effort has been expended trying to ensure that the careers of professional women are held back as little as possible by motherhood. But child care subsidies to make a swift return to work possible are not always the priority of more traditionally minded women or women in lower socioeconomic groups. They would often prefer more support to stay at home for a few years when children are very young rather than having to leave them in the care of a stranger and return to low-paid work.

Surveys in the United Kingdom show that a modified form of the male breadwinner support role is still wanted by most women when they have young children, and they also show that most women would stay at home longer when children are preschool age if they could afford it. A 2019 UK government survey found that 37 percent of mothers with young children would prefer to stay at home full-time when the children are young, and 65 percent would work fewer hours to spend more time looking after them.[38]

Indeed, more generally, opinion surveys find support for gender equality *sitting happily alongside* support for a modern version of domesticity. A British Social Attitudes survey in 2012 asked how much people agreed with the statement "Most mothers with young children prefer having a male partner who is the main family earner rather than working full time themselves." Only 15 percent of respondents disagreed (and only 1.6 percent strongly). And the proportion of people thinking the role of housewife is just as fulfilling as the role of worker actually rose slightly from 41 percent in 1989 to 45 percent in 2012. "Watching children grow up is life's greatest joy" has remained at more than 80 percent agreement for more than three decades.

Yet in the United Kingdom, and to a lesser extent the United States, the tax system prevents the full transfer of tax allowances from one partner to the other and so punishes the single-earner household and fails to recognize or reward the role of the domestic parenthood *partnership*.

"The demands made by vocal, elite women, and the pre-occupations of politicians seeking the 'female vote' have become extraordinarily divorced from majority concerns . . . Different women have very different lives and interests, like men, and policy-makers should not just listen to the voices from the female summit," writes Wolf.[39]

Care and gender equality should not be in conflict. Yet one of the unintended consequences of the priorities of that "summit" is that equality in the public domain of work, professions, and politics seems to have been pitted *against* the private domain of care and nurture. But if the Heart is to take its place as an equal partner with Head and Hand in the future, this must be seen as a false divide.

The American philosopher Virginia Held puts it like this in her book *The Ethics of Care: Personal, Political, and Global*: "If women, in their justifiable quest for equality, pursue justice at the expense of care, morality will suffer. For those previously engaged in care to become more and more like the free and equal, rational and unencumbered individuals of theories of justice will leave no one to nurture the relations of family and friendship, and to cultivate the ties of caring."[40]

And when Anne-Marie Slaughter gave up her dream job working for Hillary Clinton at the State Department in 2009 because of family demands, and returned to a less-pressured job in academia, she was dismayed to see herself widely portrayed as having betrayed the cause of female professional achievement. She wrote a book, *Unfinished Business*, in which she argues for higher status for child-rearing so choosing it over paid work is not seen as a defeat. After all, effective child-rearing requires many talents including discipline, patience, and imagination.

Is a more family-friendly, pluralistic form of feminism likely to emerge that acknowledges the large variety of female (and male) preferences from wholly career oriented to wholly family and care focused? And how can the priorities of the Heart be better embedded in our societies and job markets? It is true that many of us, male and female, do not have the sensibility or skills to care for our own relatives, let alone anyone else. Adult care responsibilities require expertise; the willing amateur can only go so far.

But the public care economy faces a double problem. For some of the cultural reasons described above there are fewer people attracted to work in the care economy. And those who do want to work in these sectors often find, after a while, that the care has been squeezed out of them and too many leave disenchanted. There are 690,000 registered nurses in the United Kingdom and only 350,000 working (300,000 in the NHS and the rest in adult social care and the private sector).[41]

Some economists argue that care is undersupplied because it generates positive externalities—positive benefits for society—that can never be properly captured by the caregiver.[42] This problem used to be solved by restricting women's opportunity to do anything else. Having relaxed those restrictions, we have not worked out an alternative solution and are today living with the consequences. But why cannot caregivers, both in the public and private realms, capture more of the honor and reward that is their due? Market signals, corporate business plans, and social priorities are not set in stone. In democratic societies they respond, sometimes swiftly, sometimes more slowly, to the mysterious fusion of elite and popular sentiment. It remains to be seen whether the Covid-19 crisis and the admiration showered on nurses and carers will do anything to make those jobs more appealing in the medium term. In the United Kingdom there are signs that demand for places in nursing courses has risen.

The Future of Nursing

It is uncontroversial to state that the historic undervaluing of work in catering, cleaning, and caring, at least economically, is because it is overwhelmingly done by women. The care economy in the United Kingdom is more than 85 percent female: 88 percent of NHS nurses, 82 percent of people working in adult social care, 85 percent of primary school teachers.[43] The numbers are similar in the United States and most other rich countries.

Patterns of reward were set decades ago when women were more likely to work part-time, were seldom the main household bread-winner, and, if married, had the family as their main focus of concern.

Nursing and teaching have been better protected in pay because they usually involve work in large units and are heavily unionized, with national pay review bodies in the United Kingdom. But although nursing is decently paid at the start, it has a flat pay structure, and mid-career pay, given the levels of stress and responsibility, is often insufficient to lure back women who have left to start families. Pay levels in nursery care and adult social care remain very low.

Patterns of esteem, too, have been heavily "gendered." Care has historically been regarded as an intuitive ability that comes more natu-rally to women. It was a given and so needed little special attention or compensation compared with the high rewards attached to cognitive achievement.

If one asks an economist why people in social care homes are paid so little, they would probably say "Because almost anyone can do it." We all know that is not true. Anyone who spends half an hour in a care home, or indeed a hospital, knows that there are, as in most occupations, good caregivers, middling ones, and poor ones.

But the economist is in fact correctly describing a low qualification threshold: many care home jobs require minimal or no qualifications for the most basic roles, even though you may be changing a catheter on your second week on the job. Care jobs end up being judged by cognitive stan-dards, or the lack of them, because there is no alternative "care" criterion.

Many care jobs are highly demanding along both a traditional cognitive dimension—requiring, in the case of nurses, increasing med-ical knowledge, enabling them to prescribe drugs, evaluate medical conditions, and even perform minor surgery—and along a distinctive caring dimension too.

"One of the most physically skillful and emotionally demanding things I ever have to do is to help a severely injured person to undress and wash," one nurse at St George's Hospital in Tooting, South Lon-don, told me.

The necessary emotional intelligence to read a face, to respond empathetically and skillfully to someone who is lonely or in pain, can be developed in people, according to Madeleine Bunting. She suggests that it is learned by example and inspired by a culture: "It combines intention—the desire to help—imagination, and cognitive ability. It requires Head and Heart."

One of the predicaments of nursing type care in an instrumentalist-utilitarian culture is that it is often about containment of pain or distress and its results are elusive and *hard to measure*. Any nurse will tell you that the least prestigious nursing role in a hospital has always been geriatric care. Compared to the technology-dependent acute specialties, it is hard to measure the success of making a very old person's day slightly less miserable or lonely.

The idea of nurse as quasi-doctor, which has driven the move to making nursing a graduate profession in many countries, sometimes sits uncomfortably alongside the impulse to see professional care as a distinctive skill and tradition in its own right.

There is no reason why, in principle, these two approaches to care should conflict; after all Florence Nightingale herself was both a caring nurse and a statistician. But the graduatization of nursing in the United Kingdom along with various neglect scandals in hospitals and care homes—most notably in the Mid Staffordshire NHS Foundation Trust in 2008—has led to a popular complaint that too many nurses are now "too posh to wash" and that old-fashioned care has gotten crowded out of the system.

There are real problems with the diminishment of care, but graduatization of nursing and other care roles is not a big factor, and, to repeat, the evidence shows that health outcomes are better in hospitals and wards where there are more graduate nurses.[44]

Yet when informal family-based care is replaced on such a large scale with more impersonal, paid care, given by people who have less emotional attachment to the toddler or elderly person in their charge, some diminution in care is probably unavoidable.

Other causes are more avoidable and are related to economic and organizational factors that we *can* do something about. When, in the summer of 2019, I spoke to a group of nurses at the giant teaching hospital, St George's, in Tooting, south London, some of them were nostalgic for a time when more time could be devoted to care and building relationships with patients. Most of them had become nurses before 2013, the year when a degree became a condition of becoming a registered nurse, but most of them had acquired degree-equivalent qualifications and none of them opposed the move to make nursing a graduate profession.

One nurse explained that it is partly the nature of the modern hospital that gives the impression of diminished care. "When my mother was a ward sister, more patients stayed for weeks, and you got to know them. Now, because of more technological medicine, there is much quicker throughput and its harder to build relationships. But I think that does mean we are less patient-centered than we used to be," she said.

Specialist wards are better, said another nurse, who also felt ambivalent about recent changes: "It's an odd mix. In the age of the graduate nurse we do have more authority and status and we can do more medical things that we could not do in the past, like prescribing drugs, cannulation, ordering X-rays and blood tests. On the other hand everything seems more rule-bound and less patient-centered, and we somehow end up with less autonomy."

As with other occupations that are moving to graduate-only entry, there seemed to be that attitude among the nurses at St George's of "If you can't beat 'em, join 'em." If deferring to the dominant cognitive motif of the age is the only way to achieve the status that registered nurses feel is their due, then so be it.

Julie Goldie, a senior nurse who is now head of professional support and development at St George's, shares the general ambivalence. She acknowledges that people are living longer and have more complex care needs and that nursing must therefore become more technically and cognitively sophisticated. "Nursing has never just been about being a nice person; obviously you have to be capable to be a good nurse. But I worry that the soft skills of communication—talking, listening, and what many nurses refer to as 'basic nursing care': addressing patients' hygiene and nutritional needs—is viewed by some as having less status. The term 'basic' denotes a devaluing of these fundamental nursing skills," she said.

Goldie also worries about a problem we have seen elsewhere: graduate expectations. "There is nothing wrong with high expectations; however, it sometimes means that ambitious nurses want to move on into other careers or continue studying straight after graduating," she pointed out.

The graduate nurse is now typical in the United Kingdom, the United States, France, and Scandinavia, but not everywhere in continental Europe—it is not common in Germany or Portugal—although equivalent competence is usually acquired via a non-university training. In the United States, people queue up to get into the top nursing schools partly because it is possible to earn a very good salary and set oneself up as an independent "nurse practitioner," a nurse equivalent of a medical GP in the United Kingdom.

So has graduatization raised the status of nursing in the United Kingdom? "It is not clear that is has, but without graduate status, the recruitment problem would probably be even worse," according to Professor Ian Norman, dean of the nursing faculty at King's College London.

To Alison Leary, professor of health care at London South Bank University, it is just common sense to think of nursing as a STEM profession and health care as a "safety-critical" knowledge industry. Her work is partly about finding ways to measure the outcomes of nursing care in the same way that we do with, for example, surgery.

Leary locates the perceived decline of care in excessive workload. She has calculated that there are 1 million episodes of care every seventeen hours in the NHS, and nurses are simply being asked to do too much. "This creates a kind of moral distress for many nurses and the only way to cope is by becoming more distant from the suffering all around them," she says.

A writer friend of mine tells a personal anecdote that supports this analysis. "I experienced a rare complication of C-section after my daughter's birth and the symptoms of my increasing illness were basically ignored by staff nurses on the postnatal ward despite my family's best efforts to get help. This was not because the nurses were indifferent or negligent, rather because they had something like fifteen mother/baby couples per nurse to keep an eye on and there was just no time to notice anything. When they finally realized something was very wrong, my daughter and I ended up back on an acute ward and the difference in care—with sometimes even the same staff delivering it who had just been ignoring me on postnatal—was astonishing. The simple difference was that the staff ratio was three beds to a nurse, not fifteen. You could do a lot to solve the failures of hospital care by just giving nurses more time."

Leary adds that because of staff turnover there is also a big "rookie" factor in too many hospitals. And pay incentives, as in so many other occupations, tend to encourage people to seek promotion into managerial posts that they may not want or be suited to instead of just being rewarded for staying put and doing a good job as a ward nurse.

Elaine Maxwell, another health academic, has a different emphasis. She says that care suffers from lack of a clear definition and that it must be seen as a discipline *distinct from medicine*. "A nurse must not be just a technical assistant to a doctor. Nursing has been dazzled by the supposed status of becoming a quasi-doctor. But a lot of these things like administering and handing out the right pills can be done by specialists like pharmacy technicians.

"Nursing must assert its autonomy," continues Maxwell. "It is about helping people adjust to their health conditions. The modern way is to distance yourself from the person and just treat the symptoms.

Nursing is about keeping the person whole and integrated." You cannot, to put it another way, put health *into* someone; you can only help them find it for themselves.

Maxwell thinks that, paradoxically, being reduced to a second-rank doctor is one of the reasons so many of the 690,000 registered nurses leave the profession. "I had more autonomy as a nurse in the 1980s," she recalls. "I could decide things such as frequency of observations and timing of medicines that are now decided by doctors."

She agrees with the St George's nurses, and Alison Leary, that the crisis of care arises in part from the way a modern hospital is managed: with a big focus on targets and bed management and with caseloads that are too high.

Maxwell wants to close the status gap between nursing and doctoring and thinks, like Leary, that finding ways of quantifying and then incentivizing relational skills will help in that process, as will acknowledging that caring is teachable, like leadership.

Jonathan Hanbury, a former associate director of nursing at Barts Health NHS Trust, agrees with Maxwell but has a different focus: "Nurses now do a lot of things that medics used to do and that is broadly good. But we are underselling nursing. Nurses essentially run the NHS. The core management of most hospitals is ex-nurses; I think about one-third of NHS trust chief execs have a medical background. Even a ward sister has a budget of millions and forty people under her.

"We are not attracting enough highly capable A students. But after you have been on the front line for a few years, a huge range of options and disciplines open up for you. There are all sorts of nursing-medical specialisms; you can manage people; if you have a mathematical bent you can go over to the data side. Indeed, the NHS has a huge shortage of data analysts who also know something about patient care," Hanbury adds.

These different perspectives, all grappling with how to raise the standing of Heart (combined with Head) in the health care sector, are not mutually exclusive. The challenge may be to attract into nursing both those who want to be quasi-doctors and those who want to care in a more holistic way. There are, for example, many different types of law and engineering, yet we tend to place nursing into one undifferentiated albeit poorly defined category.

Jonathan Hanbury has now left the NHS and set up his own social enterprise, Atlas Respite and Therapy, to help individuals and families living with dementia. Dementia has been rising almost everywhere because of rising life expectancy. The Alzheimer's Society says there are some 850,000 dementia patients in the United Kingdom, which will rise to over 1 million by 2025 (although, in the United Kingdom, it has actually been falling recently among males in the sixty-five-to-seventy-five age group). But mild to severe dementia is estimated to impact nearly half of all seventy-five- to eighty-five-year-olds and three-quarters of all those over eighty-five in the United Kingdom in the coming years.[45]

Hanbury complains that one of the problems with the underfunding of adult social care in England—Scotland and Northern Ireland have merged it into the NHS—is that there is very little innovation: "Innovation tends to follow the money, and a sector that consists of lots of small companies and lots of charities and volunteers tends to stick with what it knows."

In Japan, in part because of a social insurance levy for elderly care paid by those over forty (in Germany everyone pays), there is plenty of innovation, from "happiness centers" for elderly people and their families to novel uses of digital technology to monitor people remotely. The Dutch have model villages for the elderly that allow them to stay independent for longer, and the Buurtzorg Nederland system of self-managed community nurses gives the nurses far more autonomy and makes the work far less bleak and pressured than it usually is in the United Kingdom. (Buurtzorg is now being trialed in the United Kingdom.)

Jenny, a sixty-year-old cousin of a friend of mine, experienced that bleakness firsthand working as a home care worker in Warwickshire, visiting people in their homes for a range of tasks from administering drugs, cooking for them, dressing and bathing them, changing incontinence pads, and so on. The training was basic.

Jenny, like any such care worker, has abundant stories of having to respond to extreme situations of distress and misery. "It was probably the toughest job I have ever done," she says. The visits were usually anything between fifteen minutes and one hour—it was reported in 2013 that 500,000 care visits a day (out of a total of 2 million) are less than five minutes—and if anything went wrong with one of the "service users," it could make the whole day a frantic catch-up. And all this for something around the minimum wage, or even less if the gasoline allowance was inadequate.

This does not make for good or consistent care. Camilla Cavendish, author of the 2013 *Cavendish Review*, which examined the training of junior health and social care staff who are not registered nurses, tells the story of one elderly man who noted the names of all the caregivers who visited him in the course of the year so he could greet them by name; at the end of the year he listed 102 different names.

Cavendish complains that people doing the most close-up care in hospitals, in care homes, or in home visit care are often looked down upon by colleagues or described as unskilled because they have talents that are not academic.

"The phrase 'basic care' dramatically understates the work of this group. Helping an elderly person to eat and swallow, bathing someone with dignity and without hurting them, communicating with someone with early onset dementia; doing these things with intelligent kindness, dignity, care and respect requires skill. Doing so alone in the home of a stranger, when the district nurse has left no notes, and you are only being paid to be there for 30 minutes, requires considerable maturity and resilience," wrote Cavendish in her 2013 *Cavendish Review*.[46]

This is care where too often there really is too little time to care. Jenny says, "I remember the first day on the job overhearing one of the managers say 'She's going to be one that cares too much.' " But she says it is not really the fault of the home care providers, who are usually doing their best with limited resources; what shocked her most was the heartlessness of some families who knew that their elderly relative should have been in a proper care home but did not want to face the cost.

Jenny also worked in a residential care home. She found that slightly less stressful than home visits but could not help noticing that the care home expended far more effort with the elderly people who were visited than those who weren't.

Even right-wing think tanks in England are now proposing that funding for the adult care system should be socialized and what is seen as the arbitrary and unfair means-tested payment system, for both home care and care home support, should be swept away and merged into the tax-funded NHS, as it has been in Scotland and Northern Ireland. The English system currently costs about £22 billion ($29 billion) a year, with a further £10 billion ($13 billion) paid by users, and employs 1.4 million people to look after around 400,000 people in care homes and 500,000 in their own homes. Socializing the costs would add an extra 1 percent to UK public spending.[47]

But whatever happens to the funding of the system, the status of the people who work in it will also remain an issue if the United Kingdom and the United States, and other rich societies are going to avoid an even more intense recruitment crisis into these jobs. The longer term response to the Covid-19 crisis will surely be not only to build more emergency capacity into our health services but also to raise the status and pay of the Cinderella parts of the care economy, above all elderly care. In much of Europe care homes for the elderly reported a disproportionate number of Covid-19 deaths as protective measures focused on health systems.

All reputable surveys of future skill requirements in rich countries focus on what Adair Turner calls the "Hi-Tech, Hi-Touch" combination, meaning higher-order cognitive and technical skills on the one hand and interpersonal skills in education and health on the other—sometimes shortened to "coders and carers." The latter skills will generate many more jobs than the former thanks above all to the fitness, care, and health needs of aging populations—health care workers, home caregivers, and physical therapists of many kinds.

The latest data on job creation in the United Kingdom bears out this assumption, with one-quarter of the twenty fastest-growing occupations since 2011 being caring jobs but the single biggest rise (160,000) coming in the category "programmers and software development professionals."[48]

And, as we have seen repeatedly, many of the caring jobs are currently low-paid and low-status. The US Bureau of Labor Statistics forecast for job creation up to 2024 finds that eight out of ten of the fastest-growing job categories pay far below the average wage, and one-third of them are care related, personal care aides (top of the list) and nursing assistants among them.[49]

Some fields of care in the United Kingdom have in fact been professionalized in recent years, notably child care. Everyone who works in a nursery school or child care center must now have relevant qualifications, and each establishment must have the right mix of qualified staff, including someone with a pediatric first aid qualification. And, unlike care homes for adults, there is a minimum child–staff ratio. Both qualifications and staffing levels are subject to regular inspection, and this seems to have raised the status of early-years work.

Jill Manthorpe, director of the health and social care workforce research unit at King's College London, says the professionalization of child care should be a model for elderly care. "Is it too much to ask that these levers of change could apply to other carers? Staff need proper training and professional pride," she says, "and care needs its own Royal College or equivalent to oversee standards."

There are many medical colleges, including the Royal College of Physicians and Royal College of Nursing and even a Royal College of Paediatrics and Child Health, but no Royal College of Child and Adult *Care*.

Camilla Cavendish's review into the 1.3 million frontline NHS health care assistants and adult social care staff, many of whom have little or no formal training, proposed new common training standards across health and social care, although Cavendish herself thinks that the professionalization of child care is *not* a model for social care and would drive too many people away.

What About Men?

What role is there for men in an upward revaluation of caring roles? According to the Centre for Time Use Research, in the United Kingdom men's share of all unpaid work in the home has risen from 27 to 38 percent since the 1970s.[50] That partly reflects the fact that women on average actually spend *less* time on cooking, cleaning, and clothes care than they did in earlier decades, presumably because of a big increase in work outside the home plus domestic appliances of various kinds.

But both men and women have spent more time on child care since the 1990s, when ideals of intensive parenting and involved fathering spread widely, especially among the highly educated.

Nearly two-thirds of all fathers in most developed countries are now classified as *involved fathers*, spending an average of almost two hours a day on child care. The highly educated often focus on activities that improve the social and cognitive skills of their children, and highly educated fathers are more likely to share the ideal of equal sharing of domestic labor.

The picture is not so clear for less educated men. The breadwinner role has historically provided status and was a form of care: wage earning as service to the family. As men are seldom today the sole earner and sometimes not even the main earner in the household, the breadwinner role has been weakened.

But the old idea that family commitments help to make men more caring people and better citizens is still borne out by the statistics that show men with partners and children are far less likely to be jobless, and prisoners who are visited by families are 40 percent less likely to reoffend.[51] Conversely, men cope much less well than women after divorce; some men just go into a spiral of decline.

Much writing about men assumes that masculinity is in crisis because men are clinging to an old model of domination that doesn't work any longer and that they need to become more feminine and emotionally attuned. That may be part of the story, but it may also be because men, particularly lower-status men, have lost male caring roles that gave them some dignity as breadwinner and protector and they have not been replaced with anything that men feel comfortable with.

The absence of physical challenges in modern life also has a corrosive effect on some men. They may take up an extreme sport or take ridiculous risks in their work or relationships to fill that gap. And one reason for the persistence of a low-level ridiculing of health and safety culture is because it seems to deny to men the capacity to judge risk for themselves as well as the opportunity to be praised and valued for their courage and initiative.

A shoot-'em-up video game is designed to scratch that primal itch of heroism, but of course there is no risk involved and young men are further distanced from any sense of the dangerous reality of physical courage.

A new model of manhood has yet to emerge for a world in which some traditional male virtues—strength, physical courage, emotional stoicism—are less valued. The feminist model, which remakes men along more feminine lines, has gained little traction, and the conservative idea of a return to a world of restraint, chivalry, and protection is even more implausible.

A disproportionate number of jobs that are out of the reach of automation are those traditionally done by women. But if the past is a guide to the future, a big move by men into nursing and other traditionally female occupations seems unlikely; one UK survey found that 85 percent of men would not consider a career in social care.[52] And Daniel Susskind, in his book *A World Without Work*, reports that most adult men in the US displaced from manufacturing roles prefer not to work at all than take up "pink collar" work.

In recent years the care sector has become more female, not less, as women have moved into medical roles. (A majority of GPs in the UK are now women.) The gender imbalance in adult care is less extreme than in nursing—about 18 percent of staff are men[53]—and there are some corners of care, such as mental health nurses and paramedics and ambulance staff, that are mainly male. And if men can increase their share of labor in the home relatively swiftly, the same *might* be possible in the public care economy.

Jamie, a twenty-five-year-old nurse at a London teaching hospital, was one of just 13 men out of 460 trainee nurses on the degree course at the University of Nottingham. Three years into the job, he finds the work rewarding and challenging, but it still sometimes feels a bit odd being a man in a very female profession, no doubt a feeling many women experience in male-dominated professions. "Some of the older nurses clearly feel a bit ambivalent about male nurses," he says.

There are historic precedents for the male nurse to draw upon, such as the Knights Hospitaller order, which became a Catholic military organization but started life providing medical care to Christian pilgrims to the Holy Land. And change can happen rapidly. In the 1960s, for example, information technology was seen as a female, secretarial function, but as it became more technical and better paid, men muscled in. The same could be true of parts of nursing and adult care.

But that then raises the so-called glass escalator issue for men that some female nurses resent—meaning the fact that men are disproportionately found in the most prestigious nursing disciplines like intensive care and in the higher ranks of nursing management.

The nurses I spoke to at St George's pointed out that three out of the top four nursing positions there are occupied by men, although it was also recognized that women have entered traditionally male-dominated senior medical positions in large numbers. A planned NHS recruitment campaign for male nurses stressing how quickly they could rise to senior positions had to be dropped after senior female nurses objected.

Jamie's ambition is to be an advanced clinical practitioner, a form of nurse that is close to being a doctor. He wants to do it because of the autonomy it grants. It is not clear whether he is a model for a future with less of a gender bias in nursing and caring jobs, but if all those jobs are to be filled in the future, he may have to be.

Counting Care

In conclusion, it is not unreasonable to assume that an aging society that values gender equality will inexorably edge toward placing a higher value on the work of carers, paid and unpaid. And this will require some change in culture and behavior from people and governments. A change that the fall-out from the Covid-19 crisis might reinforce.

One way to honor dedicated caring work in the United Kingdom is through the official honors system. The kind of self-effacement that is often characteristic of care is, as Madeleine Bunting points out, not generally admired in mainstream culture. And in 2012 the British Empire Medal was reinstated specifically to recognize people, often volunteers, away from the public eye in places like hospices.

If the honors system is about signaling what society values, then it should be used more overtly to reward the things that really matter. So should our system of measuring the economy. The economist Paul Ormerod told me that: "We could easily put a value on unpaid domestic labour and put the numbers into GDP, there are already a lot of non-market transactions in GDP figures."

Thanks to the existence of time-use data, we now have good measures of the hours devoted to market work and non–market work. The Centre for Time Use Research calculates that including domestic labor would add nearly £500 billion a year to GDP.[54] The ONS estimated the value of *all* unpaid work in the United Kingdom in 2014 at £1.01 trillion ($1.4 trillion).[55]

It would, of course, not change living standards at all or the status of care roles in the short term but it would give a more accurate account of what is happening in society and help people to see and value the productive Heart work going on in the unpaid private realm.

It might also help to connect GDP more closely to well-being, since one reason that people often sense a disconnect between rising measures of GDP wealth and their own levels of contentment or stress is that economic growth is sometimes directly linked with *reductions* in caring work in the home.

Jooyeoun Suh and Christopher Payne, researchers at the Centre for Time Use Research, explain: "Fifty three per cent of women aged 16 to 64 in the UK engaged in paid work in 1971, but this figure had risen to 74 per cent by 2014. As women increased their average hours of paid work, they also decreased their average hours of unpaid work. While men were doing a bit more unpaid work over the same period, this increase has not been sufficient to fully take up the slack created by women's decrease in unpaid work."[56]

The authors conclude that improvements in families' living standards as measured through GDP may have been overestimated—although it is surely more accurate to say that their economic living standards will indeed have risen as a result of a higher second income, but their standard of life and well-being may have declined because of the loss of the productive care labor that is no longer taking place.

This overestimation is the product of an economistic-measurement bias that does not value whatever cannot be measured for GDP purposes and regards care as simply unpaid work. It also reflects a collective amnesia about the contribution of the stay-at-home wife and mother of past decades. She was not sitting at home twiddling her thumbs. She was undertaking productive labor in caring for children and the elderly as well as often playing a vital role in community organizations. The decline of such labor has not been cost-free to families or society at large. (Between 2005 and 2015 alone, there was a 15 percent drop in the number of hours dedicated to volunteer work in the United Kingdom.)[57]

Family care work in the home can be experienced as crushingly dull and limiting—a "comfortable concentration camp," as Betty Friedan put it—and many women have eagerly swapped it for paid employment. This is Marilyn French in her 1977 feminist classic *The Women's Room*: "Years of scraping shit out of diapers with a kitchen knife, finding places where string beans are two cents less a pound . . . intelligence in figuring the most efficient, least time-consuming way to iron men's white shirts or to wash and wax the kitchen floor . . . these not only take energy and courage and mind, but they may constitute the very essence of a life.

". . . I hate these grimy details as much as you do."[58]

In recent decades this has generally been the dominant narrative underpinning the shift of female labor from the home into the public economy. But domestic and care work is also experienced by others as meaningful. In the United States about one in seven adults provide unpaid care of some kind to another person and, according to the Pew Research Center, the US polling organization, the vast majority regard it as very meaningful.[59]

And educated young mothers raised in a gender-egalitarian culture are often shocked at the raw, inescapable gender-differentiation of motherhood. Here is Mary Harrington, the British political blogger, writing for the magazine *UnHerd*:

> A breastfeeding mother needs to stay physically close to her baby, and runs on the baby's timetable for months . . . The other partner, meanwhile, can support the mother in practical ways but is considerably more free to maintain a normal daily schedule or return to work, as most fathers typically do following the legally-allotted two weeks . . .
>
> Reports lament the poor uptake of shared parental leave, but given that males cannot breastfeed, it should not come as a surprise . . .
>
> This in turn shapes how housework is divided. There is no doubt

that socialization plays some role in a differential distribution of housework between men and women, but the rubber really hits the road when children arrive, and this is to no small degree because of a mother's desire to be close to her baby. It will feel logical for a mother to take on the lion's share of house and child management during maternity leave.

By the time she returns to work—and over three-quarters of mothers with dependent children in the UK now work—it is highly likely that a pattern will have emerged in which this is normalized, and the mother has become more oriented toward managing the household while her partner is more focused on work.[60]

Every woman, like every man, is different, and—given greater choice—an enormously varied balance of work and family would be chosen. But according to Catherine Hakim, adult women in Britain can be loosely divided into three broad groups: 20 percent are overwhelmingly work focused, 20 percent overwhelmingly family focused, and 60 percent are adaptive, meaning they want to combine the two in varying ways.[61] The happiest group of people in the United Kingdom, according to well-being data from the end of the twentieth century, are women with young children who work part-time.[62]

Better funded adult care from the state, combined with more moral stigma and possibly even some financial sanctions directed at people who do not care for their elderly parents, is perfectly imaginable in the coming years.

I recently met a senior official from the United Kingdom's Department of Health and Social Care and asked her: If she were granted one wish to improve the functioning of the NHS, what would it be? Her reply was more interesting and challenging than I expected: "I would want people to have the same moral and legal responsibilities for looking after their elderly relatives that they have for their children."

This could be reinforced by the potentially benign influence on Western societies of tradition-minded minorities with stronger family obligations (although the cultural influence can also flow the other way).

Add to that the evolution of a new form of feminism that honors women's caring role in the private domain as well as success in the public one; an increased movement of younger men into caring jobs at all levels, including more stay-at-home fathers; plus a less dominant role for higher cognitive aptitudes in the labor market of the future, and a better Head, Hand, Heart balance becomes not just possible but probable.

Often what we really value becomes clear only when it is too late and we are regretting on our deathbed. People seldom wish they had done more paid work or got more promotions at work. Social psychologists have actually measured this, researching what people say when close to death, and found that the regrets of the dying are overwhelmingly linked to our sense of belonging, to love and to family, and hardly at all to work or achievement in the public realm.[63] A woman I know who runs a hospice told me that men in particular invariably ask for forgiveness from those close to them for not being a more loving or caring husband or father.

PART FOUR

THE FUTURE

Chapter Nine

The Fall of the
Knowledge Worker

*The urban, educated people who voted against populism
will have a whole new attitude when globalization and
automation get up close and personal.*

Richard Baldwin

There are two fundamental reasons why cognitive ability has
become so central to status and reward in modern societies.

First, the industrial and then postindustrial economy and society
has simply demanded more highly qualified professional people with
above-average levels of cognitive ability.

Second, appointing, promoting, and rewarding people according
to their cognitive ability seems fair. This fairness, it is true, is qualified
by the fact that cognitive ability is partly inherited and the IQ tests
and exams we use to measure it may not be fully measuring what we
want them to measure, as discussed in Chapter Three.

Ken Charman, knows this landscape. He is an Oxford postgrad
who conducted undergraduate admissions interviews at Oxford and is
the CEO of a subsidiary in a big multinational. He is often involved in
recruitment and promotion decisions and says that all the gatekeepers
are looking for is "fair enough."

"Everyone likes to think that they can spot the very best people
but, in reality, so long as you fill graduate positions with people who
you can prove are in the top X per cent of IQ or degree class you are

in the clear," Charman says. "You have an objective yardstick that avoids disaster and is above criticism of bias."

Charman himself is a highly capable and successful businessman from an ordinary background and points out that he left school with no math, science, or language qualifications, and at senior school only got As in PE, art, and metalwork. (He failed math repeatedly and was not allowed to take a science or language exam.)

"Under the grade-based *must-be-seen-to-be-fair* selection criteria we use these days . . . with my exams? I wouldn't get close to an interview," he says. In 1968 he went to the then brand-new Abbs Cross Technical High School, in east London, with smart engineering and science labs from which you could see the Ford factory at Dagenham. It now specializes in the performing arts.

"Even people with weak grades like me were pushed into the professions in those days," Charman recalls. "But it seems that getting a TV talent show audition, or having your own YouTube channel, is now the main career aspiration, especially for the white kids who don't come from aspirational families." He also has strong views about fairness and social mobility:

Putting the best people in the most important and difficult jobs is just common sense, but, so far as we are able to do that, that is the easy part. The bigger problem comes when they get rewards and status that places them too far above everyone else. Then the people in the top jobs fear that their children will drop down and they do everything possible to help them. I know because I have done it myself.

But that has the effect of blocking off other peoples' perhaps more deserving children. If the differences in reward and status in the hierarchy were less dramatic, then perhaps people would relax more and not try to game the system.

I know this sounds egalitarian and Scandinavian, but I'm not talking so much about income as status, and I say this because I know so many good people who don't want to strive and don't want to have to join the middle class in order to have a decent life. I don't myself! I don't like art, opera, middle-class dinner parties. I never did parents' socials at the private schools my children went to. I never felt comfortable there.

Becoming middle-class enabled me to lead a safer, more comfortable life and provide security for my children. But those seem like things that everyone should have without having to go to university or change class. Why shouldn't people who work in supermarkets or drive lorries experience that too?

When I meet my friends from my time at the university in Bradford, many of whom have done very well from a working-class background, we turn to this subject often. In the safety of each other's company we prefer working-class warmth, wit, cynicism, pragmatism, stoicism, wryness, rude honesty, crude humor, lack of pretension, dryness, simplicity, humanity, flaws, vulgarity . . . Obviously it doesn't make us inferior or superior. These are just social manners. And I don't want to give them up as the price of being respectable and worthy of my place where the big decisions are made.

His desire for a less jagged distribution of status may have history, and economics, on its side, for that first fundamental reason that cognitive ability has been so central to status and reward in recent decades—economies and companies have simply demanded more and more cognitively trained staff—is drawing to a close.

Consider, again, the bigger picture of Head, Hand, and Heart. Andy Haldane, chief economist at the Bank of England, put it like this when I visited him at the Bank: "During the first three industrial revolutions the skills workers needed to keep one step ahead of the machine were largely cognitive. So institutions emerged to nurture thinking skills, in children and young adults, to increase the chances of successful transition to the cognitively intensive future world of work." Hence mass primary, then secondary, then higher education.

The so-called fourth industrial revolution, meaning robots and artificial intelligence, will mean, as Haldane puts it, "humans will no longer have the cognitive playing field to themselves." Thinking and other nonroutine tasks will increasingly be taken over by machines. They will be able to process more quickly, more cheaply, and with fewer errors than their human counterpart, at least in some activities.

Two big shifts in working life are imminent. The first is a demographic one. Someone born today can be expected to live to one hundred. That means multiple changes of career, not just job, are likely during a lifetime. The second shift is in the demand for skills. In the past, this skill shift has been all one way. Demand for skills of the Head have dominated those of the Hand and, to lesser extent, those of the Heart. "This may be about to go into reverse," says Haldane.

The thin, intense Haldane was born in Sunderland and educated at a Leeds comprehensive school and speaks with a mild Yorkshire accent. He is one of the most creative and respected economic thinkers in the country. To the extent that the Bank of England has tried to listen to the concerns expressed in the Brexit vote, he is the man responsible.

He seems a bit out of place in the mandarin splendor of the Bank of England, where I talked to him. But, enthusing to his theme, he explained to me the future role for humans: "My guess is that there are three areas where humans will preserve some comparative advantage over robots for the foreseeable future. The first is cognitive tasks requiring creativity and intuition. These might be tasks or problems whose solutions require great logical leaps of imagination rather than step-by-step hill climbing . . . And even in a world of superintelligent machine learning, there will still be a demand for people with the skills to program, test, and oversee these machines. Some human judgmental overlay of these automated processes is still likely to be needed . . ."

The second area of prospective demand for humans skills, says Haldane, is bespoke design and manufacture. Routine technical tasks are relatively simple to automate and are already well on their way to disappearing. But the same is not true of nonroutine technical tasks—for example, the creation of goods and services that are distinctive in their design, manufacture, or delivery. A new artisan class is emerging to satisfy this demand.

The third and perhaps the biggest potential growth area of all, argues Haldane, is social skills—that is, tasks requiring emotional intelligence (such as sympathy and empathy, relationship-building and negotiation skills, resilience and character) rather than cognitive intelligence alone. These are skills a robot is likely to find it hard to replicate. And even if they could replicate them, humans might still prefer humans to carry them out.

The future could see a world of work in which EQ rivals IQ for supremacy, he continues. Professions involving high degrees of personal and social interaction—such as health, caring, education, and leisure—will see demand rise. Indeed, it is possible the balance between cognitive and social skills might change significantly, even in jobs that traditionally have been cognitively intense.

"Take medicine. The doctors of the future might be valued far less for their clinical competence in diagnosing illness and prescribing solutions. In a world of individual medical records and data-hungry diagnostic algorithms, much of the process of diagnosis and prescription might fall to a machine rather than a human. But that is unlikely by itself to eradicate the need for doctors. Patients are still likely to want to discuss their diagnosis and prescription. And they will want this advice delivered personally and empathetically. In surveys of patient satisfaction, it is a doctor's bedside manner, rather than clinical competence, that matters most. In future, that balance between social and clinical skills may shift further. And, most likely, those social skills will be demanded from flesh-and-blood rather than robo-doctors."

Haldane sees that the future requires a better balance between the cognitive, technical, and social—Head, Hand, and Heart. He is not alone. In fact, Paul Krugman, whom I quoted in Chapter One, spotted back in 1996 (pretending to look back from the end of the twenty-first century) that high returns to education might not last long:

"In the 1990s, everyone believed that education was the key to economic success [for both individuals and nations]. A college degree, maybe even a postgraduate degree, was essential for anyone who wanted a good job as one of those 'symbolic analysts.'

"But computers are very good at analyzing symbols; it is the messiness of the real world that they have trouble with . . . So, over the course of the 21st century many of the jobs that used to require a college degree have been eliminated."[1]

Richard Baldwin, author of the *Globotics Upheaval* and one of the leading experts on the impact of robotics, also agrees with Haldane about a future in creativity, craft, and caring:

Machines have not been very successful at acquiring social intelligence, emotional intelligence, creativity, innovativeness, or the ability to deal with unknown situations.

Experts estimate it will take something like fifty years for AI to attain top-level human performance in social skills that are useful in the workplace . . .

The sheltered sectors of the future will be those where people actually have to be together doing things for which humanity is an edge. This will mean that our work lives will be filled with far more caring, sharing, understanding, creating, empathizing, innovating, and managing people who are actually in the same room.[2]

So the knowledge economy is likely to need fewer knowledge workers in the future. Indeed, according to Phillip Brown, Hugh Lauder, and David Ashton, that future is already here. In their book *The Global Auction: The Broken Promises of Education, Jobs and Incomes*, they argue that the notion that Western societies will be the global Head and developing countries will be content to remain the global Hand is now just a historical curiosity. Thanks to improvements in technology and education, it is now much easier for people in poorer countries to do the knowledge work that was once the preserve of Western graduates.

"Since the late 1990s, we've been investigating the changing contours of the global economy, talking to corporate managers and executives, along with national policy advisers, in several countries including the United States, Germany, China and India. The compelling conclusion to emerge from over 250 face to face interviews with these leaders, public and private, is that the relationship between education, jobs and incomes is being transformed in ways that cast doubt on the traditional rhetoric that 'learning equals earning' and the crucial role education plays in creating middle-class jobs."[3]

German carmakers—who, as recently as the late 1990s, thought it would be impossible to make top-end cars outside Baden-Württemberg, let alone Germany—are now building their entire product range in emerging economies. They were among the last to succumb to the globalization of industry, which is now an old story. But now in *services* it is increasingly the same story: emerging economies are no longer restricted to data entry and call center functions. Brown and Lauder cite a global law firm headquartered in New York that has moved some of the work previously given to newly qualified lawyers in London or New York with annual salaries of around $100,000 to law graduates in the Philippines, where the same work is done for less than $15,000.[4]

The barriers to higher education that previously protected the Western middle class are falling. "China and India are succeeding in 'leap-frogging' decades of technological development in the West to compete for high-skilled, high-value work, including research and development," according to Brown and Lauder. China is heading towards 200m graduates in its workforce and is currently graduating three times more students every year than the United States.[5]

This is not just about more global trade in services following in the footsteps of manufacturing. Both of these trends could in theory be reversed by protectionism, maybe driven by fear of future pandemics.

But the same technology that is helping to create a single global market in services is undermining the Western knowledge worker at home, too, via so-called Digital Taylorism.

"If the twentieth century brought mechanical Taylorism—mass production where the knowledge of craft workers is captured, codified and re-engineered in the shape of the moving assembly line—the 21st century is the age of Digital Taylorism. This involves codifying, standardising and digitising knowledge into software prescripts, platforms and packages that can be used by others regardless of location," write Brown and Lauder.[6]

New technologies, they point out, have increased the potential to translate knowledge work into *working knowledge*, leading to the standardization of an increasing proportion of technical, managerial, and professional jobs. Managerial jobs look likely to be increasingly deprived of discretion and analytical content by new technology.

The classic example is the local bank manager who used to use his judgment and knowledge of local businesses to decide whether to lend the bank's money. In many banks a software package now automatically assesses a loan application according to standard criteria. Only in appealing the software's judgment does the manager have a role. Another example is the travel agent who made a decent living getting you nifty special deals who has been replaced by Expedia and online booking of flights.

Brown and Lauder show that many big corporations have adopted a narrow view of talent management, severely limiting the numbers of employees recognized for their cognitive or problem-solving ability, leaving many other employees with a graduate education performing increasingly routinized tasks.

They break down service jobs into three categories—overlapping to some extent with the modern multinational's three layers of core, periphery, and contingent that we met in Chapter Five. Brown, Lauder, and Ashton in *The Global Auction* call them developers, demonstrators, and drones.

People in developer roles, which are no more than 10 to 15 percent of a typical organization's workforce, are given "permission to think" and include senior researchers, managers, and professionals. People in demonstrator roles are the second-level, partially de-skilled professionals who are invariably graduates but whose main job is to execute or implement existing knowledge. Communicating well is usually their main function. People in drone roles are involved in monotonous work and are not expected to think.

The swift decline of the professions has also been predicted in an influential book by father and son Richard and Daniel Susskind titled *The Future of the Professions: How Technology Will Transform the Work of Human Experts*. They write: "Our focus is on doctors, lawyers, teachers, accountants, tax advisers, management consultants, architects, journalists, and the clergy (amongst others) . . . Our main claim is that we are on the brink of a period of fundamental and irreversible change in the way that the expertise of these specialists is made available in society."[7]

They give some examples of what they mean. There are more unique visits each month to the WebMD network, a collection of health websites, than to all the doctors working in the United States. In the legal world, three times as many disagreements each year among eBay traders are resolved using "online dispute resolution" than there are lawsuits filed in the entire US court system.

The key question, as they see it, is how do we share expertise in society? "In what we term a 'print-based industrial society,' the professions have played a central role in the sharing of expertise. They have been the main channel through which individuals and organizations have gained access to certain kinds of knowledge and experience. However, in a 'technology-based Internet society,' we predict that increasingly capable machines . . . will take on many of the tasks that have been the historic preserve of the professions."[8]

One of the main objections to this argument is that people will still want the reassurance of an empathetic human expert. Their response:

"We do not deny for a second that great comfort can be given from one person to another. Indeed we identify the 'empathizer' as an important future role. However, our experience suggests that many of the recipients of professional advice are in fact seeking a reliable solution or outcome rather than a trusted adviser *per se*."[9]

Like Haldane and Baldwin, the Susskinds advise young people either to look for jobs that either favor human capabilities over artificial intelligence—above all, creativity and empathy—or become directly involved in the design and delivery of these increasingly capable systems as a data scientist or knowledge engineer.

Less Room at the Top

There is plenty of plausible skepticism about how swiftly AI is going to advance. Yet even if some of the predictions turn out to be overenthusiastic, there is other evidence for the *decline and fall of the knowledge worker* all around us: the decline in the graduate pay premium, especially in the United Kingdom; the increasing number of graduates in nongraduate jobs; and even the shrinkage, or at least slower growth, of the top managerial and professional social class.

It is obvious that as the number of graduates increased dramatically over recent decades that the prestige and economic returns associated with going to university would dip. A recent OECD report found that, on average across OECD countries, the earnings premium associated with higher education for fifty-five- to sixty-four-year-olds was 70 percent, twice that of younger adults at just 35 percent. And the same report found the decline to be accelerating.[10]

Looking more closely at the story in the UK in 2018: at age twenty-nine the average man who attended university earns around 25 percent more than the average man, with five good GCSEs, who did not. For women the gap is more than 50 percent, thanks to the fact that nongraduate women are more likely to be working part-time or in lower-paying, often care-related sectors.

However, once you control for differences in pre-university char-acteristics, the average impact of attending university on earnings at age twenty-nine is much less: 28 percent for women and just 8 percent for men. Moreover, when making that adjustment, as many as one-third of male British graduates get effectively no higher return from going to university.[11]

Anna Vignoles, one of the leading researchers in this field, shows that the median earnings of men from the bottom twenty-three universities were *less* than the median earnings for non-graduates.[12] And there are twelve institutions for which she estimates *statistically significant* negative returns for men at age twenty-nine.[13]

There is a brutal hierarchy among universities that partly determines the size of the premium, with Oxbridge, the top London colleges, and the Russell Group all linked with much higher returns and most of the former polytechnics producing significantly lower or nonexistent premiums. In fact, fully half of students now attend a UK university with an average income uplift of less than 10 percent.[14]

Male Russell Group graduates earn over 40 percent more than those who attended the former polytechnics (35 percent more for women). When controlling for pre-university factors, a Russell Group university degree still confers a 10 to 13 percent increase in earnings over non–Russell Group universities.[15]

Subject choice has a big impact on the premium too. Medicine and economics degrees have the highest returns—around 20 percent higher than the average degree (and 25 percent more than English or history)[16]—and business, computing, and architecture degrees all offer relative earnings uplift.[17] Creative arts, which enrolls more than 10 percent of all students, has very low returns: around 15 percent less than the average degree.[18] Other low scorers, partly reflecting pay levels in their sectors, include social care, sports science, communications, English, sociology, psychology, and education.[19]

Social class also plays a role in graduate premium outcomes. After controlling for all other characteristics, degree subject, and institution, graduates from private schools earn around 7 to 9 percent more than those graduates from the lowest socioeconomic backgrounds.[20] In the United States, attending the most selective state university causes earnings to be about 30 percent higher than the white male average. The Ivy League graduate earns on average twice as much as graduates of other colleges.

In some ways it is remarkable how the so-called graduate premium has held up to the extent that it has. That is partly because, at least until recently, the economy has been generating more graduate-level jobs. But it is also because of occupational "filtering down."

As Ken Mayhew, professor of education at Oxford, explains: "Imagine a hierarchy of jobs. Top of the hierarchy is the best-paying job and as we move down the hierarchy pay gets lower and lower. Graduates occupy the jobs at the top of the pay hierarchy but as more and more of them enter the labour market some of them occupy jobs further and further down the hierarchy. Thus the average pay of graduates falls. But so does the average pay of *non-graduates*. So, the average graduate wage premium can remain unchanged despite the fact that lots of young people have been to university only to enter jobs once occupied, as it were, by their non-graduate mothers and fathers.

"From an individual's economic point of view it makes sense for them to attend university given the current structure of the education and training system and the incentives presented to young people. However that does not mean that it makes sense for society, which has to ask whether, for many people, higher education is the most cost effective way of preparing them for the labour market."[21]

This describes exactly what has been happening in the United States in recent years. In the last two decades male earnings between the 50th and 80th deciles (so just below the top 20 percent) have been static. But the graduate premium over those with just a high school diploma remains significant—averaging over $30,000 a year—albeit flattening out in recent years, so it still makes economic sense to go to college if you can.[22]

The premise on which the whole expansion of higher education (and social mobility policy) has been based—more and more well-paid, professional middle-class jobs with a high cognitive content—no longer holds.

This is beginning to filter through into the choices that young people make as more people share either their negative experiences of university and their disappointing post-university careers or, alternatively, the positive experiences of even middle-class young people who decided not to take the expected path to higher education, thereby avoiding the double blow of significant debt followed by disappointment in the job market.

In the United Kingdom all the incentives still push young people down the university path, as I spelled out in Chapter Four, but politicians and newspaper columnists are also starting to think and talk more positively about non-university post-school paths such as high-level apprenticeships.

In the United Kingdom the returns to a high-level but sub-degree STEM qualification—level 4 or 5 in the jargon of international education—are higher than the returns to most degrees outside Russell Group universities.[23] Stefan Speckesser of the National Institute of Economic and Social Research in London has established that the average income for those who obtained a degree from a non-Russell institution is 11 percent lower by the age of thirty than it would have been had those same individuals achieved higher-technical qualifications instead.

A big part of the fall of the knowledge worker story is just how many graduates *are now doing nongraduate jobs*. Looking at the bigger picture for rich countries, the OECD Skills Survey finds that around one-third of *all* workers think that they have underutilized skills. Looking just at graduates, the figure was also around 40 percent for the United Kingdom and averaging around 35 percent for graduates across all OECD countries.[24]

A 2015 LinkedIn survey of users found 37 percent of mainly professional people said their current jobs did not fully use their skills.

Relying on workers' own perceptions of their skill potential may be too subjective, but the United Kingdom's statistical body, the ONS, which uses a more objective job classification methodology, reports similar numbers. In 2017 it noted that the number of recent graduates working in no-graduate jobs had risen from 37 percent in 2001 to 47 percent in 2013 and 49 percent in 2017. The percentage of non-recent graduates (more than five years) working in nongraduate jobs is 35 percent.[25]

As one might expect, the proportions tend to be highest in poorer regions of the country where there are fewer graduate jobs. The labor economist Peter Elias has gone even further and declared that *over half* of graduates were in jobs unlikely to be requiring, using, or rewarding their investment in higher education.[26]

The ONS also uses another concept of "overeducation," meaning having more education than required to do the job. In 2017 around 16 percent of all those in employment ages sixteen to sixty-four were overeducated; the corresponding figure for graduates was around 31 percent.[27]

Those with postgraduate qualifications are not immune. About half (51 percent) worked in a job that required such a qualification, another quarter (26 percent) worked in a job for which a first degree would have sufficed, and the rest were in positions that required no higher education, according to the UK Skills and Employment Survey of 2017.[28]

Ken Mayhew and Craig Holmes have also looked at jobs categorized as graduate jobs but where the skills people acquired doing their degrees are largely irrelevant. They examined twenty-nine occupations, which account for almost a third of total employment. The report concludes that while for many of these jobs the number of graduates has increased sharply over the last thirty years, *the skills required for the job have not appreciably changed.*[29]

Examples of this include managers in manufacturing, transport, and communication; health associate professionals; nursery nurses;

and a number of examples from clerical work. Also technicians in manufacturing, managers and senior administrators in the public services, and sports coaches and fitness instructors.[30]

Graduates who drop down the job hierarchy often end up doing jobs that they are not suited to and become bored with very quickly; recall in Chapter Four the graduates whose expectations make them poor at relatively routine technician-type jobs.

Ken Mayhew, whose name has cropped up frequently in the preceding paragraphs, is a reassuring guide through this corner of the maze. He is the son of a tailor who went on a full scholarship to Manchester Grammar School and for a high-ranking academic and government adviser has an attractively vivid way of talking about labor markets, often drawn from his own life or extended family.

I am sitting with him in a Café Rouge restaurant in north London, picking his brain about the rise of the nongraduate-job graduate. He looks around to illustrate his point and says: "A junior purchasing manager working for a restaurant chain like Café Rouge will now be required to have a degree, but this is mainly a screening/signaling effect; they are very unlikely to use anything they have learned doing a three-year bachelor's degree."

All in all, many of today's graduates are entering occupations, which at least by their title, are, as Mayhew puts it, just the same as the ones entered by their nongraduate mothers and fathers. Forty-one percent of new recruits to property, housing, and estate management are now graduates compared with just 3.6 percent in 1979, and 35 percent of new bank and post office clerks are now graduates compared with 1979, when just 3.5 percent were.

The increase in the graduate mix within financial services (from the 1990s) has had little effect on skills upgrading for the roles: it has been estimated that 45 percent of recently employed graduates in finance were working in jobs suitable for high school graduates, that had not been upgraded at all.[31] Studies of estate agents, press officers, software engineers, financial analysts, and laboratory technicians have suggested only limited use of specifically graduate skills in jobs that have recently become dominated by, or exclusive to, those with degrees.[32]

The fall of the knowledge worker can also be glimpsed in non-repayment of student loans. After all, if graduates are mainly going into decent graduate jobs, why are so many struggling to repay those loans? Under current repayment terms the majority of graduates will never earn enough to fully repay their debts—with the IFS estimating that 77 percent will have some of their debt written off after the end of the thirty-year repayment period.[33]

How does this picture compare with the United States and France and Germany? Although graduate filtering down is common across Europe, it is rather less so in France and Germany, and both countries have fewer graduates who believe they aren't using their skills.[34] According to one academic paper the figure for the United States of graduates in nongraduate jobs is a little bit below the United Kingdom at 32 percent, France stands at 28 percent, and Germany at 16 percent.[35] Daniel Susskind, in *A World Without Work*, says that one-third of Americans working in the fast food industry have some college education and one-third of Americans with degrees in STEM subjects are now in roles that don't require those qualifications.[36]

The result of all these trends is that the increase in the number of people in the top occupational classes is starting to slow down and even stop, at least in the United Kingdom. After continuous expansion since the categories were first invented, it appears that, according to the leading social mobility researcher John Goldthorpe, there has been "less room at the top" in recent years.[37]

As noted, education policy and social mobility policy in most rich countries have been premised on the assumption of an ever-growing cognitive class of people in professional jobs. This has, indeed, been a big part of the story over recent decades. Even now, taking the top three occupational classes (in the ONS nine class schema) in the United Kingdom, there appears to be some continuing growth. The proportion of people in those top three groups—managers, directors, and senior officials; professional occupations; and associate professional and technical occupations—has risen from 39 to 45 percent between 2001 and 2018.[38]

The government classifies these top three groups as graduate-level jobs. But if you look more closely at the classification system, it turns out that the third group, associate professional and technical occupations, has many occupations that are explicitly nongraduate, requiring only higher-level vocational qualifications. They include police community support officers, fitness instructors, marketing associates, managers in retail, and property and estate managers.

According to Anna Vignoles there are genuine classification problems here: "Is a web designer the equivalent of a managing director or a binman?" But she agrees with Goldthorpe that there has been a slowdown or even a complete halt to the increase in the number of well-paid, higher professional jobs, which means that downward mobility has become greater than upward mobility at the top of the occupational hierarchy.

All of this suggests that the human capital theory idea of higher returns to individuals and higher productivity for economies flowing from more higher education is no longer working. The idea has been very popular among politicians as well as economists as it seemed to solve both the economic problem and the fairness problem by placing educational meritocracy at the center of progressive politics, both for center-left and center-right. It was given a further boost at the end of the 1980s with the invention of the idea of the knowledge economy (a term that seems to have gone out of fashion in recent years).

Yet forecasts about the jobs of the future provide more support for the idea of the decline and fall of the knowledge worker, especially at the middling and lower level. The demand for Head jobs will still be there, but it will focus on the most able and creative, and the sharpest rise in demand will be for Heart and certain kind of technological jobs that combine Hand and Head.

A cottage industry has emerged over recent years estimating gross job loss from automation as anything between 10 and 50 percent. Most analysts agree that many jobs will go but few whole occupations. Some of the potentially powerful effects of automation on jobs and wages are already apparent. According to McKinsey, 18 percent of all hours worked in the United States are devoted to "predictable physical activities" and half of these hours could be automated away even with current technology.

That McKinsey report looked at the prospects for twenty-five different skills across five broad categories in the United States: physical and manual, basic cognitive, higher cognitive, social and emotional, and technological skills. The conclusion is that between 2016 and 2030 the hours worked on old school *physical and manual* skills will decline 11 percent (although at 26 percent of hours worked in the economy it will remain the largest sector in 2030), hours worked on *basic cognitive* skills will fall 14 percent, *higher cognitive* skills will increase by 9 percent (but not increase its overall share in 2030, which will remain at 22 percent), *social and emotional* skills will rise by 26 percent, and *technological* skills by a whopping 60 percent (although still only 16 percent of total hours in 2030). A similar trend is expected in Western Europe.[39]

It is not all bad news for the knowledge worker, even though there will be fewer of them. According to the McKinsey report: "The growing need for creativity is seen in many activities, including developing high-quality marketing strategies. Other types of higher cognitive skills—such as advanced literacy and writing, and quantitative and statistical skills—will not see a similar increase in demand, and indeed our analysis suggests the need for them could remain stable or even decline to 2030. In writing and editing, computer programs already produce basic news stories about sporting results and stock market movements for many newspaper chains. Of course, the decline in this skill does not imply that there will be no authors, writers, or editors in the future—but as in many other occupations, some of the more basic aspects of the work will shift to machines."[40]

And that bank manager whose judgment has been replaced with a loan approval algorithm is emblematic of a broader shift in lower-level financial service jobs, which is likely to have a big impact on heavily financialized economies like the United States and the United Kingdom. As the report says: "A range of back-office functions to be automated, include financial reporting, accounting, actuarial sciences, insurance claims processing, credit scoring, loan approval, and tax calculation. Computer algorithms and 'robotic process automation' can drastically reduce the time and manpower devoted to these activities."[41]

Capitalism in the Age of Robots

What does all this mean? The knowledge economy needs fewer knowledge workers than expected. The recent expansion of higher education in much of the West will stop or even go into reverse as the demand for the middling and lower-rung jobs of the knowledge economy will decline.

And companies, partly out of bitter experience, will place less confidence in the signaling effect of a degree, even from a good university, and revert to offering more apprenticeships, including degree apprenticeships, to capable high school graduates. This is already happening in several big employers and appears to be more than a fad.

The big consultancy firm EY made a splash in the UK in 2015 with the announcement that it would drop degree classification from the entry criteria for their hiring programs and you would not need to be a graduate to apply for even their top entry-level training program.[42]

The firm said it would focus on a "strengths-based assessment" and would look for people who are "strong communicators, team players, adaptable, analytical, numbers savvy, in the know."[43] Other big UK consultancies like KPMG and Deloitte and banks, including Barclays, have made similar announcements.

Opening up different routes into high-status cognitive-analytical jobs is not in itself tilting the balance away from Head, although it could weaken the grip of degree credentialism. But the indications are that the pendulum of prestige will gradually swing, at least somewhat, away from the cognitive-analytical and toward the "high-touch" jobs, often face-to-face, in care and education and fitness, and to some higher Hand niches, too, both technical and artisanal.

There will also be a renewed interest in the old generalist tradition, often seen as an English gentlemanly indulgence in the nineteenth and early twentieth centuries compared with continental specialization, although now it will be celebrated as "cross domain" competence. The model for this is something like the website designer who requires both technical know-how and some aesthetic-design ability.

But hanging over this potentially benign evolution is the specter of inequality. The knowledge economy will lose many of its rank-and-file soldiers but it will still have an officer corps of highly skilled individuals, both those managing the machines of the fourth industrial revolution and the superstar professionals of the winner-takes-all markets. Soaring corporate pay packages in recent decades have already led to chief executives of the top 500 US companies earning on average 379 times more than their average employee; the figure is 149 times for the top 100 companies in the United Kingdom. [44]

Some very sober, mainstream commentators, like Adair Turner, former chairman of the Financial Services Authority in London, worry a great deal about the further deep inequality they see built into the economic trends. At the top end of the income distribution, returns to high skill will, he thinks, be very big and very concentrated.

Here is Turner from his 2018 paper *Capitalism in the Age of Robots*:

> In a world of ever increasing automation possibilities, we only need a very small number of very clever IT literate people to write all the code we need for all the robots, all the apps, and all the computer games, and we need only a miniscule fraction of the global population to drive inexorable progress towards ever more profound artificial intelligence and super intelligence.

Three decades or more since we first began to talk of living in a computer age, the total number of workers employed in the development and production of computer hardware, software and applications, is still only 4 per cent of the total workforce in the US, and the US Bureau of Labor Statistics predicts just 135,000 new jobs in software development over 2014 to 2024, versus 458,000 additional personal care aides, and 348,000 home health aides. Total employment in the giant mobile phone, software and Internet companies which dominate global equity values is a minute drop in the global labour market. Facebook, with a market capitalization of $500 billion, employs just 25,000 people.[45]

Turner takes issue with Tyler Cowen's book *Average Is Over: Powering America Beyond the Age of the Great Stagnation* in which he argues that rising income inequality is inevitable but will not lead to social revolt, because low earners will still enjoy adequate living standards as long as housing costs are kept low.

Cowen imagines a future in which "say 10 to 15 per cent of the citizenry is extremely wealthy and has fantastically comfortable and stimulating lives" while "much of the rest of the country will have stagnant or maybe falling wages in dollar terms, but a lot more opportunities for cheap fun and cheap education" because of the free or near free services that the Internet makes available.[46]

The average citizen will not be able to afford to live well in the successful big cities . . . but will migrate to those parts of the United States, such as Texas, where plentiful land and easy zoning rules make housing affordable. Meanwhile, talented bohemians who want nothing to do with the rat race competition of the top 10 to 15 percent will tend to congregate in those cities, like Berlin and Detroit, where past economic changes have left surplus housing and where fulfilled and less stressful lives can be financed from modest incomes derived from artistic or craft activities. The future may therefore be highly unequal but cheap houses, clothes, food, video entertainment, and computer games will ensure that there is no social revolt.

Turner does not like this view of the future but thinks Cowen is probably right that inequality in the future could be combined with a reasonably high floor and need not be coupled with widespread poverty; he also agrees that the cost of housing and transport will drive most low earners out of big, successful, cosmopolitan cities; and the consequence of that will be increasing spatial segregation between the top 15 percent and the rest.

This segregation is less likely to happen on a significant scale in more densely populated Europe, but in both the United States and Europe we are already starting to see economic-cum-cultural residential divisions, partly to do with the movement of graduates.

The Cowen prophecy is avoidable if the current Head-Hand-Heart balance can be recalibrated. Yet we are still promoting and subsidizing cognitive-analytic aptitudes in ever-expanding university sectors in the false belief that feeding more graduates to the economic machine will miraculously create more comfortable, high-status, professional jobs.

Raising the rewards and prestige attached to Hand and Heart will happen only slowly over generational time, and some of the policies required—chipping away at concentrations of Head wealth, raising wages for care services, celebrating craft skills, education for life—I will consider in the final chapter.

Chapter Ten

Cognitive Diversity and the Future of Everything

Not everything that counts can be counted, and not every-thing that can be counted counts.

Albert Einstein

The title of this book is misleading. It implies that Head, Hand, and Heart, or thought, craft, and feeling, are distinct domains. They are not, of course, and too rigid a division between the three is one of the pathologies of the cognitive era.

Many Hand occupations require a great deal of Head. Matthew Crawford, the American philosopher whom I have cited several times, left a think tank to set up a motorcycle repair shop and says he found skilled Hand work more mentally engaging than working on policy questions. He lovingly describes the kind of diagnostic reasoning he uses to locate the fault in the engine of a vintage Italian motorbike—requiring logic, experience, and, sometimes, imagination.

Similarly with the Head and Heart. As we saw in Chapter Eight, many of the Heart caring and nursing jobs in modern societies also require significant degrees of Head. Conversely an overreliance on just one of the triumvirate—a narrow Head utilitarianism devoid of Heart—is one of the abiding weaknesses of modern liberal politics.

Politics is an argument about what we value, and public life, just like private lives, can get things out of balance. In recent decades public life has been too dominated by a cognitive class that has been trained to value the cognitively complex and quantifiable, and too often this has led to a narrow rationalism and economism. David Brooks, the *New York Times* columnist, reports that, according to Google, over the last thirty years there has been a sharp increase in the use of economic words and a decline in the use of moral words: "gratitude" down 49 percent, "humility" down 52 percent, and "kindness" down 56 percent.[1]

In the summer of 2019, I heard David Miliband, the former British foreign secretary, talking about Brexit, and when asked whether Labour in power (1997–2010) might have contributed to the alienation expressed in that vote, all he could talk about was economic growth and issues of inequality—nothing about identity or immigration, nothing about national sovereignty, nothing about the rapid change that makes many people feel that the past was better than the present. This exceptionally talented man seemed to have learned nothing about emotions in politics in the three years since the Brexit vote.

Privileged or highly successful people often have less incentive to ask big questions about value; there can be a blandness and invulnerability about them. But loss and failure are important teachers. James Stewart in *It's a Wonderful Life* sees the true value of his life and his family only when he's at his lowest point.

In the course of writing this book, I had a sharp lesson in loss when a love affair ended unexpectedly. Someone with whom I had felt a deep connection decided to end the relationship after a few months. It knocked me back for a time and was compounded by a back injury that made me physically lame.

Before this happened, I had recently established a contented new life for myself. I had moved into a new flat after an amicable separation from my wife of twenty-five years and had published a bestselling book a couple of years before. I was healthy and had no financial worries, I felt in a good place, and I was perhaps a bit *too* sure of myself.

Crashing back down to earth made me think about why I had invested so much in this one person. All of us are on a journey to finding a kind of wholeness, especially as we get older. Was my life a bit out of kilter? Was it too dominated by professional success and the invulnerable ways of the Head? Had this prevented me from paying attention to the other things that matter: close friendships, meaningful conversations with my children, an absorbing hobby, volunteering in my community, making more effort to see myself as others see me?

At the same time that I was thrown off balance emotionally, I happened to be reading Iain McGilchrist's remarkable book *The Master and His Emissary: The Divided Brain and the Making of the Western World*, about the radically different worldviews of the left and right brain hemispheres.[2] "The hidden story of Western culture, as told by the author, is about how the abstract, instrumental, articulate, and assured left hemisphere has gradually usurped the more contextual, humane, systemic, holistic but relatively tentative and inarticulate right hemisphere," as the philosopher Jonathan Rowson sums it up.[3]

We live in a left-brain, Head world. The way that McGilchrist talks about the abstraction, instrumentalism, and utilitarianism of the left hemisphere, its love of certainty and its inflated sense of its own autonomy and cleverness, seems a perfect metaphor for the pathologies of the Anywhere cognitive class. The right hemisphere, by contrast, is the domain of a sense of wholeness and mystery, with a religious tolerance for what can't be said or understood: "It is what it is / says love" in the words of Erich Fried's famous poem.

The two hemispheres need each other, just as Head and Heart need each other. But, as this book has been arguing, we also need a better balance between them. To some readers this little detour might be a rather unwelcome lurch into personal anecdote and mysticism. But McGilchrist is an accomplished psychiatrist whose arguments are certainly contested yet are rooted in hard science.

And I have become more convinced in the course of writing this book that a better Head-Hand-Heart balance is an unsentimental political requirement, even more so after the Covid-19 crisis. When I started writing at the beginning of 2019, I saw a better balance as a desirable ambition but a somewhat "new age" one, reinforced by learning that "Head, Hand, and Heart" is the motto of that most new age of schools, the progressive English private school Bedales!

As I have read and researched, I have increasingly concluded that the rebalancing is not just desirable but necessary, and probably inevitable, not just because of the economic trends that will eat into much cognitive employment, as described in the last chapter, but also because of the fundamental questions of meaning and value that national and global politics needs to address.

Western society has been dominated in the past two generations by *centrifugal* forces that have extended individual freedom but weakened collective bonds and the power of tradition, and in the process allowed cognitive ability to claim undue economic and political rewards. The cognitively blessed have become more powerful but many others feel they have lost place and meaning. The end of the Cold War and the emergence of postindustrial societies has weakened collective national and class identities; ethnic and value diversity has reduced trust and common social norms; while social media has created conditions of "connected isolation" promoting narrow tribal identities and individualistic identity politics. And all the while depression and mental illness has increased.

Recent political trends, surely reinforced by the pandemic, suggest we are moving into a more *centripetal* phase, in which the nation state will be consolidated and economic and cultural openness will be a little more constrained. This phase will place more stress on social stability and respect for the wisdom ingrained in institutions; it will be more skeptical of the claims of the Head and more sensitive to the humiliations and mass resentment built into modern, achievement societies.

The American historian Christopher Lasch argued many years ago that a democratic society should not aim to create a framework for competition, where the most able succeed and the others fail. Yet this is precisely what we have achieved in recent decades as the ideology of meritocracy and social mobility, endorsed by the rise of the university-educated cognitive classes, has swept all before it.

Competition is a vital force in inspiring innovation and challenging entrenched economic and political power. But too much competition and comparison at the individual level can generate a permanent state of anxiety and make it harder for people to align their expectations with their actual capacities—perhaps the best route to personal happiness.

There will always be hierarchies of competence in all domains of human aptitude, and we need to preserve meritocratic selection procedures for important jobs, from running the country to captaining the local football team, while at the same time exploring ways of spreading respect and status more evenly.

The centripetal push-back against twenty-five years of centrifugal opening is democracy working, not failing. But Brexit, Trump, and European populism are *value* challenges to the previous political mainstream, and as the long Brexit impasse showed, we have not been very good at negotiating fundamental questions of value, as discussed in Chapter Six.

Modern liberalism is supposed to support value pluralism, but many liberals struggled to do so when their own values were challenged. And it turned out that several decades of pushing back the boundaries of individual freedom, of encouraging a generous diversity of goals and Gods and ultimate ends, had left us in the United Kingdom—in the Brexit argument—with diminished psychological and institutional capacity to come together and compromise over some version of the common good.

As the British philosopher John Gray has argued, value pluralism is now a permanent feature of liberal democracies, but to function well it turns out that we also need a bedrock of shared norms, rules of the road, that everyone can stand on—peaceful and respectful disagreement, the rule of law, accepting majority decisions tempered by minority rights, and so on. The more solid that bedrock, the easier it will be to conduct robust public arguments about value *differences*— arguments that have been suppressed by Charles Murray's "ecumenical niceness"—and negotiate some other big challenges that are looming.

The most obvious one is climate change and the future of the planet. The left hemisphere–Head worldview treats the body as a machine and the natural world as a heap of resources to be exploited. This has had inevitable consequences, and if technology cannot come to our aid, it is going to require some very hard conversations within and between countries about burden sharing. There has been some shift in awareness about the heaviness of the human footprint, David Attenborough's *Blue Planet* changed the way that many of us think about plastic. But the pious consensus in most rich countries about the threat of climate change is not at all reflected in our behavior as citizens and is unlikely to be so until the threat to us is very much more immediate.

And even if there were an authority we could all trust who could spell out the relative risks of different courses of action, there is every likelihood that there would be fundamental disagreements between people of different temperaments as to which course to take, as there was at the height of the Covid-19 crisis. The same applies to how much we should forgo current consumption to invest in minimizing the threat from future pandemics and the threat of antibiotic resistance.

Another imminent value challenge concerns human enhancement and "playing God." Already there are many pharmacological ways of temporarily enhancing brain functioning, and in the future we might be able to manipulate our own DNA to improve cognitive ability or select the embryos of our babies to favor only those with the highest innate ability.*

The more optimistic accounts see cognitive improvement technology as narrowing the current cognitive divides in the way that glasses level out the optical playing field for those with good and poor

---

* Some people think the Rubicon has already been crossed when the Chinese biophysicist He Jiankui announced that he had edited an immune system gene in early embryos leading to the birth of twin girls resistant to HIV. This so-called germ line editing lasts indefinitely into the future, unlike the ordinary manipulation of an individual's genes for some medical purpose, and has therefore been almost universally condemned. But it is hard to see how the knowledge can be suppressed.

eyesight. There are also many dystopian accounts of rising cognitive and income inequality and how cognitive manipulation might open the way to a caste society divided between the normals and the super-intelligent who are able to afford the expensive treatments.

The regulation of social media ought to be a more manageable challenge. The institution is still in its infancy and will surely emerge from the "Wild West" period both in terms of the spiteful culture it has bred and in the neurotic anxieties it generates, thanks to the culture of mass comparison (as described by Jean Twenge and others).

It is increasingly hard to make the argument that there should be one law for old media and another for new media, but it will take time to work out how to suppress the damaging aspects of this new technology without undermining the beneficial. As Richard Layard has pointed out, in 1930 the car killed 7,300 people in Britain; by 2016 that had been reduced to 1,700—despite a huge increase in car ownership—largely thanks to regulation.[4] But individuals will also need to develop healthier habits for using the technology.

We have succeeded in tackling big problems in the past both nationally and internationally—from smallpox eradication to ozone layer depletion and chemical weapons treaties. But the negotiation of *value* differences is harder than dealing with the *interest* clashes of the socioeconomic politics that dominated the postwar world. And it is harder to split the difference on value questions than it is on, say, the desired level of public spending or taxation.

For this reason we need a far greater appreciation of *cognitive* diversity. The idea that the top 15 percent of the IQ bell curve should dominate all top jobs and run society was never a good one, as I argued in Chapter Three. Meritocracy of various kinds has a central place on the sports field, in the concert hall, in the science lab, maybe even in the higher ranks of officials in government departments, but the super-bright should be our servants, not our masters. This is not an argument for stupid politicians, but where the big decisions are made a breadth of human perspectives are required.

We have taken our time, but after several decades of debating the virtues of race and gender diversity, we are finally talking about cognitive diversity too. Matthew Syed, the influential British commentator, now argues in his latest book *Rebel Ideas: The Power of Diverse Thinking* that the shared training of the higher end of the cognitive class in abstract reasoning and analytical intelligence is not sufficient to tackle the complex problems heading our way.

Syed defines cognitive diversity as "about differences in perspectives . . . and the models and heuristics we deploy to make sense of the world . . . and also perhaps differences in thinking styles . . . [S]ome of us are analytical thinkers and other more holistic and contextual thinkers." He quotes countless papers on how cognitive diversity produces better outcomes in business, government, and research.[5]

One paper on diverse thinking styles by researchers at Carnegie Mellon University in the United States defines three different cognitive styles: "Verbalizers, spatial visualizers, and object visualizers . . . Journalists and lawyers tend to be verbalizers; engineers and people in other math-driven professions are spatial visualizers, who think analytically; and artists are object visualizers, who tend to think about the bigger picture."[6]

A lot of the attention on cognitive diversity is linked to "collective intelligence." Collective intelligence is a much-debated concept but is essentially about how people "pool" their different intelligences so that something emerges that is more than the sum of the parts of individual intelligences. The jury system at its best acts as a kind of collective intelligence. A friend of mine recalls the very different styles of thinking at work on a jury he served on a few years ago, on the way to making the right decision. "Some people used their intuition and ability to judge character. Others were happier with a more skeptical, evidence-based approach. Together we ended up balancing Heads and Hearts all round, it was a lesson in trusting people to do the right thing."

Diversity must also apply to ideology and political values as highlighted by the Heterodox Academy in the United States, founded by social psychologist and author Jonathan Haidt as a counter to the dominance of secular, leftist ideas on US campuses. Writing on the Heterodox Academy website, the sociologist Musa al-Gharbi puts it like this: "If we care about demographic diversity and inclusion . . . we also must care about *ideological* (political, religious, etc.) diversity and inclusion. To the extent that we attempt to pursue one to the exclusion, or at the expense, of the other—we are setting ourselves up for failure."

He also makes the point that white liberals are often unaware of how culturally specific the idea of "making the best of yourself" is and how off-putting that can sometimes be to the very people they claim to be looking out for. "US institutions of higher learning are dominated by white, Protestant, bourgeois norms of independence, meritocracy, and a focus on the self. First-gen and minority students often struggle to adapt, flourish or feel they 'belong' in these spaces in part because their own cultures, values and priorities tend to stress duties to others, mutual aid and interdependence—and are generally less self oriented (perspectives strongly associated with conservativism and religion)."[7]

These initiatives and new forms of thinking all sound like variations on a theme of bringing McGilchrist's left and right hemispheres into a more harmonious working relationship. They also overlap with a new interest in the concept of *wisdom*, about which more below, and expanding that base of shared assumptions on which pluralism can more comfortably rest.

Robin Wales, the former Labour mayor of the London borough of Newham, a super-diverse east London borough of more than 300,000 people, is an enthusiastic supporter of cognitive diversity based on his experience of running a large bureaucracy.

"I have done a lot of work looking at different ways to manage large organizations. Our Newham small-business initiative encouraged entrepreneurialism and generated substantial savings, and it was partly based on an analysis of the failings of large organizations run by the highly educated people you are writing about."

A crucial aspect of the failure of management in large organizations, argues Wales, is that more educated people are effectively trained in the ability to explain away evidence that contradicts their view—rationalization versus rationality (as discussed in Chapters Three and Six). Or, to put it more simply, people who have achieved academic success tend to acquire a lot of confidence in their own ability and then tend to assume that they are always right.

The transparency requirements of modern institutions also encourage a performative, virtue-signaling political culture that makes it harder for people to identify as insiders and come to reasonable compromises. We live in low-trust societies, especially in the United States and United Kingdom, with declining respect for professional judgment, yet we have, rightly, high requirements for accountability and measurable impact. The volume of legal regulations and instruments governing everyday activities therefore grows every year, a sign of the disappearance of the implicit understandings found in more cohesive cultures. It all makes work for the cognitive class to do.

One good example is the comparison between the Glass-Steagall Act of 1933 in the United States, which prevented banks from undertaking risky and speculative activities, and the Dodd-Frank Act of 2010, which was similarly designed to prevent future banking crises. Glass-Steagall was 37 pages long and written in relatively comprehensible English; Dodd-Frank was 848 pages supplemented with 398 pieces of rulemaking running to some 30,000 pages. It is estimated that altogether Dodd-Frank was about 1,000 times longer than Glass-Steagall.[8]

Achieving a Better Balance

This is more of a diagnosis than a policy book, but people expect that a book suggesting a different direction for society should provide at least a few thoughts on how to get there. So, in this final section, I want to pick up some threads and offer some ideas on how the Head, Hand, and Heart—the human triumvirate—can be achieved.

There is a substantial body of cross-society support for raising Hand and Heart, as the opinion poll in the last chapter indicated. There are also, to underline again, some deep trends that are already nudging rich countries in this direction: technology's elimination of so many middling cognitive jobs and the end of the golden age of mass higher education; the aging of society and the rising visibility of care functions of many kinds, especially in the light of the pandemic; the greater concern for place, ecology, and belonging—thanks to those odd bedfellows, the green movement and the populist revolt.

And we also know just how swiftly social norms can change. As Cass Sunstein has pointed out, neither the French nor the Russian nor the Iranian revolutions were expected. Norms and expectations can shift very fast when people discover that many others share their views. If it is possible for new norms on gender equality, homosexuality, smoking, animal rights—even voting Conservative in former Labour constituencies—to be established in relatively short periods of time then why not new assumptions about Head, Hand, and Heart?

So here are some ideas in five domains: inequality and the cognitive meritocracy; place and mobility; upgrading care; celebrating craft; and education for life.

Inequality and the cognitive meritocracy. Market forces are starting to adjust some of the inflated returns to Head of recent decades as the graduate premium shrinks and the shortage of both skilled and unskilled manual workers pushes up Hand wages, at least in some sectors.

At the very top there remains an inequality issue thanks to the "war for talent," the gaming of executive pay incentive systems, winner-takes-all markets, and the way that first-mover advantage, especially in digital markets, can confer enormous rewards on people without having to go through the sweat of decades building a business.

Many commentators believe that the default setting for modern liberal societies is ever higher levels of inequality and the emergence of a class of the meritocratic superrich, who may even, with the help of the latest science, evolve into some new strand of humanity.

I think this danger is somewhat exaggerated, partly because this super-class needs to live somewhere and will be subject to old-fashioned social democratic tax and regulation (including of their medical experiments with extending the lifespan) in most places, certainly in the United Kingdom and Europe. But as Adair Turner argues: "When much new wealth derives from uncreated increases in the relative price of land, and where without intervention differential inheritance will have a huge influence on life chances, there is a strong case for increasing the effective taxation of property wealth, capital gains, and inheritance."

Restrictions on the breadth of application of intellectual property rights and for shortening the length of copyright protection to reduce the super-rents enjoyed by some first movers in the digital and other market places are also feasible. The economist Mariana Mazzucato has pointed to how much apparently private innovation builds upon public support for basic research.

As I argued in Chapter Three, very clever people remain of great value to society, even if the cognitive class as a whole has taken too much reward and prestige for itself in recent decades. More big brains make technical problems easier to fix, especially with the connectivity of the Internet, as we have seen with the scientific collaborations associated with the Covid-19 crisis.

In premodern agrarian societies, the community needed warriors to protect them against other warriors. Hence monarchy and aristocracy. In those societies, strength and bravery were esteemed, and the Head played only a minor role. As societies became more sophisticated and required more intricate management, Head started to come into its own and develop its own centers of training, above all the universities. Henry I had no need for them; Henry VIII could not have managed without them.

If there is a postapocalyptic dystopia and we revert to the Dark Ages, the strongman will replace the nerd again at the apex of the hierarchy and would have to be bribed into protecting rather than plundering the community by some combination of tribute and flattery.

In a science and commerce based postindustrial society, there is a similarly utilitarian argument for rewarding the very able to ensure they are socially useful. But how they are rewarded, and how much they are rewarded, is of course where the argument begins.

How much money does a smart CEO need to do a good job? Must it be money? Why not honor? Public honor can work up to a point in parts of the public sector. It is why, in the United Kingdom, we have an honors system and some very clever people remain in the civil service, awaiting their knighthoods, on middle-management salaries way below what they could earn in the private sector. Could this also work in the private sector? It seems unlikely, but a negative version: naming and shaming overpaid business people by shareholder activists and others does seem to have had some impact. Public dishonor might be a surprisingly powerful weapon in constraining the superrich. The very public distribution of their fortunes to charity by some of the digital billionaires shows how seriously some of them take their public standing. From 2020 all UK public companies with more than 250 employees will have to reveal the ratio between the pay of the CEO and the average employee, which is a step in the right direction.

Another way in which the very pinnacle of the cognitive meritoc-racy can be regulated is to make the jobs as temporary as possible and strictly rewarded according to performance. In these circumstances, as Nicholas Lemann puts it, there would be as little lifelong tenure on the basis of youthful promise as possible: "Successful people would have less serene careers than they have now, and this would give them more empathy for people whose lives don't go smoothly."[9]

Place and mobility. The Brexit vote was, among other things, a vote for localism on an international scale. In the UK context it was a vote against London as well as Brussels, as Boris Johnson acknowl-edged in a speech in Manchester on his second day as prime minister.

But most rich countries are ambivalent about community. We want security, familiarity, and belonging, all the warm things we associate with settled communities, but we also want freedom, individual autonomy, ambition, and social mobility, which weaken settled communities by encouraging people to leave them—particularly the most able. Just as America has divided between red states and blue states, France between France périphérique and France d'en haut,[10] and Germany between west and east, so the United Kingdom is increasingly divided between London (plus the other metropolitan centers and university towns), and the rest. In some places this is not just a wealth divide but a cultural worldview divide.

The double goal is clear enough: to invest sufficiently in the expensive metropolitan centers to allow poorer people to stay put with a reasonable quality of life and, at the same time, to prevent people from the smaller towns and suburbs feeling like resentful second-class citizens.

Adair Turner argues that for even the low-paid to enjoy a reasonable standard of life in the metropolitan centers, the provision of good public services—health, education, public transport, public spaces—and, as important, affordable housing is a higher priority than Universal Basic Income (UBI).

UBI potentially disconnects people from work, which for many is an important source of meaning and companionship. Indeed, happiness researchers, like the British economist Richard Layard, argue that the state guarantee of a minimum-wage job for anyone unemployed for more than six months—even accompanied with the stick of having benefits withdrawn for those who reject the offer—is a better safety net for generating well-being. That is especially true for jobs that have an obviously beneficial purpose, such as insulating homes or installing solar panels.

A less ugly built environment has belatedly become a political issue in some countries, partly in response to the brutalist postwar developments in both Europe and America, which usually ran completely counter to mainstream aesthetic feelings. Nicholas Boys Smith, who is co-chair of the UK government's Building Better, Building Beautiful Commission, says that there are still too many shocking examples of ugly town planning from recent years in the United Kingdom "such as the malign Pathfinder Programme which tried to revive northern cities by knocking down Victorian homes, or the investment in out of town shopping centers which promptly drained the life out of the town center.

"Many of the proudest structures in England's towns and cities are 19th century civic buildings, such as Rochdale Town Hall or St George's Hall in Liverpool. Somehow, somewhere, we have lost not just the ability but even the desire to create public buildings of beauty and moral worth. We need to rediscover that confidence and ability."[11]

Boys Smith was struck by the evidence one architect gave to the Building Beautiful Commission earlier this year, who recounted how working on a hospital project he was "told by the contractor to put in a more expensive material that looked cheaper because there was real sensitivity about anything in the NHS looking expensive."

Hospitals should be our new cathedrals. Noble buildings, built for a noble cause. In many towns they are the biggest and most important buildings for miles around, and it is a great sadness that they so often look shoddy and disposable. I am lucky enough to live in Hampstead in north London, and as I write this I am looking out on the Royal Free Hospital, an ugly blot in one of the most architecturally precious corners of London.

And what about the smaller towns and suburbs and country areas that so often feel unloved and left behind by the center? This happens in all rich countries but is a particular problem in England because so many young people move away to residential universities, plus that London factor.

The obvious answers—but far easier said than done—include better post-school education options that allow people to stay at home, or at least in their home town; a more even spread of decent jobs, or the transport infrastructure to commute to them in a reasonable time; and town centers and local civic life, and media, that help instill some local pride. Many places have these things already, but too many don't and can enter a spiral of decline that is hard to break. Despite the sense of living in the shadow of the metropolis people in towns and villages often have a higher quality of life and stronger sense of community. Leveling up the towns and giving people good reasons to stay could thus contribute to national well-being. Around 70 percent of the German population live in towns of less than 100,000. It contributes to a sense of a more settled society than in the United Kingdom.

Mobility is not, of course, a vice. And it is very different today than in the nineteenth century. Then you seldom saw or spoke to your family again. Now that you can phone, email, skype, WhatsApp, and maybe return home from London at the weekend, moving doesn't seem as daunting. And a successful, London-based journalist I know who comes from Bury, near Manchester, likes to challenge people who talk too passionately about communitarian values by asking: "So, do you think I should have stayed in Bury, then?"

The technology of connection that makes it easier for leavers to stay in touch should also make it easier for stayers to feel they do not need to leave to avoid feeling marginalized. The Internet has opened up many new possibilities for small-town and rural businesses to transcend distance and to build local networks in more remote places so long as broadband connections are good enough.

A recent *New Yorker* report titled "The one traffic-light town with some of the fastest internet in the US" underscored this point. Keith Gabbard, the man behind the fast internet in the town of McKee, is quoted thus: "I don't think having broadband is necessarily going to make a 500-job factory move in, but it certainly can make people's lives better and keep them from having to drive 100 miles a day, back and forth, to work . . . It can help education, it can help entertainment, it can help the economy, it can help health care. And I even think that people's mind-set can be improved."[12]

In recent decades we have subsidized (via higher education and higher incomes in metropolitan centers) and applauded leavers;

perhaps it's time we subsidized and applauded stayers. Of course, not everything can stay the same, some communities are not sustainable, and the story moves on. But many people in rich countries feel that change has been happening too fast in recent decades, from national politics to their local neighborhoods.

Is it too much to ask that if a popular local pub that acts as a focus for community is having to close—like one I went to recently in Swindon—that it receives support from some national community fund or receives a refund from the high duties it has to charge or a lower business rate? After all, in the 1990s, huge sums were channeled from middle- and lower-income people via the lottery into creating new museums, many of which subsequently closed.

The only way for many pubs to survive is to diversify, but in practice that means being reinvented for prosperous middle-class young people. Local newspapers, which are a focus for local identity, are often dying too. They are sometimes replaced by lively local bloggers who help to keep local politicians accountable, but in many places they are replaced by nothing.

Upgrading care. The slow upward revaluation of Heart jobs will happen as politics redirects even more resources to health, social care, and education. Just as hospitals are often the most imposing buildings for miles around, health care is a central industry in many parts of the country. It is decentralized by its nature, unlike global banks or factories. And people need hospitals in all regions. Health care employs lots of people of all classes and ability levels and generates local economic development. And it is a fiscal equalizer, redistributing income from the metropolitan centers with their cognitive elites to the rest of the country.

But caring more about caring is not only about spending more money—although in the United Kingdom adult care and adult care workers' pay certainly needs investment.

Returning to nursing some of its autonomy and giving care itself a more central role in our technocratic health systems is part of the answer to the crisis of nurse recruitment. Technology is not itself the problem; indeed, when used properly, it releases doctors and nurses to listen to the whole patient, not just a bundle of symptoms.

The training for nurses and indeed all medical professionals needs to change. There needs to be more focus on emotional and human interactions with patients, alongside the traditional practical and cognitive skills needed for qualifications. If health systems are to deliver patient-centered care and equip staff to manage complex patient and family interactions, it requires a rethink of the balance of the curriculum and how grades and outcomes are judged.

In a society that runs on quantifying everything of value, care has suffered both in the hospital and the home because it has not been adequately measured. It is high time that unpaid labor in the home was included in GDP figures (or parallel GDP figures). It is estimated that it would add about £500 billion ($650 billion) a year in the United Kingdom. It would not make us any richer, but it would give a more accurate account of what is happening in everyday life and help people to value more the productive work going on in the private realm.

One cause of the pressure on adult care services and the NHS is weaker family ties and fewer intact couples to look after each other or elderly parents. Helping more families to stay together and rewarding partnership and care in the home is just common sense, especially as technology enables more frail, elderly people to be cared for at home. Yet state support for young families is very sketchy in the United Kingdom and the United States. (And marriage as an institution is dramatically weaker in lower-income households in both countries: in the United Kingdom, 90 percent of parents with young children in the top income quintile are married compared with just 25 percent in the lowest quintile.)

Why not make marriage counseling free? Even if it only helped 5 percent of couples stay together it would be a big win for the state and society. More important, why not ease the economic pressure on couples by making it easier for one parent to stay at home when children are very young? If going to work is supported with subsidized child care, why not support staying at home too? Is that not also useful work? Allowing the stay at home parent to transfer their full tax allowance to the worker, thus recognizing *partnership* in the tax system, is considered normal in much of continental Europe and even in the United States (for married couples).

Indeed, the idea of a transferable tax allowance for stay-at-home caregivers *of all kinds*, not just caregivers of young children, would further support partnerships and encourage more care to remain in the home. The Carer's Allowance in the United Kingdom for looking after an old or disabled person (who may or may not be a relative) is just £66 ($86) a week for at least thirty-five hours' care. That works out at less than £2 ($2.60) an hour, yet it costs many hundreds of pounds to look after someone for one night in a hospital.

Rebooting domesticity for an age of gender equality might also mean changing planning rules to encourage the return of "cottage industry," small enterprises run from the home that make it easier to combine care and work. Writers, childminders, therapists, beauticians, and many others have traditionally worked from home, and decent broadband connections opens the possibility to many more occupations. Many people experienced the potential of more home working during the Covid-19 crisis and became more adept at managing the technology.

The public care economy is more than 85 percent female. Men are doing more domestic labor than in the past, and nearly two-thirds of all fathers are now classified as "involved fathers," but there has been little gender de-segregation of nursing, adult social care, or primary school teaching.[13] Indeed, as more women have moved into medical roles, hospitals are becoming more not less female. Some *positive discrimination* toward young men in some of these jobs could help create a critical mass of male employment where it remains largely absent. (And maybe we need some new words to think about a typical caregiver. The word "nurse" inevitably conjures up the image of a woman.)

A limited degree of automation in adult care might help increase pay and status in the care home and thus attract more men. Aging Japan is experimenting with robots that can perform social care functions such as lifting an elderly person into a bath. One of the key social care roles of the future may be a male technician in charge of twenty robots.

Volunteering cannot fully make up for weaker families, but it has as yet unrealized potential when combined with the convening power of the Internet. The appetite for volunteering was underlined in many countries during the Covid-19 crisis. Why not build on that experience and establish a version of the United Kingdom's territorial army for health and adult care systems, a reserve army of people with some basic training who can step in to help during a crisis. This could even be extended to some noncrisis situations to help out in vital social services so long as the volunteer roles do not undermine proper paid employment. Corporate social responsibility programs could also usefully focus more on the local and on old people by encouraging staff to simply visit old people, read to them, shop for them, and take them out on trips.

Teaching, especially at primary level, is at least as much a Heart as a Head job. I am struck by how many teachers I know talk about loving their kids (and sometimes finding them intolerable too). A friend who has become a primary school teacher in middle age says this: "The best part of primary teaching is just building real relationships with the children. To do the job properly you have to love them; you have to become emotionally involved."

The latest research on good teaching confirms this. Andreas Schleicher, head of the OECD's influential PISA program of cross-country educational assessment, says that the relationship between pupil and teacher is more important than curriculum content. The child learns anything, *everything*, better when they think the teacher knows and cares about them—one of those things our grandmothers could have told us for nothing, and something our schools should try to reflect!

Care, like craft, is what many people do in their spare time, both as duty and pleasure. It can be a chore doing the shopping for Granny or taking a child to a playground, but most people know that the time spent with dependent family members is part of the real, valuable stuff of life. If I was bored or distracted or talking on my mobile phone when taking one of my children to the park, as I often was, that was my failing, my inability to be fully in the moment. Parents then often end up lamenting how quickly children grow up. Where does all the time go?

Caring and craft are linked to one another in that both depend on paying attention—deeply—to what is there in front of you, to the needs of the moment. In the case of craft, it is paying attention to the needs of the material, and in care, to the needs of the person. The feeling that a Head-dominated world does not pay sufficient attention to many of the things that really matter is one reason for the growing interest in mindfulness and meditation. Paying attention is the essence of mindfulness and meditation: trying to see what is really of value; living slow rather than fast. The number of yoga teachers in the United States has been growing at more than 10 percent a year for many years.

Celebrating craft. One of the things that might prevent open, semi-meritocratic societies degenerating into genetic caste societies is that with the reduction of economic insecurity for most people, more highly able people will choose to do more rewarding things than work as a high-flying lawyer or banker. There will increasingly be no single hierarchy of wealth and status. Perhaps we are beginning to see this in privileged families where at least one of the children becomes a chef or takes up an artisanal calling of some kind.

Jobs that have a high level of satisfaction but not necessarily a high level of pay, such as working as a National Trust park ranger, are already highly sought after. And in the countryside, as conventional farming is increasingly replaced by organic farming, with its more labor-intensive concern for nature and animal welfare, new agricultural Heart jobs will be created.

Public policy, so far as possible, should have a bias toward work that produces high job satisfaction. That often means working in a team solving problems together against a common adversary.

Many of the craft jobs that disappeared over the course of the twentieth century, such as stonemason or thatcher, are now making a comeback. Beautiful old buildings require a skilled workforce to keep them standing. The art of weaving was showcased for the first time at the Frieze London art show in 2019. Over the coming century more people are likely to find satisfying jobs as artists, gardeners, surfboard designers, cooks, small organic farmers, and beekeepers than as software developers or AI technicians.[14]

The UK organic food market is now said to stand at £2.5 billion ($3.25 billion) a year. Craft breweries are growing fast; there are now 5,000 in the United States, 2,000 in the United Kingdom, and a comparable growth in much of Europe. Today there are more than three hundred independent British cheese makers, up from just sixty-two in the mid-1970s.[15] (There is also some evidence that people are now cooking from scratch more often, and sales of raw ingredients are rising.)[16]

As noted in Chapter One, when people retire, they usually take up something embodied and rooted, a sporting or musical or "making" hobby of some kind. And with retirements stretching longer, the young-old and their Hand-Heart concerns will loom ever larger in our culture.

Also, assuming we take at least some of the benefits of the next stage of automation in the form of increased leisure, everyone will have more time to develop sporting, musical, and craft skills, which is why it is so important that the arts and music are taught as rigorously as possible to as many children as possible in school.

And why not require everyone in school by the age of eighteen to learn at least one manual-technical skill to a basic level, from carpentry to coding? And there is a good case for teaching these skills away from school at special youth skill centers, which would also provide an opportunity for social and ethnic mixing. A mini-version of national service.

Education for life. It sometimes feels that we are more schooled but less educated than ever before, as the writer Joanna Williams puts it. And it is absurd that so much higher education is focused on those aged eighteen to twenty-two. The conveyor belt that has been sending millions of young people into three or four years of higher education at the age of eighteen or nineteen should be slowed down. Many of them have acquired useful life experience and grown into young adults away from home for an extended period for the first time. Many have also acquired useful professional skills or pursued intellectual interests for the sheer joy of it. But far too many have learned little of value, and what they have learned they have quickly forgotten, their degree acting primarily as a signal to a future employer that they have the right personal characteristics to enter the bloated cognitive class.

Many of them would do better to follow the advice a friend of mine gave to his nephew who was wondering whether to continue a social science degree, having failed his second-year exams: "Rather than plowing on with something you are either not very good at or not very interested in, and acquiring at least £50,000 ($65,000) of debt, you would do far better to borrow £15,000 ($19,000) to spend on a six-month coding course that guarantees a reasonably well-paid job in a tech company. If in five or ten years' time you get a hunger to go deeper into computer science or just want to understand Byzantium, you will get far more out of it then."

The American venture capitalist Peter Thiel has been offering money to would-be entrepreneurs to leave university and focus on Web-based start-ups instead, and some British private schools are encouraging pupils to take vocational qualification in business, hospitality, and so on with a view to going straight into jobs. Northeastern University in Boston has pioneered a hybrid form of learning somewhere between an apprenticeship and a conventional degree, with students signing up for three six-month internships as part of their degree course.[17]

In Israel, young people tend to go to university later because of national service when they are more mature and often get more out of it. One way to encourage people to go to university later would be to charge older students lower tuition fees.

Part of my critique of the expansion of higher education in Chapter Four was that it was driven by a cultural bias toward academic forms of knowledge that are often economically dysfunctional, when what business want is shorter, more practical courses. This is going to become even more the case as AI eats into cognitive occupations. "Colleges are continuing to generate 20th century professionals . . . to undertake tasks for which machines are now better suited," as Richard and Daniel Susskind put it.

But, looking to the future of the university, and of education at all levels, we need more hard thinking about education for life and lifelong learning. This has become a cliché. We talk endlessly about lifelong learning but do very little about it; indeed, in the United Kingdom in recent years, we have been going backward, thanks to the current financial incentives, with fewer mature students or people returning part-time to college to re-skill.

Rather than the life-cycle model of the past couple of hundred years, with a fixed period of education and a fixed period of work, we need a "rotation model" in which work and education are rotated over the course of a career. But, as Andy Haldane of the Bank of England points out, existing universities in most countries are not designed for this, and the future university will need to be a very different kind of creature.

"It may need to cater for multiple entry points along the age distribution, rather than focussing on the young," Haldane notes. "And it may need to cater for multiple entry points along the skills spectrum, rather than focussing on the cognitive. Those skills will be social and technical every bit as much as cognitive, with Head, Hand and Heart sharing equal billing. It would, in short, need to be plural rather than singular—a 'multiversity,' rather than a university."[18]

Massive open online courses—so called MOOCs—have not taken off as some people expected outside niche areas; it seems that people like human contact when learning. But some combination of online and classroom is likely to prove increasingly popular, and one of the home-working success stories of the Covid-19 lockdown was higher education, with many courses moving online.

And the spirit of the old autodidact, who just had an urge to read up on everything about, say, botany, has not disappeared even in a more educated society. There will always be a substantial minority with a thirst for knowledge for its own sake, as can be seen from the reach of intellectual popularizers like Brian Cox and Martin Rees in the United Kingdom, Steven Pinker and Jared Diamond in the United States, and Yuval Noah Harari across Europe and North America.

Also coming back into its own is the old generalist model of the nineteenth-century educated person. This is now called "cross-domain knowledge" and often combines both scientific and artistic forms of thinking, as has always been the case with architecture. Subjects like digital literacy, entrepreneurship, and emotional intelligence will become less "soft" and more relevant.

As this implies, in a world where rapid productivity growth can be driven by a very small number of people who program the robots and occupy the top layer of the professions, the rest of us will need to nurture aptitudes for caring, craft, and creativity, both for the jobs of the future and to fill the countless hours we are no longer at work. The idea of the individual learning account or "opportunity grant"— in which the state invests a fixed sum in every individual that can be drawn down for any kind of post-compulsory education—is an old idea that deserves revisiting.

The focus on raising the academic floor for all young people in secondary education has in some places been at the cost of breadth of education. But most forms of creativity can be taught rigorously, just like math and biology can be.

The same can apply to craft skills. In addition to the youth skill centers proposed above, those sixteen-year-olds not in the academic stream at school should be encouraged to undertake a part-time skill pupilage with a local "master" (car mechanic, baker, social care manager, hairdresser, local authority clerical officer, and so on). The master would get some inexperienced free labor and in return for that, and a tax allowance from the government, would supervise good work habits and the foundations of a useful skill. Where the system works well, the pupil could start work proper from the day they leave school.

And what about education for life and citizenship? Our conversations about education, including in this book, are far too economy oriented; the intense discussions about education in the nineteenth century were hardly ever about the economy despite our societies being much poorer then.

There is, in particular, a largely missing conversation about educating people for democracy and for mental and physical well-being. The American educationalist E. D. Hirsch says a democratic republic can't exist without an educated citizenry who are equipped to distinguish fact from fiction, to respect other people's arguments, and to understand the complexity of some of the challenges we face. Studying history, for example, should not just be about the exam result you get. Indeed, it is not a disaster if someone gets a D in history so long as they leave school knowing more about their country's history than they did when they started.

Recalibrating the balance between Head, Hand, and Heart is partly about reimagining what we mean by skill and valuing the skills associated with Hand and Heart as well as cognitive ability and manipulating data. This is starting to happen in some corners of education such as the innovative School21 in London's East End, founded by Peter Hyman, Oli de Botton, and Ed Fidoe. And to end this section, here is an appealing Head, Hand, and Heart list from Iain McGilchrist of what he would like children to learn in school on top of the academic foundations: "All children should learn practical embodied skills in the crafts and arts, working not just with machines and ideas, but with actual materials, such as wood, metal and fabric, to make things that are both useful and beautiful. All children should be taught mindfulness and some form of spiritual exercise. They should learn some sort of practical life-skills, such as how to recognise cognitive distortions in oneself and others, and how to mediate in disputes. These are practical things that can easily be taught, and transform lives."

To Boldly Go

I have scarcely mentioned religion in this book. I am not a religious man, but in the course of writing it I have become more sympathetic to aspects of the religious worldview. And the notion of spiritual revival certainly flickers around the edge of the Head-Hand-Heart readjustment.

The Head world is generally a secular one, with little feel for the mysteries of life, which is why so many of us today seek a substitute for it in everything from yoga and meditation to the green movement. Yet it is striking what a disappointing failure humanism has been. It has been an effective critic of religion but has provided no convincing alternative set of ideas on how to live well.

John Maynard Keynes, writing about a world in which economic necessity has been largely overcome in his essay "Economic Possibilities for Our Grandchildren," sees a return to religious principles. "I see us free, therefore, to return to some of the most sure and certain principles of religion and traditional virtue . . . We shall once more value ends above means and prefer the good to the useful. We shall honour those who can teach us how to pluck the hour and the day virtuously and well, the delightful people who are capable of taking direct enjoyment in things, the lilies of the field who toil not, neither do they spin."[19]

I recently visited St Edmundsbury Cathedral in Bury St Edmunds, where the tour guide told us about the carved angels looking down, wings spread, upholding the roof. Apparently, the backs of the angels are carved in just as much intricate detail as the front even though no one can ever see the backs (without scaffolding).

The medieval craftsmen were doing their work for God. In a self-centered age it is hard not to be impressed. But God can be stripped out of that process: in today's language a craftsman could be working "to be the best that he can be."

Many secular people are suspicious of the religious impulse for its dogmatism. Surely in our more divided and tribal age the last thing we need is a more religious sensibility. How do we conduct the more public debates we need to have about ultimate values if the religious people already know the answer?

But it has also become a truism to argue that even liberal secularists have never fully escaped religious ways of thinking.[20] Religion is born of the need to face death, and we secular people face death too. Moreover, the still revolutionary idea of the moral equality of all people regardless of talent or wealth—an idea bequeathed by Christianity—is the core inspiration behind the wish to rebalance human value away from Head towards Hand and Heart.

We will need wisdom along the way, and wisdom is at least as much a religious as secular idea. It is due for a comeback. The American author Jonathan Rauch argues in his book *The Happiness Curve: Why Life Gets Better After 50* that while wisdom may be struggling in our civic and political culture, it is coming into its own in medicine, psychology, and neuroscience.

Rauch interviewed one of the pioneers in wisdom research, the US-based Indian psychiatrist Dilip Jeste, who argues that it is a distinct and measurable human quality that has remained surprisingly constant across regions and civilizations. "Again and again, modern scholarly definitions mention certain traits: compassion and prosocial attitudes that reflect concern for the common good; pragmatic knowledge of life; the use of one's pragmatic knowledge to resolve personal and social problems; an ability to cope with ambiguity and uncertainty and to see multiple points of view; emotional stability and mastery of one's feelings; a capacity for reflection and for dispassionate self-understanding," Rauch writes.[21]

"You might think that people with the fastest mental processors would bring more cognitive power to bear on reflection and therefore would be wiser; but voluminous research finds that raw intelligence and wisdom simply do not map to one another, at least not reliably. In fact, on some dimensions, such as wise reasoning about intergroup conflicts, cognitive ability and wisdom, seem to be negatively related."

Wisdom expresses itself, often, in counterpoint to ideology. Whereas ideology pushes us toward certainty, purity, and adversarialism, wisdom prizes humility, multiplicity, and compromise. And it is a package: "On *Star Trek* . . . a recurrent theme is that the most blazingly intelligent character, the Vulcan Spock, lacks the instinctive empathy of Dr. McCoy and the pragmatic decisiveness of Captain Kirk. None of the three alone is wise. Wisdom arises from the (sometimes tense) interaction of the triumvirate."[22]

Head, Hand, and Heart brought into harmony on the Starship *Enterprise*.

Endnotes

Chapter One: Peak Head

1 James Flynn, *Are We Getting Smarter?: Rising* IQ *in the Twenty-First Century* (New York: Cambridge University Press, 2012).
2 "Income Inequality," OECD, https://data.oecd.org/chart/5NKF.
3 Nikou Asgari, "One in Five UK Baby Boomers are Millionaires," *Financial Times*, January 8, 2019, https://www.google.com/amp/s/amp.ft.com /content/c69b49de-1368-11e9-a581-4ff78404524e.
4 David Lucas's website, www.paradoxographia.com.
5 Randall Collins, Credential Inflation and the Future of Universities," *Italian Journal of Sociology of Education*, 2, 2011.
6 Damian Hinds, secretary of state for education, technical education speech, December 6, 2018.
7 Speech to the UK Social Mobility Commission, March 30, 2017.
8 Michael Lind, *The New Class War: Saving Democracy from the Managerial Elite* (New York: Portfolio/Penguin, 2020), 16.
9 Sir Peter Lampl, foreword to Michael Donnelly and Sol Gamsu, *Home and Away: Social, Ethnic, and Spatial Inequalities in Student Mobility*, Sutton Trust/University of Bath (February 2018), 2, 7, http://dro.dur.ac.uk /27367/1/27367.pdf?DDD34+drmg83.
10 Press release from Harvard Business School Press for Joan C. Williams, *White Working Class: Overcoming Class Cluelessness in America* (2019).
11 Michael Lind, *The New Class War: Saving Democracy from the Managerial Elite* (New York: Portfolio/Penguin, 2020), 16.
12 Abhijit V. Banerjee and Esther Duflo, *Good Economics for Hard Times: Better Answers to Our Biggest Questions* (Penguin, 2019).
13 Nicholas Carr, *The Shallows: What the Internet Is Doing to Our Brains* (New York: W. W. Norton, 2010).

14 Paul Krugman, "White Collar Workers Turn Blue," *New York Times Magazine*, September 29, 1996, https://web.mit.edu/krugman/www/BACKWRD2.html.

15 *Economist*, June 22, 2019, 65.

16 "Woman and Work: Do Attitudes Reflect Policy Shifts?," British Social Attitudes 36, https://www.bsa.natcen.ac.uk/media/39297/4_bsa36_women-and-work.pdf.

Chapter Two: The Rise of the Cognitive Class

1 Kirby Swales, "Understanding the Leave Vote," NatCen, December 2016, http://natcen.ac.uk/our-research/research/understanding-the-leave-vote/.

2 OECD Family Database, http://www.oecd.org/social/family/database.htm.

3 "Populations Past—Atlas of Victorian and Edwardian Population," University of Cambridge, updated May 29, 2018, https://www.populationspast.org/about/.

4 David Brooks, "The Nuclear Family Was a Mistake," *Atlantic* (March 2020).

5 Guy Routh, *Occupations of the People of Great Britain 1801–1981* (London: Macmillan, 1987); French Occupational Census of 1911, *Monthly Review of the U.S. Bureau of Labor Statistics* 5, no.1 (July 1917); US Census Bureau, *Part II: Comparative Occupation Statistics, 1870–1030: A Comparable Series of Statistics Presenting a Distribution of the Nation's Labor Force, by Occupation, Sex, and Age*; "Employment by occupation—ILO modelled estimates," International Labor Organization, November 2018.

6 Geoffrey Millerson, *The Qualifying Associations: A Study in Professionalism* (London: Routledge & Keegan Paul, 1964).

7 Alison Wolf, *Does Education Matter?: Myths About Education and Economic Growth* (London: Penguin, 2002), 51.

8 Geoffrey Millerson, *The Qualifying Associations*.

9 Ibid.

10 Michael Sanderson, "Education and the Economy, 1870–1939," *ReFRESH* 17 (Autumn 1993).

11 Robert Anderson, *British Universities: Past and Present* (London: Bloomsbury, 2006).

12 Matthew Crawford, *The Case for Working with Your Hands: Or Why Office Work Is Bad for Us and Fixing Things Feels Good* (London: Penguin, 2009), 161–62.

13 David F. Labaree, *A Perfect Mess: The Unlikely Ascendancy of American Higher Education* (Chicago: University of Chicago Press, 2017), 25.

14 Nicholas Lemann, *The Big Test: The Secret History of the American Meritocracy* (New York: Farrar, Straus and Giroux, 1999), 347.

15 Michael Sanderson, "Education and the Economy."

16 Ibid.

17 Frederick Jackson Turner, *The Significance of the Frontier in American History* (American Historical Association, 1893).

18 Charles Murray on Coming Apart, Uncommon Knowledge, interview with Peter Robinson (Hoover Institution), YouTube, April 10, 2012, https://www.youtube.com/watch?v=6q3zy4NRzz4.

Chapter Three: Cognitive Ability and the Meritocracy Puzzle

1 Polly Mackenzie, "The Myth of Meritocracy," *UnHerd*, April 17, 2019, https://unherd.com/2019/04/the-myth-of-meritocracy/.

2 Linda S. Gottfredson, "Mainstream Science on Intelligence: An Editorial with 52 Signatories, History, and Bibliography," *Intelligence* 24, no. 1 (1997), 13.

3 Carol Dweck, *Mindset: The New Psychology of Success* (New York: Ballantine, 2007).

4 See for example, Robert Plomin and Sophie Von Stumm, "The New Genetics of Intelligence," *National Review of Genetics* 19, no. 3 (2018), 148–59.

5 Nicholas Lemann, *The Big Test: The Secret History of the American Meritocracy* (New York: Farrar, Straus and Giroux, 1999), 23.

6 Tomas Chamorro-Premuzic, "Ace the Assessment," *Harvard Business Review* (July/August 2015).

7 Interview with Dr. Scott Barry Kaufman, Psychology Podcast, June 2015.

8 James Flynn: *Are We Getting Smarter?: Rising IQ in the Twenty-First Century* (Cambridge, UK: Cambridge University Press, 2012).

9 James Flynn, "Massive IQ Gains in 14 Nations: What IQ Tests Really Measure," *Psychological Bulletin* 101, no. 2 (1987), 171–91.

10 James Flynn, "The Mean IQ of Americans: Massive Gains 1932 to 1978," *Psychological Bulletin* 95, no. 1 (1984), 29–51.

11 Toby Young, "The Fall of the Meritocracy," Quadrant Online, September 7, 2015, https://quadrant.org.au/magazine/2015/09/fall-meritocracy/.

12 David Robson: *The Intelligence Trap: Why Smart People Make Dumb Mistakes* (New York: W. W. Norton, 2019).

13 Apenwarr blog, https://apenwarr.ca/log/?m=201407.

14 Quoted in Julia Ingram, "Cardinal Conversations Speaker Charles Murray Stirs Campus Debate," *Stanford Daily*, January 30, 2018.

15 Robert Plomin, *Blueprint: How DNA Makes Us Who We Are* (London: Allen Lane, 2018).

16 Niki Erlenmeyer-Kimling and Lissy Jarvik, "Genetics and Intelligence: A Review," *Science* 142, no. 3590 (1963), 1477–78.

17 Daniel W. Belsky, Benjamin W. Domingue, Robbee Wedow et al., "Genetic Analysis of Social-Class Mobility in Five Longitudinal Studies," *PNAS* (*Proceedings of the National Academy of Sciences of the United States*) 115, no. 31 (2018), 7275–84, https://www.pnas.org/content/115/31/E7275.

18 James Bloodworth, *The Myth of Meritocracy* (London: Biteback, 2016), 102.

19 Erzsébet Bukodi and John H. Goldthorpe, *Social Mobility and Education in Britain: Research, Politics and Policy* (Cambridge, UK: Cambridge University Press, 2018).

20 Alice Sullivan, "The Path from Social Origins to Top Jobs: Social Reproduction via Education," *British Journal of Sociology* 69, no. 3 (2018), 782–84.

21 Jo Blanden, Paul Gregg, and Stephen Machin, *Intergenerational Mobility in Europe and North America: A Report Supported by the Sutton Trust*, Centre for Economic Performance, London School of Economics/Sutton Trust (2005).

22 Peter Saunders, *Social Mobility Myths* (London: Civitas, 2010), 69.

23 Michael Young, *The Rise of the Meritocracy, 1870–2033* (London: Thames & Hudson, 1958).

24 Charles Murray, "The Bell Curve Explained: Part 1, the Emergence of a Cognitive Elite,", American Enterprise Institute, May 12, 2017, https://www.aei.org/society-and-culture/the-bell-curve-explained-part-1-the-emergence-of-a-cognitive-elite/.

25 For summary, see Toby Young, "The Fall of the Meritocracy," Quadrant Online, September 7, 2015, https://quadrant.org.au/magazine/2015/09/fall-meritocracy/.

26 "The Rise and Rise of the Cognitive Elite: Brains Bring Ever Larger Rewards," *Economist*, January 22, 2011.

27 "Modern Women Marrying Men of the Same or Lower Social Class," IPPR May 4, 2012, https://www.ippr.org/news-and-media/press-releases/modern-women-marrying-men-of-the-same-or-lower-social-class.

28 David Willets, *The Pinch: How the Baby Boomers Took Their Children's Future—and Why They Should Give it Back* (London: Atlantic, 2011).

29 Charles Murray, *Coming Apart: The State of White America, 1960–2010* (New York: Crown Forum, 2012), 59.

30 Richard Reeves, *Dream Hoarders: How the American Upper Middle Class Is Leaving Everyone Else in the Dust, Why That Is a Problem, and What to Do About It* (Washington, DC: Brookings Institution, 2017).

31 Daniel Markovits, *The Meritocracy Trap: How America's Foundational Myth Feeds Inequality, Dismantles the Middle Class, and Devours the Elite* (London: Allen Lane, 2019).

32 James Bloodworth, *The Myth of Meritocracy*, 67.

33 Richard Breen, *Social Mobility in Europe* (Oxford, UK: Oxford University Press, 2004).

34 Andrew Hacker, "The White Plight," *The New York Review of Books*, 10 May 2012.

35 David Robson, *The Intelligence Trap*.

36 Dalton Conley and Jason Fletcher, *The Genome Factor: What the Social Genomics Revolution Reveals About Ourselves, Our History, and the Future* (Princeton, NJ: Princeton University Press, 2017).

37 Kwame Anthony Appiah, "The Myth of Meritocracy: Who Really Gets What They Deserve?," *Guardian*, October 19, 2018, https://www.theguardian.com/news/2018/oct/19/the-myth-of-meritocracy-who-really-gets-what-they-deserve.

38 Michael Young, *The Rise of the Meritocracy*, 135–36.

39 Kwame Anthony Appiah, *The Lies That Bind: Rethinking Identity* (London: Profile Books, 2018), 178.

Chapter Four: The Era of Educational Selection

1 Mark Bovens and Anchrit Willie, *Diploma Democracy: The Rise of Political Meritocracy* (Oxford, UK: Oxford University Press, 2017), 21.

2 Terry Wrigley, "The Rise and Fall of the GCSE: A Class History," History Workshop Online, December 1, 2012.

3 Mike Hicks, "The Recruitment and Selection of Young Managers by British Business, 1930–2000," St. Johns College, Oxford, D.Phil. 2004, 109.

4 US Department of Education, https://nces.ed.gov/programs/digest/d19/tables/dt19_103.20.asp?current=yes.

5 David Willets, "Abolishing Private Schools Is Not the Education Fight We Need," *Financial Times*, September 27, 2019, https://www.ft.com/content/3f77e02c-e101-11e9-b8e0-026e07cbe5b4.

6 David Soskice and Torben Iversen, *Democracy and Prosperity* (Princeton, NJ: Princeton University Press, 2019).

7 Nicola Woolcock, "Vocational Courses Get a Makeover," *Times*, July 8, 2019.

8 Michael Shattock, *Making Policy in British Higher Education* (London: Open University Press/McGraw-Hill Education, 2012).

9 Robbins Report (*Higher Education: Report of the Committee appointed by the Prime Minister under the Chairmanship of Lord Robbins*), Committee on Higher Education, October 1963, paragraph 26, http://www .educationengland.org.uk/documents/robbins/robbins1963.html.

10 John Pratt, *The Polytechnic Experiment, 1965–1992* (London: Open University Press, 1997).

11 Chris Belfield, Christine Farquharson, and Luke Sibieta, *2018 Annual Report on Education Spending in England* (IFS, September 2018), 10.

12 Based on data from Robert C. Feenstra, Robert Inklaar, and Marcel P, Timmer, "The Next Generation of the Penn World Table," *American Economic Review* 105, no. 10 (2015), 3150–82.

13 "Tuition Fees Changes 'to Save Students £15,700,' " BBC News, October 3, 2017.

14 Post-18 Education Review, Augar Review, May 2019.

15 Ibid.

16 Alison Wolf, "We Must End 'the One Degree and You're Out' Education System," *Financial Times*, June 1, 2019.

17 Will Tanner and James O'Shaughnessy, *The Politics of Belonging: What Is Driving the Sea Change in Our Politics and Why We Must Embrace Conservatism for the Common Good*, Onward, https://www.ukonward .com/wp-content/uploads/2019/10/Politics-of-Belonging-FINAL.pdf.

18 Paul Lewis, "The Missing Middle: How to get more young people to level 3-5," paper delivered at Policy Exchange seminar, London, June 6, 2019.

19 Francis Green, Alan Felstead, Duncan Gallie et al., "What Has Been Happening to the Training of Workers in Britain?," LLAKES research paper 43, 2013, https://www.llakes.ac.uk/sites/default/files/43.%20Green%20 et%20al.pdf.

20 Paul Johnson, "My Son Taught Me a Lesson About University," *Times*, January 5, 2018.

21 "Many Recent Graduates Are Unconvinced That University Was Worth the Cost," YouGov, June 23, 2017.

22 Damian Hinds speech.

23 Richard Reeves, "Yes, Capitalism Is Broken. To Recover, Liberals Must Eat Humble Pie," *Guardian*, September 25, 2019, https://www.theguardian .com/commentisfree/2019/sep/25/broken-capitalism-liberals-economy -politics.

24 Daniel Markovits, *The Meritocracy Trap: How America's Foundational Myth Feeds Inequality, Dismantles the Middle Class,* and *Devours the Elite* (London: Allen Lane, 2019).

25 *Demos Quarterly*, Winter 2014–15.

26 Matthew Crawford, *The Case for Working with Your Hands: Or Why Office Work Is Bad for Us and Fixing Things Feels Good* (London: Penguin, 2010), 19.

27 Ibid., 20.

28 Laura Bridgestock, "How Much Does It Cost to Study in the US?," Top Universities, May 17, 2019.

29 Erin Duffin, "Community Colleges in the United States—Statistics and Facts," *Statista*, February 6, 2020, https://www.statista.com/topics/3468 /community-colleges-in-the-united-states/.

30 Ibid.

31 Nat Malkus, "The Evolution of Career and Technical Education, 1982–2013," American Enterprise Institute, May 1, 2019, https://www.aei.org/research -products/report/the-evolution-of-career-and-technical-education -1982-2013/

32 Claudia Goldin and Lawrence F. Katz, *The Race Between Education and Technology*, Harvard University paper, July 2007.

33 Nicholas Lemann, *The Big Test: The Secret History of the American Meritocracy* (New York: Farrar, Straus and Giroux, 1999), 351.

34 Apprenticeship Toolbox, https://www.apprenticeship-toolbox.eu/. Higher Education and Research in France, Facts and Figures, https://publication .enseignementsup-recherche.gouv.fr/eesr/10EN/EESR10EN_RESUME -higher_education_and_research_in_france_facts_and_figures_sum mary.php. Euroeducation.net.

35 John Lichfield, "French Universities Crisis: Low Fees and Selection Lotteries Create Headaches in Higher Education," *Independent*, September 25, 2015.

36 HochschulKompass, https://www.hochschulkompass.de/en/study-in -germany.html. Destatis Statistisches Bundesamt, https://www.destatis .de/DE/Home/_inhalt.html.

37 Most of the information about the German apprenticeship system comes from an interview with Dr. Michael Meister of the German Federal Ministry for Education and Research in Berlin, September 2019.

38 Alison Wolf, The Kings Lectures: Making Higher Education Policy, Lecture III: "Falling Productivity and Slowing Growth: Do Our Post-2008 Problems Have Anything to Do with Universities?," March 25, 2019, https://www.kcl.ac.uk/events/series/kings-lectures-2019.

39 See this analysis of the negative correlation between more graduates and increased productivity from the German economic research institute DIW: https://www.diw.de/sixcms/detail.php?id=diw_01.c.672546.de.

40 Peter Walker, "Rising Number of Postgraduates 'Could Become Barrier to Social Mobility,'" *Guardian*, February 7, 2013, https://www.theguardian.com/education/2013/feb/07/rising-number-postgraduates-social-mobility.

41 Bryan Caplan, *The Case Against Education: Why the Education System Is a Waste of Time and Money* (Princeton, NJ: Princeton University Press, 2018).

42 Richard Arum and Josipa Roksa, *Academically Adrift: Limited Learning on College Campuses* (Chicago: University of Chicago Press, 2011), 2.

43 Jean Twenge, W. Keith Campbell, and Ryne A. Sherman, "Declines in Vocabulary Among American Adults within Levels of Educational Attainment, 1974–2016," *Intelligence* 76 (September 2019).

44 HEPI Student Academic Experience Survey, 2019.

45 *Demos Quarterly*, Winter 2014/2015 issue.

46 Andrew Hindmoor, *What's Left Now?: The History and Future of Social Democracy* (Oxford, UK: Oxford University Press, 2018).

47 Fraser Nelson, "'I'll Eat You Alive'—Angela Rayner Interview," *Spectator*, January 6, 2018.

48 Paul Swinney and Maire Williams, "The Great British Brain Drain," Centre for Cities, November 21, 2016, https://www.centreforcities.org/reader/great-british-brain-drain/migration-students-graduates/.

49 Sarah Knapton, "British Industrial Regions Suffer 'Gene Drain' with the Healthier and More Academically Gifted Moving Away," *Daily Telegraph*, October 21, 2019, reporting on a paper in the journal *Nature Human Behaviour*, https://www.telegraph.co.uk/science/2019/10/21/british-industrial-regions-suffer-gene-drain-healthier-better/.

50 Andy Haldane speech at St James's Park, Newcastle, September 24, 2019, cited by David Smith, *Times*, December 4, 2019, 43.

51 Ken Mayhew and Craig Holmes, *Over Qualification and Skills Mismatch in the Graduate Labour Market*, CIPD Policy Report, August 2015, 3.

52 Sally Weale, "Levels of Distress and Illness Among Students in UK 'Alarmingly high,'" *Guardian*, March 5, 2019.

53 William Whyte, *Somewhere to Live: Why British Students Study Away from Home—and Why It Matters*, Higher Education Policy Institute Report 121, November 2019, 9.

Chapter Five: Rise of the Knowledge Worker

1 See, for example, Claudia Goldin and Robert A. Margo, "The Great Compression: The Wage Structure in the United States at Mid-Century," *Quarterly Journal of Economics* 107 (February 1992), 1–34.

2 Richard Baldwin, *The Globotics Upheaval: Globalization, Robotics, and the Future of Work* (New York: Oxford University Press, 2019), 33.

3 Ibid., 35.

4 David Autor, "Work of the Past, Work of the Future," *AEA Papers and Proceedings* 109 (2019), 1–32, https://economics.mit.edu/files/16724.

5 Ibid.

6 Ibid.

7 Ibid.

8 Sir Angus Deaton, "Why Is Democratic Capitalism Failing So Many? And What Should We Do About It?," Keynote Address, Tri-Nuffield Conference, May 16, 2019, https://www.nuffieldfoundation.org/news /why-is-democratic-capitalism-failing-so-many-sir-angus-deatons-key note-lecture-to-the-tri-nuffield-conference.

9 Gary S. Becker, "Investment in Human Capital: A Theoretical Analysis," *Journal of Political Economy* 70, no. 5 (1962).

10 John Burton, *Leading Good Care: The Task, Heart and Art of Managing Social Care* (London and Philadelphia: Jessica Kingsley, 2015), 13–14.

11 New Earnings Survey, Annual Survey of Hours and Earnings UK; Statistical Abstract of the United States 1976, Bureau of Labour Statistics May 2017 National Occupational Employment and Wage Estimates US.

12 David Autor, "Work of the Past, Work of the Future."

13 Federal Statistical Office of Germany; INSEE (National Institute of Statistics and Economic Studies).

14 Robert J Samuelson, "Where Did Our Raises Go? To Healthcare," *Washington Post*, September 2, 2018.

15 Guy Michaels, Ashwini Natraj, and John Van Reenen, "Has ICT Polarized Skill Demand? Evidence from Eleven Countries over Twenty-Five Years," *Review of Economics and Statistics* 96, no.1 (2014), 60–77.

16 "UK Labour Market: December 2018," Office for National Statistics, https://www.ons.gov.uk/releases/uklabourmarketstatisticsdec2018.

17 "Employment by Occupation—ILO Modelled Estimates," International Labour Organisation, November 2018.

18 "The Decline of Blue Collar Jobs, in Graphs," CEPR Blog, February 22, 2017.

19 "Trade Union Statistics, 2018," Department for Business, Energy & Industrial Strategy, https://www.gov.uk/government/statistics/trade-union -statistics-2018.

20 Resolution Foundation, Ibid., 6.

21 Stephen McKay and Ian Simpson, "Work," British Social Attitudes 33, Natcen, 2016, https://www.bsa.natcen.ac.uk/media/39061/bsa33_work .pdf.

22 Golo Henseke, Alan Felstead, Duncan Gallie, and Francis Green, *Skills Trends at Work in Britain: First Findings from the Skills and Employment Survey 2017,* Economic and Social Research Council, Cardiff University, and the Department for Education Mini-Report, 2018, Section 5.

23 Calculated by Mark Williams using New Earnings Survey, Annual Survey of Hours and Earnings UK; Statistical Abstract of the United States 1976, Bureau of Labour Statistics May 2017 National Occupational Employment and Wage Estimates US.

24 "Education at a Glance 2018," OECD Publishing, 2019, https://www .oecd-ilibrary.org/education/education-at-a-glance-2018_eag-2018-en.

25 Chris Belfield, Jack Britton, Franz Buscha et al., *The Impact of Undergraduate Degrees on Early-Career Earnings*, Institute for Fiscal Studies, 2018, 5.

26 Hugh Hayward, Emily Hunt, and Anthony Lord, *The Economic Value of Key Intermediate Qualifications: Estimating the Returns and Lifetime Productivity Gains to GCSEs, A Levels and Apprenticeships*, Department for Education, December 2014, https://assets.publishing.service.gov .uk/government/uploads/system/uploads/attachment_data/file/387160 /RR398A_-_Economic_Value_of_Key_Qualifications.pdf.

27 "Education at a Glance 2018."

28 Philip J. Cook and Robert H. Frank, *The Winner-Take-All Society: Why the Few at the Top Get So Much More Than the Rest of Us* (Virgin Books, 2010).

29 Robert Frank and Philip Cook, UK Employment Policy Institute report, January 1997.

30 Phillip Brown, Hugh Lauder, and David Ashton, *The Global Auction: The Broken Promises of Education, Jobs and Incomes* (New York: Oxford University Press, 2011).

31 Henseke et al., *Skills Trends at Work in Britain*, Section 3.
32 Peter Cheese interview with author
33 Ken Mayhew and Craig Holmes, *Over Qualification and Skills Mismatch in the Graduate Labour Market*, CIPD Policy Report, August 2015, 3.
34 Ibid.
35 Ibid.
36 *Quality with Compassion: The Future of Nursing Education; Report of the Willis Commission 2012*, https://www.macmillan.org.uk/documents/newsletter/willis-commission-report-macmail-dec2012.pdf.
37 Linda H. Aiken, Douglas M. Sloane, Luk Bryneel et al., "Nurse Staffing and Education and Hospital Mortality in Nine European Countries: A Retrospective Observational Study," *Lancet* 383, no. 9931 (May 24, 2014), 1824–30, https://www.ncbi.nlm.nih.gov/pmc/articles/PMC4035380/.
38 "Nursing to Become Graduate Entry," BBC News, November 12, 2009, http://news.bbc.co.uk/2/hi/health/8355388.stm.
39 UK Department for Education, Graduate Labour Market Statistics 2018, https://assets.publishing.service.gov.uk/government/uploads/system/uploads/attachment_data/file/797308/GLMS_2018_publication_main_text.pdf.
40 Ken Mayhew and Craig Holmes, *Alternative Pathways into the Labour Market*, CIPD Policy Report, October 2016, 11.
41 "All New Police Officers in England and Wales to Have Degrees," BBC News, December 15, 2016, https://www.bbc.com/news/uk-38319283.
42 https://www.college.police.uk/News/College-news/Documents/Proposals_for_Education_Qualification_Framework.pdf.
43 *Policing Education Qualifications Framework: Consultation*, College of Policing, February 2 to March 29, 2016, 8, https://www.college.police.uk/What-we-do/Learning/Policing-Education-Qualifications-Framework/Documents/PEQF_consultation_final_290116.pdf.
44 "Chronic Lack of Clear Career Routes for Non-Graduate Workers Stranding Many in Low Pay," Resolution Foundation, May 11, 2016, https://www.resolutionfoundation.org/press-releases/chronic-lack-of-clear-career-routes-for-non-graduate-workers-stranding-many-in-low-pay/.
45 Conor D'Arcy and David Finch, *Finding Your Routes: Non-Graduate Pathways in the UK's Labour Market*, Resolution Foundation Report, May 2016, 50, https://www.resolutionfoundation.org/app/uploads/2016/05/Non-grads-2.pdf.
46 Ibid.
47 Henseke et al., *Skills Trends at Work in Britain*.

48 Alison Wolf, *The XX Factor: How Working Women Are Creating A New Society* (London: Profile Books, 2013).

49 Jenny Chanfreau, Cheryl Lloyd, Christos Byron et al., *Predicting wellbeing*, NatCen, 2008, 10, http://natcen.ac.uk/media/205352/predictors-of-well being.pdf.

Chapter Six: The Diploma Democracy

1 See Jonathan Sumption, "Shifting the Foundations," *The Reith Lectures*, May 5, 2019, https://www.bbc.co.uk/programmes/m00060vc.

2 Ibid.

3 Mark Bovens and Anchrit Wille, *Diploma Democracy: The Rise of Political Meritocracy* (Oxford, UK: Oxford University Press, 2017), 1–2.

4 Jennifer E. Manning, *Membership of the 113th Congress: A Profile*, Congressional Research Service Report, November 24, 2014, 5.

5 Much of the data on the educational background of politicians and other matters in this chapter is taken from Mark Bovens and Anchrit Willie, *Diploma Democracy: The Rise of Political Meritocracy* (Oxford, UK: Oxford University Press, 2017).

6 Bovens and Wille, *Diploma Democracy*, 112.

7 Belgium, Denmark, France, Germany, Netherlands, and the UK.

8 Bill Bishop, *The Big Sort: Why the Clustering of Like-Minded America Is Tearing Us Apart* (New York: Houghton Mifflin Harcourt, 2008).

9 Martin Gilens, *Affluence and Influence: Economic Inequality and Political Power in America* (Princeton, NJ: Princeton University Press, 2012); David C. Kimball, Frank R. Baumgartner, Jeffrey M. Berry et al., "Who Cares About the Lobbying Agenda?," *Interest Groups & Advocacy* 1 (2012), 5–25.

10 Will Dahlgreen, "50 Years on, Capital Punishment Still Favoured," YouGov, August 13, 2014, https://yougov.co.uk/news/2014/08/13/capital-punishment-50-years-favoured/.

11 Anthony Wells, "Where the Public Stands on Immigration," YouGov, April 27, 2018, https://yougov.co.uk/topics/politics/articles-reports/2018/04/27/where-public-stands-immigration.

12 "What UK Thinks: EU," NatCen Social Research, https://whatukthinks.org/eu/.

13 YouGov poll, January 2011.

14 YouGov poll, October 2016,

15 YouGov poll, February 5–6, 2018.

16 2018 American Values Survey, Public Religion Research Institute.

17 John Baxter Oliphant, "Public Support for the Death Penalty Ticks Up," Pew Research Center, June 11, 2018.

18 CBS News–Refinery29 survey conducted by YouGov, available in "Young Women: What's on Their Minds as Midterm Elections Approach?" August 13, 2018, https://www.cbsnews.com/news /young-women-whats-on-their-minds-as-midterm-elections-approach/.

19 Daniel Cox, Rachel Lienesch, and Robert P. Jones, "Beyond Economics: Fears of Cultural Displacement Pushed the White Working Class to Trump," PRRI/Atlantic Report, September 5, 2017, https://www.prri.org /research/white-working-class-attitudes-economy-trade-immigration -election-donald-trump/.

20 2018 American Values Survey, PRRI.

21 Tony Blair, "British Prime Minister Tony Blair's Speech to the Polish Stock Exchange in Warsaw 6 October 2000," EUobserver.com.

22 Alison Wolf, *Have Middle Class Women Captured Family Policy?* (Society Central, 2015).

23 Geoff Dench, "Putting Social Contribution Back into Merit," in *The Rise and Rise of Meritocracy*, Geoff Dench, ed. (Oxford: Blackwell Publishing, 2006).

24 David Runciman, *How Democracy Ends* (London: Profile Books, 2018), 179.

25 John Gray, "The Dangers of a Higher Education," *A Point of View*, BBC Radio 4, February 23 and 25, 2018, https://www.bbc.co.uk/programmes /b09rzxh7.

26 Fareed Zakaria, *The Future of Freedom* (New York: W. W. Norton, 2003).

27 Alan S. Blinder, "Is Government Too Political?," *Foreign Affairs*, November/December 1997.

28 Peter Mair, *Ruling the Void: The Hollowing-Out of Western Democracy* (London: Verso, 2013), 99.

29 Will Hutton and Andrew Adonis, *Saving Britain: How We Must Change to Prosper in Europe* (London: Abacus, 2016).

30 Talk given at Cumberland Lodge, April 29, 2017.

31 Robert D. Putnam, *Bowling Alone: The Collapse and Revival of American Community* (New York: Simon & Schuster, 2000).

32 Bovens and Wille, *Diploma Democracy*.

33 US General Social Survey.

34 Paul Johnson, "My Son Taught Me a Lesson About University," *Times*, (London), January 5, 2018.

35 Cited in Bovens and Wille, *Diploma Democracy*, 143.

36 Matthew Smith, "Are MPs Elected to Exercise Their Own Judgement or Do Their Constituents' Bidding?," YouGov, August 13, 2019.

37 Cited in Bovens and Wille, *Diploma Democracy*.

38 Nicholas Carnes and Noam Lupu, "What Good Is a College Degree? Education and Leader Quality Reconsidered," *Journal of Politics* 78, no. 1 (2016), 35–49.

39 YouGov Profiles data, courtesy of YouGov.

40 Bovens and Wille, *Diploma Democracy*, 172.

41 Stephen Hawkins, Daniel Yudkin, Miriam Juan-Torres, and Tim Dixon, *Hidden Tribes: A Study of America's Polarized Landscape*, a study by the social cohesion think tank More in Common, New York, 2018, https://hiddentribes.us/pdf/hidden_tribes_report.pdf.

42 Charles Murray, *Coming Apart: The State of White America, 1960–2010* (New York: Random House, 2012).

43 Charles Murray, *Coming Apart* (New York: Crown Forum, 2012), p. 293.

44 George Orwell, *Politics and the English Language* (London: Penguin Modern Classics, 2013).

Chapter Seven: Whatever Happened to Hand?

1 The connection is made by Kwame Anthony Appiah in his book *The Lies That Bind: Rethinking Identity* (London: Profile Books, 2018), 168.

2 Michael Young and Peter Wilmott, *Family and Kinship in East London* (Abingdon, UK: Routledge, 2013), 14.

3 Mike Savage, Fiona Devine, Niall Cunningham et al., "A New Model of Social Class? Findings from the BBC's Great British Class Survey Experiment," *Sociology* 47, no. 2 (2013), 219–50.

4 Michael Hout, "Social and Economic Returns to College Education in the United States," *Annual Review of Sociology* 38 (2012), 379–400, https://www.annualreviews.org/doi/pdf/10.1146/annurev.soc.012809.102503.

5 Michael Hout, private correspondence.

6 Christoph Lakner and Branko Milanovic, "Global Income Distribution: From the Fall of the Berlin Wall to the Great Recession," *World Bank Economic Review* 30, no. 2 (2016), 203–232.

7 David Bailey, Caroline Chapain, and Alex de Ruyter, "Employment Outcomes and Plant Closures in a Post-Industrial City: An Analysis of the Labour Market Status of MG Rover Workers Three Years On," *Urban Studies* 49, no. 7 (2011), 1595–1612.

8   Tara Tiger Brown, "The Death of Shop Class and America's Skilled Work-
    force," *Forbes*, May 30, 2012, https://www.forbes.com/sites/tarabrown
    /2012/05/30/the-death-of-shop-class-and-americas-high-skilled-work
    force/#7ba6e3a0541f.

9   Conversation with the author.

10 See, for example, Office for National Statistics, *Construction Statistics,
    Great Britain: 2017.*

11 "Self-Employment Jobs by Industry," Office for National Statistics.

12 https://www.gov.uk/government/statistical-data-sets/fe-data-library
    -apprenticeships.

13 https://www.citb.co.uk/documents/research/tns-2016-2017_final%20
    20-10-17.pdf.

14 "Migrant Labour Force Within the Construction Industry," Office for
    National Statistics, June 2018.

15 "Employer Skills Survey 2017: UK Finding," Department for Education,
    https://www.gov.uk/government/publications/employer-skills-survey
    -2017-uk-report.

16 Ibid.

17 Ibid.

18 *Educating for the Modern World*, CBI/Pearson, 2018, 16–17.

19 Alexia Fernández Campbell, "The US Is Experiencing a Widespread
    Worker Shortage. Here's Why," Vox, March 18, 2019.

20 For the United States, see Daniel Zhao, "Local Pay Reports: Pay Growth
    Steady at 2.3 Percent in January," Glassdoor Economic Research, January
    29, 2019, https://www.glassdoor.com/research/january-2019-local-pay
    -reports/. For the United Kindom, see "UK Employer Skills Survey: 2015,"
    Department for Education, https://www.gov.uk/government/publications
    /ukces-employer-skills-survey-2015-uk-report.

21 Harriet Agnew, "France Faces Growing Threat of Skills Shortages," *Finan-
    cial Times*, October 17, 2018.

22 Paul Vickers, *International immigration and the labour market, UK:
    2016*, Office for National Statistics, April 12, 2017, https://www.ons.gov
    .uk/peoplepopulationandcommunity/populationandmigration/interna
    tionalmigration/articles/migrationandthelabourmarketuk/2016.

23 Noam Gidron and Peter A. Hall, "The Politics of Social Status: Economic
    and Cultural Roots of the Populist Right," *British Journal of Sociology*
    68, no. 51 (2017), 10, https://onlinelibrary.wiley.com/doi/full/10.1111
    /1468-4446.12319.

24 Michele Lamont, *The Dignity of Working Men: Morality and the Boundaries of Race, Class, and Immigration* (New York: Russell Sage Foundation, and Cambridge, MA: Harvard University Press, 2000), 177, 178.

25 Ibid.

26 Justin Gest, *The New Minority: Working Class Politics in an Age of Immigration and Inequality* (New York, Oxford University Press, 2016), 16, 17, 21.

27 Arlie Russell Hochschild, *Strangers in Their Own Land: Anger and Mourning on the American Right* (New York: New Press, 2016).

28 "Dataset A01: Summary of Labour Market Statistics," ONS, December 17, 2019.

29 *Megatrends: Is Work in the* UK *Really Becoming Less Secure?*, CIPD report, July 2019, 8, https://www.cipd.co.uk/Images/7904-megatrends-insecurity-report-final_tcm18-61556.pdf.

30 "Dataset EMP17: People in Employment on Zero Hours Contracts ONS," August 12, 2019.

31 "Contingent Work and Alternative Employment Arrangements—May 2017," US Bureau of Labor Statistics, Press Release, June 7, 2018.

32 See "Employment Rate, Labour Market Statistics," OECD.

33 Nye Cominetti, Kathleen Henehan, and Stephen Clarke, *Low Pay Britain 2019*, Resolution Foundation Report, May 2019, 4.

34 Francis Green, *Demanding Work: The Paradox of Job Quality in the Affluent Economy* (Princeton, NJ: Princeton University Press, 2007), 1.

35 *Megatrends: Is Work in the* UK *Really Becoming Less Secure?*, 9–10.

36 Stephen Clarke and Nye Cominetti, *Setting the Record Straight: How Record Employment Has Changed the* UK, Resolution Foundation, January 2019.

37 "Employment by Sex and Occupation," ILO modelled estimates, International Labour Organisation, November 2018.

38 Stephen McKay, "Work," in *British Social Attitudes 33* (NatCen, 2015), 1

39 "The State of American Jobs," Pew Research Center, October 6, 2016, 13, https://www.pewsocialtrends.org/2016/10/06/the-state-of-american-jobs/.

40 Stephen McKay, "Work," 14.

41 Ibid., 17.

42 Christian Welzel, "Change in Materialist/Post-Materialist Priorities in 5 EU Countries Including UK, 1970 and 2000," in Dalton and Klingemann, *The Oxford Handbook of Political Behaviour* (Oxford, UK: University Press, 2007).

43 StephenMcKay, "Work," 7.

44 "The State of American Jobs," Pew Research Center, 56.

45 Ibid., 57.

46 Ibid.

47 "37% of British workers think their jobs are meaningless," YouGov, August 12, 2015.

48 See Noam Gidron and Peter A. Hall, "The Politics of Social Status: Economic and Cultural Roots of the Populist Right," *British Journal of Sociology* 68, no. S1 (November 2017), S74.

49 Private analysis of ISSP Data.

50 Gidron and Hall, "The Politics of Social Status," S75.

51 Tak Wing Chan, "Understanding the Social and Cultural Bases of Brexit," UCL Institute of Education 2017.

Chapter Eight: Whatever Happened to Heart?

1 New Earnings Survey UK, Annual Survey of Hours and Earnings; Statistical Abstract of the United States 1976, Bureau of Labour Statistics May 2017 National Occupational Employment and Wage Estimates United States.

2 Yuval Noah Harari, *Homo Deus: A Brief History of Tomorrow* (London: Harvill Secker, 2016), 199.

3 Daniel Cox and Robert P. Jones, "America's Changing Religious Identity: Findings from the 2016 American Values Atlas," Public Religion Research Institute, September 6, 2017.

4 Conrad Hackett, "U.S. Public Becoming Less Religious," Pew Global Research Center, November 3, 2015.

5 "When Americans Say They Believe in God, What Do They Mean?" Pew Global Research Center, April 25, 2018.

6 David Voas and Steve Bruce, *Religion*, British Social Attitudes 36, Natcen, 2019, https://www.bsa.natcen.ac.uk/media/39293/1_bsa36_religion.pdf.

7 "Being Christian in Western Europe," Pew Global Research Center, May 29, 2018.

8 Yuval Noah Harari, "Why Technology Favors Tyranny," *Atlantic*, October 2018, https://www.theatlantic.com/magazine/archive/2018/10/yuval-noah-harari-technology-tyranny/568330/.

9 Sir Angus Deaton, "Why Is Democratic Capitalism Failing So Many? And What Should We Do About It?" Keynote Address, Tri-Nuffield Conference, May 16, 2019, https://www.nuffieldfoundation.org/news/why-is-democratic-capitalism-failing-so-many-sir-angus-deatons-keynote-lecture-to-the-tri-nuffield-conference.

10 Richard Layard, *Happiness: Lessons from a New Science* (London: Penguin, 2005).

11 David Brooks, "The Nuclear Family Was a Mistake," *Atlantic*, March 2020.

12 Ibid.

13 Harry Benson, *Family Stability Improves as Divorce Rates Fall* (Marriage Foundation, January 2019)

14 *Why Family Matters*, Centre for Social Justice, March 2019, 5.

15 *Health Survey for England 2016: Well-Being and Mental Health*, ONS/NHS Digital, December 13, 2017.

16 *Antidepressants Were the Area with Largest Increase in Prescription Items in 2016*, NHS Digital, June 29, 2017.

17 *Mental Health Bulletin 2017–18 Annual Report*, NHS Digital, November 29, 2018.

18 NatCen, University of Leicester, Department of Health, *Mental Health and Wellbeing in England: Adult Psychiatric Morbidity Survey 2014*, NHS Digital, September 2016.

19 Edmund S. Higgins, "Is Mental Health Declining in the U.S.?," *Scientific American*, January 1, 2017.

20 *The State of Mental Health in America 2019*, Mental Health America, https://www.mhanational.org/issues/state-mental-health-america.

21 Stephen Ilardi, "Depression Is a Disease of Civilisation," Ted Talk, May 2013.

22 "An Epidemic of Loneliness," *Week* (US), January 6, 2019.

23 Louise C. Hawkley, Rebeccah Duvoisin, Johannes Ackva et al., *Loneliness in Older Adults in the USA and Germany: Measurement Invariance and Validation*, NORC Working Paper Series WP-2015-004, 2016.

24 Kantar Public, "Trapped in a Bubble: An Investigation into Triggers for Loneliness in the UK," British Red Cross/Co-op, December 2016.

25 *The Forgotten Role of Families*, Centre for Social Justice, 2017.

26 David Brooks, "The Nuclear Family Was a Mistake," *Atlantic*, March 2020.

27 Harry Benson, *The Myth of "Long-term Stable Relationships" Outside Marriage*, Marriage Foundation, May 2013, https://marriagefoundation.org.uk/wp-content/uploads/2019/09/MF-paper-Myth-of-long-term-stable-relationships-outside-marriage.pdf.

28 Branko Milanovic, *Capitalism, Alone* (Cambridge, MA: Harvard University Press, 2019).

29 Madeleine Bunting, *Labours of Love: The Crisis of Care* (London: Granta, 2020 [forthcoming]).

30 Interview with the author.

31 Tom De Castell, "Rise in Nurse Vacancy Rate in England Prompts Fresh Warnings," *Nursing Times*, September 12, 2018; Stephanie Jones-Berry, "Why as Many as One in Four Nursing Students Could Be Dropping Out of Their Degrees," *Nursing Standard*, September 3, 2018; "What Are the Vacancy Trends in the Public Sector?" ONS, August 6, 2019.

32 "Is Staff Retention an Issue in the Public Sector?" ONS, June 17, 2019.

33 See for example, "German Opposition Slams Government for 36,000 Vacant Jobs in Care Industry," *Deutsche Welle*, April 25, 2018.

34 Barra Roantree and Kartik Vira, *The Rise and Rise of Women's Employment in the* UK, IFS Briefing Note BN234, April 2018.

35 "Women Shoulder the Responsibility of 'Unpaid Work'" ONS, November 10, 2016.

36 Interview with the author.

37 Alison Wolf, *The XX Factor: How Working Women Are Creating a New Society* (London: Profile Books, 2013).

38 https://www.gov.uk/government/statistics/childcare-and-early-years-survey-of-parents-2019.

39 Alison Wolf, "Have Middle Class Women Captured Family Policy?" *Society Central*, 2015.

40 Virginia Held, *The Ethics of Care: Personal, Political, and Global* (New York: Oxford University Press, 2006), 64.

41 "The Number of Nurses and Midwives in the UK," Fullfact, January 23, 2018.

42 Amy Wax, *Caring Enough: Sex Roles, Work and Taxing Women*, Villanova University, 1999, https://digitalcommons.law.villanova.edu/cgi/viewcontent.cgi?article=3042&context=vlr.

43 UK Quarterly Labour Force Survey.

44 Linda H. Aiken, Douglas M. Sloane, Luk Bruyneel et al., "Nurse Staffing and Education and Hospital Mortality in Nine European Countries: A Retrospective Observational Study," *Lancet* 383, no. 9931 (2014), 1824–30.

45 Professor Charles Goodhart, "Dementia Plus Demography Equals Care Crisis" (unpublished paper).

46 *The Cavendish Review: An Independent Review into Healthcare Assistants and Support Workers in the* NHS *and Social Care Settings* (July 2013), 7, https://assets.publishing.service.gov.uk/government/uploads/system/uploads/attachment_data/file/236212/Cavendish_Review.pdf.

47 Warwick Lightfoot, Will Heaven, and Jos Henson Gric, "21st Century Social Care," Policy Exchange, May 2019.

48 Fabian Wallace-Stephens, "What New Jobs Will Emerge in the 2020s?" Royal Society of Arts, January 8, 2020.

49 "Occupational Employment Projections to 2024," Bureau of Labor Statistics, December 2015.

50 Jonathan Gershuny and Oriel Sullivan, eds., *What We Really Do All Day: Insights from the Centre for Time Use Research* (London: Pelican, 2019), 113.

51 See, for example, *Reducing Re-offending: Supporting Families, Creating Better Futures: A Framework for Improving the Local Delivery of Support for the Families of Offenders*, Ministry of Justice, Department for Children, Schools and Families, 2009.

52 Anchor, Care England survey, June 21 2018.

53 *The State of the Adult Social Care Sector and Workforce in England*, Skills for Care, September 2017.

54 Jonathan Gershuny and Oriel Sullivan, *What We Really Do All Day*, 143.

55 "Women Shoulder the Responsibility of 'Unpaid Work,'" ONS, November 10, 2016.

56 Jonathan Gershuny and Oriel Sullivan, eds., *What We Really Do All Day*, 135.

57 "Billion Pound Loss in Volunteering Effort," ONS, March 2017.

58 Marilyn French, *The Women's Room* (London: Virago Modern Classics, 1977).

59 Gretchen Livingston, "Adult Caregiving Often Seen as Very Meaningful by Those Who Do It," Pew Research Center, November 8, 2018.

60 Mary Harrington, "How Motherhood Put an End to My Liberalism," *UnHerd*, October 9, 2019, https://unherd.com/2019/10/how-motherhood-put-an-end-to-my-liberalism/.

61 Catherine Hakim, "A New Approach to Explaining Fertility Patterns: Preference Theory," *Population and Development Review* 29, no.3 (2003), 349–74.

62 British Social Attitudes Survey, 1989.

63 Bronnie Ware, *The Top Five Regrets of the Dying* (London: Hay House, 2019).

Chapter Nine: The Fall of the Knowledge Worker

1 Paul Krugman, "White Collar Workers Turn Blue," *New York Times Magazine*, September 29, 1996, https://web.mit.edu/krugman/www/BACKWRD2.html.

2 Richard Baldwin, *The Globotics Upheaval Globalization, Robotics, and the Future of Work* (New York: Oxford University Press, 2019), 12–13.

3 Phillip Brown and Hugh Lauder, "Auctioning the Future of Work," *World Policy*, June 10, 2013.

4 Ibid.

5 Ibid.

6 Ibid.

7 Richard and Daniel Susskind, *The Future of the Professions: How Technology Will Transform the Work of Human Experts* (Oxford, UK: Oxford University Press, 2015), 1.

8 Ibid., 2.

9 Ibid., xi.

10 OECD (2018), "How Does the Earnings Advantage of Tertiary-Educated Workers Evolve Across Generations?," *Education Indicators in Focus*, no. 62 (2018).

11 Anna Vignoles, Ian Walker, et al., *The Impact of Undergraduate Degrees on Early-Career Earnings* (Institute for Fiscal Studies, 2018).

12 *Treating Students Fairly: The Economics of Post-School Education*, House of Lords, Economic Affairs Committee, 2nd Report of Session 2017–19, June 2018, 25.

13 They are University College Falmouth, Goldsmiths, Glamorgan, Bath Spa, Leeds City, Middlesex, Bolton, University of the Arts London, West London, Ravensbourne, Wolverhampton, and Bangor. (Some of these are art and design colleges, which for most graduates is a precarious and low-paid sector.)

14 Vignoles et al., *The Impact of Undergraduate Degrees*, 50–51.

15 Chris Belfield, Jack Britton, Laura van der Erve, et al., *The Relative Labour Market Returns to Different Degrees* (IFS, 2018).

16 Vignoles et al., *The Impact of Undergraduate Degrees*, 6

17 Ibid., 61–62.

18 Belfield, Britton, and van der Erve, *The Relative Labour Market*, 6, 61.

19 Vignoles et al., *The Impact of Undergraduate Degrees*, 19.

20 Bellfield, Britton, and van der Erve, *The Relative Labour Market*, 34.

21 Ken Mayhew, "Human Capital, Growth and Inequality," *Welsh Economic Review* 24 (2016), 23–27.

22 Jared Ashworth and Tyler Ransom, *Has the College Wage Premium Continued to Rise? Evidence from Multiple US Surveys*, IZA Institute of Labor Economics, July 2018.

23 Stefan Speckesser and Héctor Espinoza, "A Comparison of Earnings Related to Higher Level Vocational/Technical and Academic Education," CVER Discussion Paper, Research Discussion Paper 019, April 2019.

24 *Skills Matter: Additional Results from the Survey of Adult Skills*, OECD Skills Studies, 2019.

25 Richard Clegg, "Graduates in the UK Labour Market: 2017," ONS, November 2017.

26 Heike Behle, Gaby Atfield, Peter Elias et al. "Reassessing the Employment Outcomes of Higher Education," in Jennifer M. Case and Jeroen Huisman, eds., *Researching Higher Education: International Perspectives on Theory, Policy and Practice* (Routledge Press, 2015), 114–31.

27 Maja Savic, *Overeducation and Hourly Wages in the UK Labour Market, 2006 to 2017,* ONS, April 2019.

28 Alan Felstead, Duncan Gallie, Francis Green, and Golo Henseke, *Skills Trends at Work in Britain: First Findings from the Skills and Employment Survey 2017,* Economic and Social Research Council, Department for Education, Cardiff University (2018).

29 Ken Mayhew and Craig Holmes, *Alternative Pathways into the Labour Market*, CIPD Policy Report, October 2016.

30 Ibid. and Ken Mayhew and Craig Holmes, *Over Qualification and Skills Mismatch in the Graduate Labour Market*, CIPD Policy Report, August 2015.

31 Geoff Mason, "Graduate Utilisation in British Industry: The Initial Impact of Mass Higher Education," *National Institute Economic Review* 156, no. 1 (May 1996), 93–103.

32 Gerbrand Tholen, *The Role of Higher Education Within the Labour Market: Evidence from Four Skilled; Occupations*, paper presented at SKOPE/ESRC Festival of Science, St. Anne's College, Oxford, November 3, 2014; Susan James, Chris Warhurst, Gerbrand Tholen, and Johanna Commander, *Graduate Skills or the Skills of Graduates, What Matters Most? An Analysis from a Graduatising Occupation*, paper presented at the 30th International Labour Process Conference, Stockholm University, Stockholm (2012)

33 Chris Belfield, Jack Britton, Lorraine Dearden and Laura van der Erve, *Higher Education Funding in England: Past, Present and Options for the Future*, IFS Briefing Note BN211, July 2017.

34 Mayhew and Holmes, *Alternative Pathways*, 4, 50.

35 Francis Green and Golo Henseke, "Should Governments of OECD Countries Worry About Graduate Underemployment?," *Oxford Review of Economic Policy* 32, no.4 (2016), 514–37.

36 Susskind Daniel, *A World Without Work: Technology, Automation and How We Should Respond* (London: Allen Lane, 2020), 103–105

37 Erzsébet Bukodi and John H. Goldthorpe, *Social Mobility and Education in Britain: Research, Politics and Policy* (Cambridge, UK: Cambridge University Press, 2018).

38 John Boys, CIPD, private correspondence using ONS Dataset EMP04: "Employment by Occupation."

39 Jacques Bughin, Eric Hazan, Susan Lund et al., *Skills Shift: Automation and the Future of the Workforce*, McKinsey Global Institute (MGI) Discussion Paper, May 2018.

40 Ibid.

41 Ibid.

42 "EY Transforms Its Recruitment Selection Process for Graduates, Undergraduates and School Leavers," press release from Ernst and Young, August 3, 2015.

43 "EY: How to Excel in a Strengths-Based Graduate Interview," Target Jobs, https://targetjobs.co.uk/employers/ey/ey-how-to-excel-in-a-strengths-based-graduate-interview-323859.

44 See UK High Pay Centre.

45 Adair Turner, *Capitalism in the Age of Robots: Work, Income and Wealth in the 21st Century*, Lecture given at the School of Advanced International Studies, John Hopkins University, April 10, 2018, 29.

46 Tyler Cowen, *Average Is Over: Powering America Beyond the Age of the Great Stagnation* (New York: Dutton, 2013).

Chapter Ten: Cognitive Diversity and the Future of Everything

1 David Brooks, Intelligence Squared lecture, October 20, 2015.

2 Iain McGilchrist, *The Master and His Emissary: The Divided Brain and the Making of the Western World* (New Haven, CT: Yale University Press, 2009).

3 Jonathan Rowson and Iain McGilchrist, *Divided Brain, Divided World: Why the Best Part of Us Struggles to be Heard*, RSA, February 2013, 4–5, https://www.thersa.org/globalassets/pdfs/blogs/rsa-divided-brain-divided-world.pdf.

4 Richard Layard, *Can We Be Happier?* (London: Pelican, 2020).

5 Matthew Syed, *Rebel Ideas: The Power of Diverse Thinking* (London: John Murray Press, 2019)

6 "Different Kinds of Thinking Make Teams Smarter," Futurity, posted July 2, 2019.

7 Musa Al-Gharbi, *On the Relationship Between Ideological and Demographic Diversity*, https://musaalgharbi.com/2019/04/29/relationship-between-ideological-demographic-diversity/.

8 Dag Detter and Stefan Folster, *Out of the Box Economics: Inventive and Little Known Ways of Tackling the World of Tomorrow Today* (forthcoming in 2021).

9 Nicholas Lemann, *The Big Test: The Secret History of the American Meritocracy* (New York: Farrar, Straus and Giroux, 1999), 347.

10 The formulation of French geographer Christophe Guilluy. See Christophe Guilluy, *Twilight of the Elites: Prosperity, the Periphery and the Future of France* (New Haven, CT: Yale University Press, 2019).

11 Nicholas Boys Smith, "How Communities Lost Their Soul," *UnHerd*, October 4, 2019.

12 Sue Halpern, "The One Traffic-light Town with some of the Fastest Internet in the US," *New Yorker*, December 3, 2019.

13 According to a YouGov poll of May 2016, only 2 percent of eighteen- to twenty-four-year-old British men felt "completely masculine" compared with 39 percent of eighteen- to twenty-four-year-old women who felt "completely feminine." Young Americans have more traditional gender identities.

14 Adair Turner, *Capitalism in the Age of Robots: Work, Income and Wealth in the 21st Century*, Lecture given at the School of Advanced International Studies, John Hopkins University, April 10, 2018, 31.

15 Wendell Steavenson, "Back to the Rind,", *FT Books*, November 9, 2019.

16 Bee Wilson, *The Way We Eat Now: Strategies for Eating in a World of Change* (London: Fourth Estate, 2019).

17 Joseph E. Aoun, *Robot-Proof: Higher Education in the Age of Artificial Intelligence* (Cambridge, MA: MIT Press, 2017).

18 Andy Haldane, *A Growth Story*, speech to the Guild Society, University of Oxford, May 23, 2018.

19 John Maynard Keynes, *Essays in Persuasion* (New York: W. W. Norton, 1963).

20 Tom Holland, *Dominion: The Making of the Western Mind* (London: Little Brown, 2019).

21 Jonathan Rauch, "A Word to the Wise: Why Wisdom Might Be Ripe for Rediscovery," *Globe and Mail*, May 11, 2018).

22 Ibid.

Bibliography

Appiah, Kwame Anthony, *The Lies That Bind: Rethinking Identity* (London: Profile Books, 2018).

Arum, Richard, and Josipa Roksam, *Academically Adrift: Limited Learning on College Campuses* (Chicago: University of Chicago Press, 2011).

Augar Review, "Review of Post-18 Education and Funding" (UK Government report, May 2019).

Autor, David, "Work of the Past, Work of the Future," Richard T Ely Lecture to the annual meeting of the American Economic Association (2019).

Baldwin, Richard, *The Globotics Upheaval: Globalization, Robotics and the Future of Work* (London: Weidenfeld & Nicolson, 2019).

Bell, Daniel, *The Coming of Post-Industrial Society: A Venture in Social Forecasting* (London: Penguin, 1976).

Bishop, Bill, *The Big Sort: Why the Clustering of Like-Minded America Is Tearing Us Apart* (New York: Houghton Mifflin Harcourt, 2008).

Blanden, Jo, Paul Gregg and Stephen Machin, *Intergenerational Mobility in Europe and North America: A Report Supported by the Sutton Trust* (Centre for Economic Performance, London School of Economics/Sutton Trust, 2005).

Bloodworth, James, *The Myth of Meritocracy* (London: Biteback Publishing, 2016).

———. *Hired: Undercover in Low-Wage Britain* (London: Atlantic, 2019).

Bovens, Mark, and Anchrit Wille, *Diploma Democracy: The Rise of Political Meritocracy* (Oxford, UK: Oxford University Press, 2017).

Brown, Phillip, Hugh Lauder, and David Ashton, *The Global Auction: The Broken Promises of Education, Jobs and Incomes* (Oxford, UK: Oxford University Press, 2011).

Bukodi, Erzsébet and John H. Goldthorpe, *Social Mobility and Education in Britain* (Cambridge, UK: Cambridge University Press, 2019).

Bunting, Madeleine, *Labours of Love: The Crisis of Care* (London: Granta Books, 2020).

Burton, John, *Leading Good Care* (London: Jessica Kingsley Publishers, 2015).

Caplan, Bryan, *The Case Against Education: Why the Education System Is a Waste of Time and Money* (Princeton, NJ: Princeton University Press, 2018).

Cavendish, Camilla, *Extra Time: 10 Lessons for an Ageing World* (London: HarperCollins, 2019).

Christodoulou, Daisy, *Seven Myths About Education* (London: Routledge, 2014).

Collier, Paul, *The Future of Capitalism: Facing the New Anxieties* (London: Allen Lane, 2018).

Cowen, Tyler, *Average Is Over: Powering America Beyond the Age of the Great Stagnation* (New York: Dutton, 2013).

Crawford, Matthew, *The Case for Working with Your Hands: Or Why Office Work Is Bad for Us and Fixing Things Feels Good* (London: Penguin, 2011).

Deaton, Angus, "Why is Democratic Capitalism Failing So Many People?" The Tri-Nuffield Conference lecture (June 2019).

Dench, Geoff (ed.), *The Rise and Rise of Meritocracy* (Oxford: Blackwell Publishing, 2006).

———. *What Women Want: Evidence from British Social Attitudes* (London: Hera Trust, 2010).

Florida, Richard, *The Rise of the Creative Class Revisited* (New York: Basic Books, 2014).

Flynn, James, *Are We Getting Smarter?: Rising IQ in the Twenty-First Century* (London: Cambridge University Press, 2012).

Gardner, Howard, *Frames of Mind: The Theory of Multiple Intelligences* (New York: Basic Books, 1983).

Gershuny, Jonathan, and Oriel Sullivan (eds.), *What We Really Do All Day: Insights from the Centre for Time Use Research* (London: Pelican, 2019).

Gest, Justin, *The New Minority: White Working Class Politics in an Age of Immigration and Inequality* (New York: Oxford University Press, 2016).

Gidron, Noam and Peter Hall, "The Politics of Social Status: Economic and Cultural Roots of the Populist Right," *British Journal of Sociology* (November 2017).

Goldin, Claudia, and Lawrence Katz, *The Race Between Education and Technology* (London: Harvard University Press, 2009).

Goleman, Daniel, *Emotional Intelligence: Why It Can Matter Than IQ* (London: Bantam, 2006).

Goodhart, Charles, "Dementia Plus Demography Equals Care Crisis," unpublished paper.

Guyatt, Richard, "Head, Hand and Heart," inaugural lecture at Royal College of Art, London, 1950.

Haidt, Jonathan, *The Righteous Mind: Why Good People Are Divided by Politics and Religion* (London: Penguin, 2013).

Haldane, Andy, "Ideas and Institutions—A Growth Story," lecture to the Guild Society, University of Oxford, May 23, 2018.

Harari, Yuval Noah, *Homo Deus: A Brief History of Tomorrow* (London: Harvill Secker, 2016).

———. *21 Lessons for the 21st Century* (London: Jonathan Cape, 2018).

Held, Virginia, *The Ethics of Care: Personal, Political and Global* (New York: Oxford University Press, 2006).

Hochschild, Arlie Russell, *Strangers in Their Own Land: Anger and Mourning on the American Right* (New York: The New Press, 2016).

———. *The Managed Heart: Commercialization of Human Feeling* (London: University of California Press, 2012).

Holland, Tom, *Dominion: The Making of the Western Mind* (London: Little, Brown, 2020).

Kahneman, Daniel, *Thinking, Fast and Slow* (London: Penguin, 2012).

Keynes, John Maynard, *Essays in Persuasion* (New York: W. W. Norton, 1963).

Labaree, David F, *A Perfect Mess: The Unlikely Ascendancy of American Higher Education* (Chicago: University of Chicago Press, 2017).

Lamont, Michele, *The Dignity of Working Men: Morality and the Boundaries of Race, Class and Immigration* (London: Harvard University Press, 2000).

Lasch, Christopher, *The Revolt of the Elites: And the Betrayal of Democracy* (New York: W. W. Norton, 1995).

Layard, Richard, *Can We Be Happier?: Evidence and Ethics* (London: Penguin, 2020).

Leadbeater, Charles, *Living on Thin Air* (London: Penguin, 2010).

Lemann, Nicholas, *The Big Test: The Secret History of the American Meritocracy* (New York: Farrar, Straus and Giroux, 2000).

Lenon, Barnaby, *Other People's Children* (London: John Catt Educational, 2018).

Lind, Michael, *The New Class War: Saving Democracy from the Managerial Elite* (New York: Portfolio/Penguin, 2020).

Mair, Peter, *Ruling the Void: The Hollowing of Western Democracy* (London: Verso, 2013).

Markovits, Daniel, *The Meritocracy Trap* (London: Allen Lane, 2019).

Marmot, Michael, *Status Syndrome: How Your Social Standing Directly Affects Your Health* (London: Bloomsbury, 2005).

Mayhew, Ken, and Craig Holmes, *Overqualification in the Graduate Labour Market* (CIPD report, August 2015).

Mazzucato, Mariana, *The Value of Everything: Making and Taking in the Global Economy* (London: Penguin, 2019).

McGilchrist, Iain, *The Master and His Emissary: The Divided Brain and the Making of the Western World* (London: Yale University Press, 2012).

Milanovic, Branko, *Global Inequality: A New Approach for the Age of Globalisation* (London: Harvard University Press, 2016).

Mumford, James, *Vexed: Ethics Beyond Political Tribes* (London: Bloomsbury, 2020).

Murray, Charles, *Coming Apart: The State of White America, 1960–2010* (New York: Crown Forum, 2013).

McKinsey Global Institute, "Skill Shift: Automation and the Future of the Workforce," discussion paper (May 2018).

Orwell, George, *Politics and the English Language* (London: Penguin, 2013).

Perry, Grayson, *The Descent of Man* (London: Penguin, 2017).

Plomin, Robert, *Blueprint: How DNA Makes Us Who We Are* (London: Allen Lane, 2018).

Pratt, John, *The Polytechnic Experiment, 1965–1992* (London: Open University Press, 1997).

Putnam, Robert D, *Bowling Alone: The Collapse and Revival of American Community* (New York: Simon & Schuster, 2000).

Rauch, Jonathan, *The Happiness Curve: Why Life Gets Better After Midlife* (New York: Green Tree, 2018).

Reeves, Richard, *Dream Hoarders: How the American Upper Middle Class Is Leaving Everyone Else in the Dust, Why That Is a Problem, and What to Do About it* (Washington: The Brookings Institution, 2018).

Reich, Robert, *The Work of Nations* (London: Simon & Schuster, 1991).

Robson, David, *The Intelligence Trap: Why Smart People Do Stupid Things and How to Make Wiser Decisions* (London: Hodder & Stoughton, 2019).

Runciman, David, *How Democracy Ends* (London: Profile Books, 2019).

Saunders, Peter, *Social Mobility Myths* (London: Civitas, 2010).

Savage, Michael, *Social Class in the 21st Century* (London: Pelican, 2015).

Seldon, Anthony, *The Fourth Education Revolution: Will Artificial Intelligence Liberate or Infantilise Humanity* (Buckingham, UK: University of Buckingham Press, 2018).

Shattock, Michael, *Making Policy in British Higher Education* (London: Open University Press/McGraw-Hill Education, 2012).

Slaughter, Anne-Marie, *Unfinished Business: Women Men Work Family* (New York, Random House, 2015).

Soskice, David, and Torben Iversen, *Democracy and Prosperity: Reinventing Capitalism Through a Turbulent Century* (Oxford, UK: Princeton University Press, 2019).

Sumption, Jonathan, *Shifting the Foundations*, BBC Reith Lectures (2019).

Susskind, Daniel, and Richard Susskind, *The Future of the Professions: How Technology Will Transform the Work of Human Experts* (Oxford, UK: Oxford University Press, 2017).

Susskind Daniel, *A World Without Work: Technology, Automation and How We Should Respond* (London: Allen Lane, 2020).

Syed, Matthew, *Rebel Ideas: The Power of Diverse Thinking* (London: John Murray, 2019).

Taleb, Nassim Nicholas, *Skin in the Game: Hidden Asymmetries in Daily Life* (London: Penguin, 2019).

Tamir, Yuli, *Staying in Control: What Do We Really Want Public Education to Achieve?* (Educational Theory, August 2011).

Turner, Adair, "Capitalism in the Age of Robots: Work, Income and Wealth in the 21st Century," lecture at the School of Advanced International Studies, John Hopkins University, Washingon DC, April 10, 2018.

Vance, J. D., *Hillbilly Elegy: A Memoir of a Family and Culture in Crisis* (London: HarperCollins, 2016).

Ware, Bronnie, *The Top Five Regrets of the Dying* (London: Hay House, 2019).

Whyte, William, *Why Do So Many UK Students Live Away from Home and Why Does it Matter?* (Higher Education Institute report, November 2019).

Willetts, David, *A University Education* (Oxford, UK: Oxford University Press, 2017).

———. *The Pinch: How the Baby Boomers Took Their Children's Future—And Why They Should Give it Back* (London: Atlantic, 2019).

Williams, Joan C, *White Working Class: Overcoming Class Cluelessness in America* (Boston: Harvard Business Review Press, 2017).

Wilson, Bee, *The Way We Eat Now: Strategies for Eating in a World of Change* (London: Fourth Estate, 2019).

Wolf, Alison, *Does Education Matter?* (London: Penguin, 2002).

———. *The XX Factor: How Working Women Are Creating a New Society* (London: Profile Books, 2013).

Young, Michael, *The Rise of the Meritocracy, 1870–2033* (London: Penguin, 1973).

Young, Michael and Peter Wilmott, *Family and Kinship in East London* (Abingdon, UK: Routledge, 2013).

Young, Toby, "The Fall of the Meritocracy," essay in *Quadrant*, September 2015.

Acknowledgments

My last book, *The Road to Somewhere,* covered themes I had been thinking about for some years, so I was able to write the book quite quickly and without much help. This book has been different. It covers many subjects, such as human intelligence and the care economy, about which I had little prior knowledge and on which I can only write as an interested generalist. This time, however, I have had invaluable research assistance from Richard Norrie and Tom Hamilton-Shaw. I have also had special support and engagement from a couple of institutions and several individuals. Above all I want to thank Dean Godson and other colleagues at the Policy Exchange think tank in London, where I work part-time, for allowing me both the time to work on the book and to explore some of its themes in my Policy Exchange work. I hope I can repay the organization's generosity over the coming years. I was also invited to spend a month at the Institut fur die Wissenshaften vom Menschen (IWM), a wonderful institute in Vienna where I was able to get the book underway in March 2019 and discuss some of its ideas with many lively minds from across Europe; special thanks to Ivan Krastev and Dessy Gavrilova for making my time there so enjoyable.

I want to say a special thanks to a further dozen people: David Lucas for having the original insight that launched the book, Toby Mundy (my agent and friend) for picking it up and running with it, to Ken Charman, Alun Francis, and Paul Morland for a constant flow of ideas and feedback, to Madeleine Bunting and Julie Goldie for insights into the world of care both domestic and institutional, to Eric Kaufmann, Matt Goodwin, Pamela Dow, Mary Harrington, and Michael Lind for vital suggestions. Thanks are also due to my publishers: to my editor at Penguin Press, Maria Bedford, for her thoughtful interventions and oversight and the same to Stuart Roberts at Free Press in the United States—and thanks too to the teams at both publishers who have worked on the book.

Then there is a much larger group of people who have been helpful in some way, apologies to anyone I have left out. Andrew Adonis, Claire Ainsley, Douglas Alexander, Jake Arnold-Forster, Ewa Atanassow, Toby Baxendale, Mark Bovens, Paul Broks, Belinda Brown, Phillip Brown, Noah Carl, Emily Carver, Camilla Cavendish, Peter Cheese, Daisy Christodoulou, Robert Colls, Paul Corby, Ian Deary, Peter Dolton, Edward Fidoe, Catherine Fieschi, Beccy Goodhart, Charles Goodhart, Rose Goodhart, Helen Goulden, Christine Goronowicz, Alexander Gray, John Gray, Manuela Grayson, Andy Haldane, Jonathan Hanbury, Nick Hillman, Craig Holmes, Paul Johnson, Allyson Kaye, Lucy Kellaway, Sam Kershaw, Mark Leach, Alison Leary, Simon Lebus, Charlotte Leslie, Oliver Letwin, Tim Leunig, Paul Lewis, Warwick Lightfoot, John Lloyd, Iain Mansfield, Jill Manthorpe, Ken Mayhew, Elaine Maxwell, Jasper McMahon, Rosie Meek, Munira Mirza, James Mumford, Joanna Newman, Orna NiChionna, Ian Norman, Tim Oates, Paul Ormerod, Edward Peck, Louise Perry, Nina Power, Jonathan Rauch, David Robson, Juliet Rodgers, Jonathan Rutherford, Freddie Sayers, Isabel Scholes, Tom Simpson, Swaran Singh, Richard Sloggett, David Soskice, Yuli Tamir, Nick Timothy, Adair Turner, Bobby Vedral, Anna Vignoles, Robin Wales, Adele Waters, Amy Wax, Simon Wessely, Joanna Williams, Mark Williams, Christopher Winch, Alison Wolf, Jon Yates, Toby Young.

Finally, I want to mention some of the podcasts I listened to regularly while writing the book either for general distraction or for ideas that informed the book (or both). LSE Public Lectures & Events; Unherd Confessions with Giles Fraser; Talking Politics; Exponential View; Rebel Wisdom; Real Talk with Zuby; Conversations with Tyler; The Psychology Podcast with Dr Scott Barry Kaufman; Making Sense, Sam Harris.

Index

About the Author

David Goodhart is founding editor of London-based *Prospect* magazine. He is currently head of the Demography, Immigration, and Integration Unit at the think tank Policy Exchange and was previously director of the center-left think tank Demos. He is the author of the bestselling book *The Road to Somewhere: The Populist Revolt and the Future of Politics*, in which he identified the value divisions in western societies that help explain Brexit, Trump, and the global rise of populism. His book *The British Dream: Successes and Failures of Post-War Immigration* was runner-up for the Orwell Prize.